NEW COVENANT and the EARLY CHURCH

THE REV. CHARLIE HOLT

New Covenant and the Early Church
The Core: Strong Foundations of Faith

© 2022 by The Rev. Charlie Holt
Published in Jacksonville, Florida by Bible Study Media, Inc.

All rights reserved. No part of this publication may be reproduced, distrib-uted, or transmitted in any form or by any means, including photocopying, recording, or other electronic or mechanical methods, without the prior written permission of the publisher, except in the case of brief quotations embodied in critical reviews and certain other noncommercial uses permit-ted by copyright law.

Unless otherwise indicated, Scripture quotations are from the ESV® Bible (The Holy Bible, English Standard Version®), copyright © 2001 by Cross-way, a publishing ministry of Good News Publishers. Used by permission. All rights reserved.

ISBN Number: 978-1-942243-63-2
Library of Congress Control Number: 2022916314

TABLE OF CONTENTS

Introduction to the Core	5
Introduction to New Covenant and the Early Church	9

Chapter 1
Salvation has Come to this House — 11

Chapter 2
The New Covenant: Story of the Early Church — 43

Chapter 3
The Jerusalem Council — 63

Chapter 4
The Day of the Lord: Theology of Hope in the Face of Persecution — 87

Chapter 5
The Cross and Resurrection: Dying and Rising in Christ — 105

Chapter 6
The Gospel of God: The Gift that Changed the World — 131

Chapter 7
The Spirit and the Church: Freedom Unchained — 157

Chapter 8
Succession: Letters from Departing Apostles — 185

Chapter 9
Discipleship: Pick up your Cross and Follow Jesus — 229

Chapter 10
The Last Apostle: The Writings of John from Patmos — 273

A woman of Canaan (colour litho), Copping, Harold (1863-1932) / Private Collection / © Look and Learn / Bridgeman Images.

INTRODUCTION TO THE CORE
Strong Foundations of Faith

The Core is a course of study designed to help the maturing Christian develop a strong foundation for lifelong learning. The mature disciple of Jesus Christ will be able to express the Christian worldview with truth and love as they witness to their faith in the world.

The Christian worldview is all-encompassing. It affirms our identity in Christ, purpose in life, character, and ethics. It develops over a lifetime. Christians are called to develop a broad, inclusive—and even sophisticated—view of life. This view has at its core a relationship with God and other people. It reflects the phenomenon of human existence as well as a person's philosophical, "moral" and religious positions based on deep reflection upon, and relationship with, God's word as revealed in the Bible.

The Christian worldview encourages deep thought about fundamental questions such as the origins of the universe, development of life, the nature of good and evil, and the ultimate destiny of all things. These first-order concepts then lead to questions, understandings and applications for the nature of individual development, family dynamics, the relationship between church and state, social challenges, and the world of politics and economics.

"The Christian worldview encourages deep thought about fundamental questions such as the origins of the universe, development of life, the nature of good and evil, and the ultimate destiny of all things."

In order to build a solid foundation for the Christian worldview, we will explore the breadth of Christian knowledge, understanding, and wisdom through a study of six key areas of Christian theology and practice.

The six classes are:

1. Old Covenant and Ancient Israel
2. New Covenant and the Early Church
3. Christian History and Theology
4. Christian Formation and Spiritual Practice
5. Contemporary Christian Ethics and Apologetics
6. Christian Vocation and Servant-Leadership

All the classes in *The Core* will combine to create a comprehensive understanding of the basics of Christianity. For example, to understand the new covenant and early church, one must have prior knowledge and understanding of the old covenant and ancient Israel. How does the exodus from Egypt help explain the cross and resurrection of Jesus? Why does Jesus redefine the Jewish passover meal to apply to his sacrificed body and blood? How does the sacrificial system of Solomon's temple relate to the new living temple in Paul's letter to the Ephesians? We will consider the importance of these questions in the modern day, and we will answer them.

From a broad grasp of the teaching of the entire Bible, we can build a theological understanding and rule of life for spiritual formation and practice. The sacramental life established by Jesus and the Apostles is manifest in the contemporary community of the Church. It leads to individual as well as communal maturity.

Finally, through *The Core*, the maturing Christian will learn how to engage in the world as a wise advocate for the Christian faith and as a compelling servant-leader. How does a mature Christian interact with the larger marketplace of ideas and religious paradigms? The call and vocation of the Christian is to consider every thought as we contend for the Gospel in a world that does not understand its value and at times is even hostile to its central message.

By working through each of *The Core's* six courses, the Christian student will gain a foundation for future study. We will offer interpretive keys to Biblical passages that will allow for far greater exploration in the future. Along the way, we will share other tools that will always be of great use to the Christian. And if this course is done in community, the participants will make friends who can share their faith journey and live shoulder to shoulder with them in the faith. Ultimately, the aim of the core curriculum is to help bring all people closer to Jesus in ways that will change their world for good.

The Core Series: The Beginning

It is natural for all human beings to try to come to a better understanding of the world around them. However, unlike God, we know very little about it; and so, we find that we need to base many of our observations upon assumptions about what those observations mean. These assumptions are *core*, because they shape the entire way we view the world.

It should be little surprise, then, that when we attempt to teach another person about a topic, there will be core assumptions that shape the content and manner of that teaching. This should be remembered by those who wish to study Christianity: many Christian learners never consider or examine the assumptions made by those who teach them. As a result, they can be led astray if their teacher has faulty beliefs about the faith.

For example, if a Biblical scholar were an atheist, then their scholarship would inevitably reflect their belief that there is no God. One such popular scholar is Dr. Bart Ehrman, James A. Gray Distinguished Professor of Religious Studies at the University of North Carolina at Chapel Hill, who offers one of his core assumptions (and its logical implication):

"I came to a point where I simply didn't believe there was a God who was active in the world, and that necessarily had implications, because there can't be a miraculous resurrection of Jesus if there's nobody who is performing miracles." [1]

Because of this assumption, Ehrman would reject the claim that an act of God could be considered, or even classified, as an historical event. His worldview is implicitly and explicitly reflected in his writings:

"You've moved from history to faith,' he objects. 'You can show historically that people claimed they saw Jesus alive afterwards, you can draw the conclusion that they probably believed it. But if you yourself agree that Jesus was raised from the dead, you are saying that was an act of God in history. What you are doing is no longer history – it's faith." [2]

Therefore, a scholar such as Ehrman will teach the miracle stories of the resurrection as mere human myth with no historic basis—a conclusion which by his own admission is governed by his starting assumption. If there is no God, then there is no way that a person could miraculously come back to life after three days. There must be some other explanation for the story.

For many secular historians, faith in the rules and conventions of modern history and science preclude any possibility of Jesus' divinity and miracles such as his resurrection. When asked why an historian would not even consider the real possibility that the resurrection actually happened, Dr. Dale Martin, Woolsey Professor Emeritus of Religious Studies, Yale University, responds:

"What can the modern historian say about the historical Jesus and not lose tenure. You can't say Jesus is divine if you are a modern historian. We can't say for example that the resurrection of Jesus is a historical fact. Nobody who accepts modern science can accept that." [3]

The scholarly expositions of the Bible by atheist scholars like Bart Ehrman and Dale Martin are shaped around explanations, propositions and conclusions that merely expand the key core assumption—that there is no God. Unreflective students of scholars like these may unknowingly accept their unspoken and unsupported assumptions. The house built on sand may be quite appealing. But a sharp, critically-minded person will not enter that house without asking some questions first!

Of course, the same argument could sometimes be applied to believing scholars. One cannot escape the fact that thought is always shaped by core assumptions. That's just how it is. And sometimes, people's assumptions change radically over time. This movement from one set of core assumptions to another is the act of *conversion*. Such conversions are often shaped by factors beyond the scope of reasonable argument and thought. As Blase Pascal famously wrote in his *Pensées*,[4] "The heart has its reasons, which reason does not know. We feel it in a thousand things. It is the heart which experiences God, and not the reason. This, then, is faith: God felt by the heart, not by the reason."[4] Bart Ehrman's conversion from believing in God to rejecting God required no less faith than C.S. Lewis' conversion, after many years of rejecting God, he surrendered to belief.

"You must picture me alone in that room at Magdalen, night after night, feeling, whenever my mind lifted even for a second from my work, the steady, unrelenting approach of Him whom I so earnestly desired not to meet. That which I greatly feared had at last come upon me. In the Trinity Term of 1929 I gave in, and admitted that God was God, and knelt and prayed: perhaps, that night, the most dejected and reluctant convert in all England." [5]

Jesus' resurrection, like it or not, is a matter of historic fact. It either happened or it didn't. Our core assumptions can do nothing to change that. Yet, the core beliefs residing deep in the human heart will influence and determine our understanding and view of the world and our significance within it. So let's go to *The Core*.

---

[1] Brierley, Justin, "The Sceptic: Why I Can't Believe The Resurrection." Premier Christianity, May 1, 2014, https://www.premierchristianity.com/Past-Issues/2014/May-2014/The-Sceptic-Why-I-can-t-believe-the-resurrection

[2] Ibid.

[3] Hinge Podcast, Interview with Dale Martin, "#1 It was my job to have answers", December 14, 2017.

[4] Blasé Pascal, Pensées, (E. P. Dutton & Co., Inc..., 1958), Of the Means of Belief, 277-278.

[5] Surprised By Joy, (Harper Collins, 1955), chapter 14, page 266.

INTRODUCTION TO NEW COVENANT AND THE EARLY CHURCH

The Bible is one of the oldest and most popular books in the world. It holds amazing stories, histories, and philosophies, but most people never get the chance to understand the Bible in context. Though the Lord still speaks through biblical passages taken out of context, being able to understand the depth and significance of a verse, chapter, or book builds a firmer foundation for further study and a deeper relationship with the Lord. The educated reader will hear the word of God more clearly and find even more meaning and significance in scripture.

This course aims to provide historical, literary, and theological context for the New Testament in order to strengthen a student's understanding. Rather than move through the books in canonical order, this study will move through the books thematically, focusing on the formation of the Gospel narrative into the early church. The timeline of the early church provided in Acts will serve as a touchstone for understanding the other books.

Nature and origin of the New Testament

Testament is a term that refers to God's special dealings with humanity. The term is synonymous with the word covenant, meaning promise. The first significant divine covenant is the covenant with Moses, which forms the framework of the Old Testament. The New Covenant (or Testament) was prophesied in Jeremiah. The believers in Jesus used the language of Jeremiah to describe the New Covenant, which was not like the covenant made with their ancestors. Instead, it was a covenant that would free humanity from the bondage of sin. While now the mainstream term for the New Covenant, Christians did not use the term New Testament until the 2nd Century.

Jesus never wrote down any of his teachings, and so for a period of time, his teachings survived as oral histories told by disciples. But as the disciples grew old and Christian persecution increased, it became clear that the memory of Jesus' words and deeds needed to be recorded in a more permanent way. The word moved through the apostles to their followers, and they wrote down the Gospel narrative of Jesus. Following the martyrdom of the apostles, there were many letters and sermons outlining and examining the theology of Christianity as well as providing testimony. By 90 A.D., the disciples and their followers had written all the material in the New Testament.

Literary Context

The books of the New Testament vary in form and function, so part of this course will examine the literary structure of each book. Though the whole New Testament revolves around the narrative of Jesus Christ and the birth of Christianity, each book is different. Some books are epistles, like Galatians and Thessalonians, written by the apostle Paul for specific congregations. Some, like James and Hebrews, are written as sermons or theological discourses. The Gospels, Matthew, Mark, Luke, and John, each tell the Gospel story of Jesus in a narrative format. Luke wrote the Book of Acts as a sequel to his Gospel. His Gospel told the story of Jesus while Acts told about the founding of Christianity. Revelation, also called the Apocalypse, was written in a genre similar to the Old Testament prophetic books.

Each book adds something different, and their individual forms inform their contents—one must wonder if the authors of the epistolary books intended their letters to end up as part of the Bible and how that impacted their contents. At first, these early letters and writings were copied and shared beyond their original recipients. As other congregations and church leaders read them, they formed authoritative collections. Then, the early church convened to decide on a specific order and canon of work to call the New Testament. The basis for inclusion in what would become the New Testament was:

- Either the work was written by an apostle or by men closely associated with apostles;

- The communities to whom they were written played a key role in winning acceptance and confirming the authenticity of Christianity.

The term canon, or norm, may have first described the standard of beliefs and practices of the Christian communities before it referred to a collection of writings that became standard. Once the early church decided on the canon for the New Testament, they did not condone any additions. There were other writings and teachings that may have fit the criteria for inclusion, but the early church often used canon rule to disregard these other writings.

Historical Context

A portion of this course will be devoted to helping students understand the complex sociological and historical context both in the time of Jesus and during the formation of the early church. While part of the Bible is historical, most of the historical detail hides in the background of the books. By examining the social tensions and political atmospheres implicit in the texts, the student will gain a greater appreciation for the struggles of the early church and a better grasp on the material itself.

Theological Context and Themes

Despite being a collection of texts written by men, the New Testament is still the word of

God. Peter calls Paul's writings scriptures, as indeed they are:

"And count the patience of our Lord as salvation,
just as our beloved brother Paul also wrote to you according to the wisdom given him,
as he does in all his letters when he speaks in them of these matters.
There are some things in them that are hard to understand,
which the ignorant and unstable twist to their own destruction,
as they do the other Scriptures."
(2 Peter 3:15-16)

The Lord granted the authors of the New Testament with the experiences and knowledge they needed to write His Son's story. Though the major focus of the New Testament is God's promise of salvation through Jesus Christ, there are other theological themes and teachings. The New Testament is more than the Gospel, more than the epistolary sermons, more than the story of the early church. It's the ultimate collection intended to instruct and inspire all those who follow Jesus. Paul writes,

"All Scripture is breathed out by God and profitable for teaching,
for reproof, for correction, and for training in righteousness,
that the man of God may be complete, equipped for every good work."
(2 Timothy 3:16-17)

As you complete this study, consider the practical application of what you learn. Deepen your relationship with the Word, and watch how your relationship with the Lord deepens as well. Take your study to heart, and open your mind to the Gospel and accompanying teachings—even the most knowledgeable student can learn something new that enhances their experience with the Lord.

CHAPTER 1
Salvation Has Come to This House

OBJECTIVE: The maturing Christian will understand the providence of the Gospel and its application to new converts of Jesus from both Jewish and Gentile world views.

CONTEXT STORY OF CORNELIUS IN ACTS

Cornelius was having a relatively normal day until he saw it: an angel of the Lord before him. His jaw dropped, and his heart somersaulted in his chest as he trembled with terror. The angel called him by name, and Cornelius sank to his knees and asked,

"'What is it, Lord?' And he said to him,
'Your prayers and your alms have ascended as a memorial before God.
And now send men to Joppa and bring one Simon who is called Peter. He is lodging with one Simon, a tanner, whose house is by the sea.'"
(Acts 10:4-7)

Then the angel left, and Cornelius called his servants. He asked two servants and one of his soldiers to find Peter, and after he explained everything the angel of God had said, the servants and soldiers set out for Joppa.

Cornelius was a faithful follower of God who gave generously to the poor and prayed daily. As a Roman centurion of the Italian Cohort, he led a hundred men, who admired him as a leader and soldier. Polybius, a Greek historian who chronicled the rise of the Roman Empire, described centurions as the backbone of the Roman army.

Fig. 1 . *Vision of Cornelius the Centurion* (oil on canvas, c. 1664), Eeckhout, Gerbrand van den (1621-1674) The Walters Art Museum, Amsterdam, Netherlands/WikiCommons.

Centurions like Cornelius were natural leaders and commanded their men logically. They weren't men who initiated attacks and opened battles rashly— they knew the cost of battle and only fought when necessary. And yet, centurions like Cornelius were prominent converts to Christianity at a time when confessing Jesus was a dangerous act. They even appear elsewhere in the New Testament: there's a centurion with a dying child who sends for Jesus; and a centurion stood at the foot of the cross as Jesus died. These men, pillars of their communities, were so open to the Gospel of Jesus Christ that the early church often referred to them as saints.

But when Cornelius saw the angel of God, he did not yet know the story of Jesus Christ, despite his reputation as a God-fearer. Instead of worshiping the popular pantheon of gods, Cornelius belonged to a group of Gentiles who worshipped the one true God. He practiced prayer and gave generously, and the Lord rewarded him by telling him to summon Peter so he might know the salvation of Jesus.

Caesarea Maritima and Joppa

Cornelius' group of messengers began their journey by leaving Caesarea Maritima, a major Roman port on the coast of Israel. This city featured public infrastructure built under the direction of Herod the Great. Excavations have revealed Roman coliseums, tracks, theaters, and bathhouses in this important provincial capital.

Fig. 2. *A cenotaph to Marcus Caelius*, a centurion of Legio XVIII, killed at the Battle of Teutoburger Wald.

The messengers traveled about thirty miles south to Joppa, which is famous as the place where Jonah departed. Joppa—now Jaffa—is a natural port, one of the oldest still in use. It is a now a suburb of Tel Aviv.

Caesarea had a less-conservative Gentile government and Joppa had an exclusively Jewish population. Caesarea was the administrative capital of the Roman Empire in the Middle East, and later became a major center of Christianity.

Clean and Unclean

By the time Cornelius' servants and the soldier made it to Joppa, Peter was praying on the roof of Simon the tanner. As he sat in the hot sun, stomach rumbling with hunger, Peter had a vision. He saw all kinds of animals, including reptiles and birds, on a sheet before him, and a voice from the heavens said,

Map 1. *Caesarea and Joppa*
https://www.bible-history.com/maps/palestine_nt_times.html

"'Rise, Peter; kill and eat" (Acts 10:13). Peter recoiled in disgust. He said, "'By no means, Lord; for I have never eaten anything that

is common or unclean.' And the voice came to him a second time, 'What God has made clean, do not call common.'"
(Acts 10:14-15)

After refusing three times, the vision left, and the voice stopped.

This was a challenge to Peter, practicing elements of Judaism despite his belief in Jesus. The Old Covenant had strict rules about food: only certain animals were considered clean enough to eat, and the preparation of food was essential to maintaining its cleanliness. Jewish people were not supposed to eat unclean animals or food lest they be sullied in the eyes of God. They weren't even allowed to interact with people who did not keep their rules, as Gentiles were considered unclean and interacting with an unclean Gentile would jeopardize their cleanliness. Peter followed these laws because he was a Jew. But Peter also saw the miracles of Jesus and believed in the Son of God. He saw that when Jesus touched unclean people, they became clean: he healed a leper with his touch, making him clean of disease. He touched a bleeding woman, and the bleeding stopped, making her clean. Peter saw that when Jesus ministered to a Gentile, that Gentile became clean as well.

Fig. 3. *Peter and Cornelius' men, Acts of the Apostles,* Schnorr von Carolsfeld, Julius (1794-1872) / Lebrecht Authors / Bridgeman Images.

As Peter pondered the meaning of his vision, the Spirit came to him again and told him to greet the messengers at the gate. He did as he was commanded, and after he introduced himself as the one they'd been looking for, the messengers told him of Cornelius' vision and asked him to return with them to Caesarea, as Cornelius was anxiously waiting to hear what Peter had to say. Though Peter knew these servants were Gentiles, he invited them in to be his guests, and the next day, they left Joppa with some of his brothers.

As Peter crossed the threshold into Cornelius' house, Cornelius fell at his feet and began to worship him. Peter pulled Cornelius up and looked at the crowd of family members and close friends Cornelius had assembled. He addressed the crowd, saying,

"'You yourselves know how unlawful it is for a Jew to associate with or to visit anyone of another nation, but God has shown me that I should not call any person common or unclean. So when I was sent for, I came without objection. I ask then why you sent for me.'"
(Acts 10:28-29)

Cornelius told Peter the story of how the angel had appeared to him, sparing no detail, and then said,

"'Now therefore we are all here in the presence of God to hear all that you have been commanded by the Lord.'"
(Acts 10:33)

Peter gathered his thoughts. He began to understand that preaching the story of Jesus would make these Gentiles clean, that if they also believed in Jesus, they would be redeemed in the eyes of God. By sending him to Cornelius, God was telling Peter that it was time to preach to the Gentiles. Peter cleared his throat and began to speak.

Worthy of Redemption

"So Peter opened his mouth and said: 'Truly I understand that God shows no partiality,
but in every nation anyone who fears him and does what is right is acceptable to him.
As for the word that he sent to Israel,
preaching good news of peace through Jesus Christ
(he is Lord of all),
you yourselves know what happened throughout all Judea,
beginning from Galilee after the baptism that John proclaimed:
how God anointed Jesus of Nazareth with the Holy Spirit and with power.
He went about doing good and healing all who were oppressed by the devil, for God was with him.
And we are witnesses of all that he did both in the country of the Jews and in Jerusalem.
They put him to death by hanging him on a tree,
but God raised him on the third day and made him to appear,
not to all the people but to us who had been chosen by God as witnesses,
who ate and drank with him after he rose from the dead.
And he commanded us to preach to the people and to testify
that he is the one appointed by God to be judge of the living and the dead.
To him all the prophets bear witness that everyone who believes in him receives forgiveness of sins through his name.'"
(Acts 10:34-43)

Fig. 4. *Peter preaches in house of Cornelius,* engraving by Gustave Dore, from Holy Scriptures containing Old and New Testaments: Translated from Latin Vulgate by Antonio Martini, with friezes by Enrico Giacomelli, Acts of Apostles 10, Volume 2, 1869-1870 edition / Veneranda Biblioteca Ambrosiana, Milan, Italy / De Agostini Picture Library / Bridgeman Images.

As Peter shared the Gospel with Cornelius, the Holy Spirit fell on all who heard. Even Peter's friends who had heard the Gospel were amazed that the Holy Spirit was given to the Gentiles.

Then Peter asked,

"'Can anyone withhold water for baptizing these people, who have received the Holy Spirit just as we have?' And he commanded them to be baptized in the name of Jesus Christ."
(Acts 10:47-48).

This amazing moment threw the Jewish Christians into a tailspin, but Peter knew God favored sharing the Gospel with the Gentiles.

"When they heard these things they fell silent.
And they glorified God, saying,
'Then to the Gentiles also God has granted repentance that leads to life.'"
(Acts 11:18)

The summary of Peter's speech in Acts is fairly short— so how would he have told the full story of Jesus? The answer lies in the Gospel of Mark.

The Synoptic Gospels

The word Gospel comes from the old English word *godspel*, meaning "glad tidings announced by Jesus," which is a translation of Latin *bona adnuntiatio*. The Latin phrase comes from the Greek word *euangelion*, meaning "reward of good tidings."[1] While it might seem like *euangelion* is also the root for the word evangelist, used now to describe those who tell the good news about Jesus Christ, it is actually derived from the Latin word *evangelista*, which came from the Greek *euangelistes*, meaning "bringer of good news." The Greek word can be broken down even further— *eu-* "good" and *angellein* "announce."[2]

The New Testament accounts of Jesus' life are called Gospels because they are truly "glad tidings." While there are four Gospels, the first

Fig. 5. *St. Peter Baptising the Centurion Cornelius* (oil on canvas), Trevisani, Francesco (1656-1746) / Private Collection / Photo © Christie's Images / Bridgeman Images

---

[1] Online Etymology Dictionary, "Gospel" https://www.etymonline.com/word/gospel

[2] Online Etymology Dictionary, "Evangelist" https://www.etymonline.com/word/evangelist

three considered synoptic gospels because of their similarity. The synoptic Gospels (Mark, Matthew, and Luke) offer a summary of Jesus' life and acts, while the Gospel of John offers a more theological account.

There were two phases of the Gospel before it was written down. Obviously, the public ministry of Jesus, from 30-33 A.D., was the first Gospel, straight from Jesus himself. Once Jesus died on the cross, the second phase began. This is when the apostles preached about Jesus, traveling far and wide to do so. This period lasted until 60 A.D. As the apostles began to die, they wrote down the Gospel themselves or had a companion do it for them. All four gospels were written before 100 A.D.

Two Gospels are attributed to apostles—Matthew and John, while the other two Gospels are attributed to apostolic men—Mark (of Peter) and Luke (of Paul). The synoptic Gospels were interdependent in their formation. They contain many similar teachings and accounts of Jesus in common. John appears to have been written last and independent of the other three Gospels.

APOSTOLIC MARK

When Peter traveled to spread the Gospel, he took a group of fellow believers with him. Among his party was a man named Mark, who often served as his interpreter and had traveled with Paul before. Mark was the son of a woman named Mary who lived in Jerusalem, and Paul fled to her house after an angel released him from Herod's prison. This is presumably when Mark became involved with the early church. Mark joined Paul and his cousin Barnabas on their first missionary journey. However, Mark deserted them during the trip and returned to Jerusalem. Disappointed with Mark's desertion, Paul would not allow Mark to rejoin them, so Barnabas and Mark then departed to minister in Cyprus while Paul chose Silas to join him in Syria and Cilicia.

Later, Mark joined Peter in Rome. The two became close as they traveled and spread the word of the Lord, and Mark became like a son to Peter. As translator, Mark heard the Gospel over and over, and every time Peter told the story, Mark internalized how Peter told it. When Mark wrote the story down in 60 A.D., it's likely that he wrote it almost exactly as Peter repeated it.

The Occasion for the Gospel

Mark wrote the Gospel of Mark to capture the preaching and teaching of the apostle Peter. The early Christians knew they would not have the apostles with them much longer, and they knew they needed to record the way the apostles spoke about Jesus.

Clement of Alexandria (150-215 A.D.) in his Hypotyposeis says the Christians in Rome asked Mark to record Peter's message: "When Peter had preached the Gospel publicly in Rome ... those who were present ... besought Mark, since he had followed him (Peter) for a long time and remembered the things that had been spoken, to write out the things that had been said; and when he had done this he gave the Gospel to those who asked him. When Peter learned of it later, he neither obstructed nor commended."

Though Clement says Peter neither obstructed nor commended Mark's writings, it is possible that Mark was commissioned by Peter to write the Gospel.

"I think it right, as long as I am in this body,
to stir you up by way of reminder,
since I know that the putting off of my body will be soon,
as our Lord Jesus Christ made clear to me.
And I will make every effort so that after my departure
you may be able at any time to recall these things."
(2 Peter 1:13-15)

Peter used assistants to write for him, including Silvanus (also translated Silas) whom Peter refers to as a "faithful brother" (1 Peter 5:2). Mark served in a similar capacity in Rome as an interpreter or translator for Peter. It's widely accepted that Mark wrote this Gospel, and sources in the early church confirm Mark as the author.

The first church father to mention Mark as author was Papias, the bishop in Asia Minor around 130 A.D. Eusebius, a bishop of Caesarea and prolific writer of early church history, quotes Papias' attribution in his Ecclesiastical History, written around 325 A.D.: "Mark, having become the interpreter of Peter, wrote down accurately, though not in order, whatsoever he remembered of the things said or done by Christ. For he neither heard the Lord nor followed him, but afterward, as I said, he followed Peter, who adapted his teaching to the needs of his hearers."

'Interpreter' likely means Mark translated Peter's Aramaic speech into Greek or Latin. In this role, Mark would have had an intimate knowledge of Peter's stories and experience with Jesus.

Fig. 6. *Eusebius* (260-340 AD), Ecclesiastical Histories II.15

Social Climate

Another reason for recording the Gospels was to encourage the Gentile Christians who were suffering persecution during Nero's reign. The 60s A.D. in Rome were a really tough time for Christians. Before Nero, Roman law recognized Judaism as a permitted religion, a *religio licita*, and Jewish Christians were not persecuted. But when the Roman authorities realized the new movement included Gentiles—non-Jews—and was a different religion than Judaism, it was no longer permitted. This ushered in a time of Christian persecution.

In the year 59, the Emperor Nero became more and more unpredictable and obsessed with asserting himself as the complete lord over his people. Paul arrived in Rome the next year, preaching that Jesus is Lord—not Nero. When a great fire burned Rome in 64, and Nero blamed the new Christian sect, increasing persecution on all who followed Christ. Mark's Gospel emphasizes the crucifixion of Jesus and the persecution of the disciples. He wanted the readers to know what it meant to take up their cross and follow Jesus.

Mark's Gospel makes it clear that Jesus had suffered the difficulties and temptations faced by the Roman Christians. He was condemned unjustly in a Roman court. He was beaten by Roman soldiers. And he was crucified on a Roman cross.

But through his suffering, Jesus was victorious. And Mark wanted to assure his readers that if they followed Jesus faithfully, they would be conquerors, too.

Original Audience

Papias, Clement, and Irenaeus all thought that Mark wrote his Gospel in Italy, and some specifically identified Rome as the birthplace of Mark's book. Irenaeus said the Gospel of Mark was written "when Peter and Paul were preaching the Gospel in Rome and founding the church there." He adds, "After their departure, Mark, Peter's disciple, has himself delivered to us in writing the substance of Peter's preaching."

In Peter's first letter, Mark is identified as a disciple of Peter in Rome:

"She who is at Babylon, who is likewise chosen,
sends you greetings, and so does Mark, my son."
(1 Peter 5:13)

Mark's Gospel explains Jewish customs to his readers, which means that his audience was likely Gentile. He needed to explain certain things, otherwise they might be confused. For example, he parenthetically explains hand washing and dish cleaning traditions, and he points out geographic details that would not be known by a largely Gentile audience.

He also translates Aramaic terms into Greek and often uses Latin words transliterated into Greek, indicating that his readers understood Latin, a language spoken almost exclusively in Italy.

Latin Translations Referenced in the Gospel of Mark

Mark 4:27: *modios* = Lat. *modius* (a measure)
Mark 5:9, 15: *legiôn* = Lat. *legio* (legion)
Mark 6:27: *spekoulator* = Lat. *speculator* (guard)
Mark 6:37: *dênariôn* = Lat. *denarius* (a Roman coin)
Mark 7:4: *xestês* = Lat. *sextarius* (container)
Mark 12:14: *kênsos* = Lat. *census* (tribute money)
Mark 15:15: *phragellan* = Lat. *fragellare* (to whip)
Mark 15:39, 44-45: *kenturiôn* = Lat. *centurio* (centurion)

In his passion narrative, Mark unnecessarily (from a literary point of view) identifies Alexander and Rufus as the sons of Simon the Cyrene (Mark 15:21). The probable reason is that his readers would recognize their names, and this recognition would make the story feel more relevant and current. The clues that point towards Mark having a Gentile audience supports the theory that his Gospel is as Peter would have told it as Peter frequently preached to Gentile groups.

Structure and Content

The Gospel of Mark

1	2 — Identity of Jesus			3 Belief	4 — Passion of Jesus			5
Gospel Prologue (1:1-13)	Cycle 1 Early Galilee (1:14-3:6)	Cycle 2 Later Galilee (3:7-6:13)	Cycle 3 Leaving Galilee (6:14-8:26)	Confession of Peter (8:27-30)	Approaching Jerusalem (8:31-10:52)	Ministry in Jerusalem (11:1-13:37)	Death in Jerusalem (14:1-15:47)	Gospel Epilogue (16)

The structure of Mark's Gospel follows the general pattern of Peter's preaching to Cornelius' Gentile household as recorded in Acts. The book begins with Jesus' baptism and his early preaching in Galilee, and like Peter's speech in Acts, Mark's Gospel focuses on the miracles of Jesus and the good works he did. Using a narrative structure, Mark tracks Jesus' travels immediately from his baptism until his resurrection. His main rhetorical choice is the use of the word "immediately," which appears some 40 times to convey the need for haste and fervency for the reader in accepting the message of the Gospel.

THE GOSPEL OF MARK

The Gospel of Mark begins very simply and profoundly with:

"The beginning of the Gospel of Jesus Christ, the Son of God."
(Mark 1:1)

The word beginning is significant. In Jesus Christ, the world is experiencing a new creation. For that reason, Mark calls his book good news (Greek: *euangelion*). The long-awaited hope of Israel for the Messianic Age is breaking forth in Jesus (see Isaiah 52:7, 61:1-3).

The title Son of God is a royal one that identifies Jesus as the messianic King of Israel. And in the context of the Roman Empire, it names Jesus as the rightful ruler of the entire world—even over Caesar!

John the Baptist

Mark dives into the story of Jesus, skipping his birth and going straight to his baptism. Because Mark's Gospel is written primarily for Gentile Christians living in Italy, Old Testament quotations are used more sparingly than in the Gospel of Matthew. However, Mark quotes a compilation of prophecies to identify John the Baptist as the divinely ordained foreteller of the messiah who would prepare the way.

The nature of John's preparation was a call to repentance through moral and spiritual transformation symbolized by re-entering the Jordan River as entrance to the Promised Land.

Jesus' baptism is the inauguration of the messianic age, and this is where the Gospel begins. Mark uses dramatic language where the heavens were torn open. Many Hebrews believed the heavens had been shut to them and that God had withdrawn. But with Jesus' baptism, the Holy Spirit was back, powerfully so. The divine voice identifying Jesus as *"my Son"* signifies that Jesus is the Son of God

Fig. 7. *Jesus dans le desert, soumis a la tentation du diable - The temptation of Christ - Satan tempted Jesus* - engraving by Gustave Dore - later colouring / © Leemage / Bridgeman Images.

by divine authority and not by the self-exalted will of man. As the Gospel unfolds, many will agree with this central claim of the Gospel that *"Truly this man was the Son of God!"* (Mark 15:39).

The Temptation

Like the dramatic language of the heavens tearing open with Jesus' baptism, Mark describes how the Holy Spirit immediately drove Jesus into the wilderness. In this case, the drama points to the war between God's son and God's adversary, Satan. As Paul wrote,

"For we do not wrestle against flesh and blood, but against the rulers, against the authorities, against the cosmic powers over this present darkness, against the spiritual forces of evil in the heavenly places."
(Ephesians 6:12)

For forty days, Jesus wandered the wilderness, tempted by Satan. He lived among the wild animals, and the angels ministered to him. The mention of wild animals could have been for very practical reasons for the Roman Christians who had seen fellow believers martyred in the Coliseum. The Roman historian Tacitus spoke of Nero's savagery in his persecution of Christians in the 60s A.D., "They were covered with the hides of wild beasts and torn to pieces by dogs." The narrative transitions from Jesus in the wilderness to the beginning of his ministry.

CYCLE ONE: Jesus' Early Galilean Ministry

Mark tells the story of Jesus' ministry in three narrative cycles—an early Galilean ministry, a later Galilean ministry, and then the withdrawal from Galilee.

Mark describes the beginning of Jesus' ministry, summarizing the content and expected response to the Gospel:

"The time is fulfilled, and the kingdom of God is at hand; repent and believe in the gospel."
(Mark 1:15)

Fig. 8. *The Calling of Four Disciples.* Illustration for The Life of the Master (Hodder and Stoughton, 1901).

Jesus' call to repentance and belief in the kingdom of God (by believing its king) is not only issued to his first hearers. It also is a sovereign summons to all who read Mark's Gospel.

The First Responders

Two fishermen, Simon (Peter) and Andrew (his brother) responded first to Jesus' call. James and John, the sons of Zebedee, followed them. Peter, James, and John would form the inner circle of 12 disciples, and their vocation of fishing would now be put to use for the kingdom.

"Follow me, and I will make you become fishers of men. And immediately they left their nets and followed him." (Mark 1:17-18)

Authority in Word and Deed

Jesus traveled with his newfound disciples to Capernaum, where he began to teach in the synagogue. The people immediately recognized a distinction between Jesus and the other religious leaders: He taught them as one who had authority. As he taught, a man with an unclean spirit pushed through the crowd and shouted at Jesus, identifying him as the *"Holy One of God"* (Mark 1:24). Jesus silenced the man and commanded the demon to leave him. As the man convulsed and cried out, the unclean spirit exited his body, and the witnesses of this exchange whispered among themselves, wondering who this amazing teacher could be. The word of mouth traveled quickly in those times, and soon everyone in Galilee had heard what happened that Sabbath in the synagogue.

The distinguishing characteristic of Jesus is authority (Greek: *exousia*). Jesus will continue to exercise this authority over the scribes, the demons, and diseases. After Jesus cast out the demon in the synagogue, he went to the house of Simon and Andrew, where Simon's mother suffered from a fever. By taking her by the hand, the fever left her, and she was healed. That night, the house was surrounded by people bringing their sick and possessed relatives to Jesus. He healed those who were ill, and he exorcised all the unclean spirits. It's interesting to note that Jesus would not allow the demons to speak—they knew he was the son of God, but he did not want people to know that yet. He knew that once his true identity was revealed, it would be difficult to preach openly.

A man riddled with leprosy approached Jesus, begging for healing. Jesus took pity on the man and healed him. He told the man not to tell anyone about his miraculous healing, but as soon as the former leper left Jesus, he told everyone he could. Because word of Jesus' power had spread, he couldn't enter a town without being mobbed by people asking for healing.

In the people's eyes, the works of authority and power overshadowed the Gospel. Jesus refocused the disciples by reasserting the primacy of preaching about God's Kingdom.

Confrontations with Religious Leaders

The talk about God's Kingdom and the displays of power became increasingly threatening to the Jewish leaders. When Jesus was preaching to a group in his home, four men lowered their paralytic friend into the room from the roof because it was too crowded to enter through the door. Jesus again asserts his divine authority in pronouncing the forgiveness of sins upon the paralytic, but he knew the scribes sitting among them were questioning his right to offer forgiveness, wondering, *"Who can forgive sins but God alone?"* (Mark 2:7). To validate his authority to forgive sins, Jesus heals the man of his paralysis with the command of royal authority: *"I say to you, rise, pick up your bed, and go home."* (Mark 2:11)

The people continued to be amazed, but this was just the beginning of the confrontation with the scribes and Pharisees. They questioned his fellowship with tax collectors and sinners, and his celebrations instead of fasting, but Jesus reminded them,

"Those who are well have no need of a physician, but those who are sick. I came not to call the righteous, but sinners."
(Mark 2:17)

Fig. 9. *Christ Heals the Paralytic*, c.1570 (oil on canvas), Tintoretto, Jacopo Robusti (1518-94) / Scuola Grande di San Rocco, Venice, Italy / Cameraphoto Arte Venezia / Bridgeman Images.

Though the scribes and Pharisees had many criticisms of Jesus, the primary confrontation came over Jesus' claim to have sovereignty over the Sabbath.

The Radical Conversion of James, the Brother of Jesus:

James, the brother of Jesus Christ, was a hardline skeptic about his brother. However, he was radically converted after witnessing the risen Jesus. In the Gospels of Mark and John, his, and his family's, position is well documented.

In Mark 3:21, Jesus' family thinks he has lost his mind. In John 7:5, we read this, **"For not even his brothers believed in him."** *See also, Mark 6:2-4 and John 19:24-27*

The conversion of James is seen in Christian apologetics as one of the most significant testimonies to the resurrection of Jesus and speaks to the historicity of the actual event. James went on to become one of the great leaders of the early church and suffered martyrdom for his belief in the divine nature of his brother, Jesus the Messiah.

Lord of the Sabbath

One Sabbath, Jesus and his disciples were walking though the grain fields. As they walked, the disciples began to pick heads of grain. The Pharisees saw this and grew angry, questioning the lawfulness of their actions, as it was considered unlawful to work on the Sabbath. Jesus began his rebuttal by reminding them of David, who, as the future king of Israel, had the authority to eat the bread of Presence in the temple (1 Samuel 21:1). The second point he makes is that the Sabbath is a gift for humanity, not oppression over humanity. But the most significant claim was this: *"The Son of Man is Lord even of the Sabbath."* (Mark 2:28)

The Lord of the Sabbath is God, and Jesus was identifying himself as God. Mark's indirect story line asserts the divinity of Jesus all along with Jesus exercising authority in teaching, preaching and healing, forgiving sins and driving out demons. The religious leaders already have accused him once of blaspheming (Mark 2:7). One day, when Jesus entered the synagogue, he saw a man with a withered hand. Noting the Pharisee's close watch, he asked them, *"Is it lawful on the Sabbath to do good or to do harm, to save a life or to kill?"* (Mark 3:4). Then he healed the man's hand. The healing of a man's withered hand on the Sabbath sealed their animosity and desire to destroy Jesus, and the Pharisees ran out to consult with the pseudo-royal establishment, the Herodians.

CYCLE TWO: Jesus' Later Galilean Ministry

Jesus continues to engage the demonic forces with power and authority. The demons know exactly who Jesus is: The Son of God. But Jesus would not have his mission thwarted by evil agendas and timing, so when great crowds of those in need of healing pressed around him, he strictly ordered the demons to be silent, to not make him known (Mark 3:12).

With the appointment of the 12 apostles, we see a tension developing between the family of birth and the family of God. Jesus' own family thinks he has gone out of his mind. The scribes accused Jesus of being a prince of demons, a possessed man, a satanic deceiver; and though Jesus rebuked them, some members of his family certainly doubted Jesus' identity.

When his mother and brothers came to talk to him, Jesus said,

"'Who are my mother and my brothers?' And looking about those who sat around him, he said, 'Here are my mother and brothers! For whoever does the will of God, he is my brother and sister and mother."
(Mark 3:33-35).

Whether calling him a lunatic or a satanic deceiver, the children of Israel were missing the Kingdom of God.

The Command to Listen!

Fig. 10. *Christ Stilling the Tempest*, illustration for 'The Life of Christ', c.1886-94 (w/c & gouache on paperboard), Tissot, James Jacques Joseph (1836-1902) / Brooklyn Museum of Art, New York, USA / Bridgeman Images.

Jesus' family and the scribes rejected him because they did not listen! The way Jesus preached required not only close listening, but thoughtfulness as well.

He used parables to convey his message, so whoever heard his teachings needed to consider seriously what he said in order to understand. The Parable of the Sower is a parable about listening— the seed is the Word, and growing conditions represent the reception of the word. It explains why some believe and respond to the Word and others do not. After he preached the Parable of the Sower, the disciples asked him about it. Jesus explained it to them, making the metaphor clear, but he seldom fully explained his parables to the disciples. The Parable of the Lamp speaks to the call of the kingdom to speak the truth— just as one would not hide a lamp under a basket, one should not keep the Gospel to themselves but instead share it. The Parable of the Mustard Seed reveals the temporal-bound and progressive nature of the kingdom of God.

The emphasis in this section of Mark is on hearing and understanding. Parables would be very helpful for spreading the kingdom in Rome, especially as Christians experienced more and more persecution. As Jesus did, the disciples would proclaim the Word through parables, secretly explaining the deeper meaning to committed disciples privately.

Divine Authority Over Nature

As Jesus and the disciples slept on the boat, a great storm arose, causing water to crash over the sides of the boat. The disciples were full of fear, and they woke Jesus. He commanded the sea and wind to be still, and the storm stopped.

The calming of the storm demonstrates Jesus' divine authority over nature. The disciples realize that the one in the boat was more fearsome than the chaotic power of wind and sea outside the boat. The reader is left to wrestle with the question: *"Who then is this, that even the wind and the sea obey him?"* (Mark 4:41)

Fig. 11. *Jesus driving out demons into a herd of swine* (wall painting), Goul, Philippos (fl.1494) / Church of St. Mamas, Louvaras, Cyprus / Sonia Halliday Photographs / Bridgeman Images.

Divine Authority Over Demons and Death

Three incidents confirm Jesus' authority over the unclean. The first is the man with the unclean spirit (Mark 5:2). There was a man who had lived among the tombs, tortured by a legion of demons. He broke out of every shackle and chain and spent his days crying out and cutting himself. When the possessed man saw Jesus, he threw himself at his feet, begging for mercy. Jesus powerfully drove the demonic legion out of the man and into a herd of two thousand pigs that rushed off a cliff and drowned in the sea. The man was healed, and everyone in the city and countryside came to see what Jesus had done. When they saw the previously possessed man sitting at peace and whole, they felt afraid. This section of Mark focuses on Jesus' war with the evil legions and his power in driving out the unclean spirits.

When Jesus crossed the sea, a ruler of the synagogue met him at the shore. He begged him to save his daughter who was nearly dead, and so Jesus went with him. On his way to save the daughter, he encountered a woman who had bled for 12 years. She had spent all her money trying to find a cure, and she recognized Jesus' power. As he walked by, she reached out and touched his garment hem, knowing that she would be healed. When Jesus called out to see who had touched him, she fearfully confessed herself to him, telling him her whole story. Jesus healed her for her faith.

But as he was talking with the bleeding woman, a messenger came from the ruler's house. He tearfully told the ruler that his daughter was dead. But Jesus pressed on toward the ruler's house, charging them all to have faith despite what the messenger had said. When they arrived at the house, the servants and family were wailing with grief, but Jesus told them the girl was only sleeping. He went to the girl and told her to get up, and she got up, as though she had only been asleep. He told them to tell no one about this miracle.

Disbelief and Dispersion

In Jesus' hometown of Nazareth, the people tried to reduce him to simply being a carpenter and son of Mary. They gossiped about him and took offense to Jesus' work. Jesus marveled at them for their unbelief (Mark 6:5).

Jesus makes a major shift in focus after the rejection in Nazareth. He sent out his disciples two by two, giving them the authority to cast out demons and heal the ill. Soon after he sent out the twelve, King Herod beheaded John the Baptist, whom he had imprisoned. The disciples took his body and laid it in a tomb. It is at this point that Jesus begins to withdraw from active ministry in Galilee. The focus is turning gradually toward intensification of persecution and the eventuality of the cross.

CYCLE THREE: Withdrawal from Galilee

Jesus began to seek a desolate place to withdraw with his disciples, but the crowds followed them. Jesus was filled with compassion, *"because they were like sheep without a shepherd"* (Mark 6:34). He taught the crowd of 5,000 people until the sun sank low in the sky, and the crowd became hungry. Though the disciples only have two fish and five loaves of bread, Jesus blessed it, and the small rations multiplied into enough to feed the whole crowd. That act of provision demonstrated that Jesus would provide for them as Yahweh provided for his people in the wilderness.

Fig. 13. *The Multiplication of loaves and fishes,* c.1575 (oil on canvas), Tintoretto, Jacopo Robusti (1518-94) / Scuola Grande di San Rocco, Venice, Italy / Bridgeman Images.

After the sermon ended, Jesus sent the disciples ahead of him to cross the sea to Bethsaida while he dispersed the crowd. The disciples sailed slowly against the wind, wondering how Jesus would get to the boat now that they were in the middle of the water. Deep in the night, they saw a figure walking on the water, and they trembled with fear, thinking it was a ghost. But as the apparition got closer, it called out, and they realized that it was Jesus. Jesus climbed into the boat, and they were astounded (Mark 6:45-52). Though they had seen Jesus' divine works, they again failed to understand that God was in their presence in the person of Jesus.

Pharisees Confronted: Clean vs. Unclean

Confrontation with the Pharisees intensified when they noticed some of the disciples not washing their hands in accordance with Jewish tradition. They accused Jesus of profaning the laws of God by refusing to follow the Jewish traditions, but Jesus replied that the Pharisees failed to understand the point of God's laws. He challenged Jewish tradition by saying that it is not what a person consumes that defiles him but what comes out. Jesus says,

"What comes out of a person is what defiles him. For from within, out of the heart of man, come evil thoughts, sexual immorality, theft, murder, adultery, coveting, wickedness, deceit, sensuality, envy, slander, pride, foolishness. All these evil things come from within, and they defile a person."
(Mark 7:20-23)

The ultimate aim was not external cleanliness but internal holiness of the heart. In the new covenant, Jesus would make all who believed clean.

Savior of All

When Jesus left the confrontation with the Pharisees, he encountered a Syro-Phonecian woman who begged him to deliver her daughter from an unclean spirit. She was a Gentile, so when she asked this, Jesus replied,

"Let the children be fed first, for it is not right to take the children's bread and throw it to the dogs.' But she answered him, 'Yes, Lord; yet even the dogs under the table eat the children's crumbs.'"
(Mark 7:27-28).

And for her faith, Jesus cleared the demon from her daughter.

He then traveled to the Decapolis where people brought him a Gentile who could not hear or speak, and they begged him to heal the man. Jesus took him away from the crowd and opened his ears and released his tongue. Though Jesus told the people to tell no one of this healing, those who saw could not contain their amazement and spread the word of Jesus' power.

With Jesus' healing of the Syro-Phoenecian woman and the deaf and dumb beggar in the Gentile Decapolis, he showed that he is Lord and Savior of all people, not just the Jews. This all would have particular significance to Mark's Roman hearers.

The disciples continued to stumble in understanding the message after Jesus feeds the 5,000 and the 4,000. Despite Jesus' ability to provide for crowds of thousands, the disciples were worried that they only had one loaf of bread on their boat. He asked them, what is the significance of the leftover baskets, 12 and then seven? But they did not understand that Jesus is the Lord of Israel and the Lord of all creation. Jesus is Yahweh, the creator and giver of life, and Mark has been providing evidence of Jesus' divinity as part of the narrative.

The Apostles' Affirmation of the Messiah

Until this point in the Gospel story, Mark has been telling the good news of Jesus' teaching, preaching, and healing. Through Jesus' words and powerful deeds, the authority and presence of God is manifest. The repeated question asked throughout the story is: Who is this?

Fig. 12. *A woman of Canaan* (colour litho), Copping, Harold (1863-1932) / Private Collection / © Look and Learn / Bridgeman Images.

Several answers are proposed: He is Elijah or he is a prophet (said the crowds, Mark 6:15), he is John the Baptist raised from the dead (said Herod, Mark 6:16), he is out of his mind (said his family, Mark 3:21), he has a demon (said the religious leaders, Mark 3:22), and he is the Son of God (said the demons, Mark 3:11).

The question raised by Jesus himself to his disciples is: Who do people say that I am? And: Who do you say that I am? Peter affirms, *"You are the Christ."* (Mark 8:29)

The affirmation of Peter is the turning point of the Gospel, when Mark explains what it means to truly see and follow Jesus.

Seeing on the Way to the Cross

As Jesus journeys to Bethsaida, Caesarea Philippi, Jericho and Jerusalem, he instructs his disciples. He begins to explain that the Son of God will suffer many things in the coming days: rejection by the elders and chief priests, state-sanctioned murder, and finally, resurrection after three days. Peter's previous confession reveals that he only has partial insight into Jesus. The disciples understand who Jesus is as the Christ, the Messiah, but what they do not perceive what Jesus came to do. Likewise, they are beginning to understand their role as Jesus' disciples, but they do not understand or see what it truly means to follow him.

This section is built around three passion predictions, each of which is followed by the misunderstanding of one or more of the disciples and further teaching by Jesus about the requirements of true discipleship.

First Passion Prediction

"And he began to teach them that the Son of Man must suffer many things and be rejected by the elders and the chief priests and the scribes and be killed, and after three days rise again."
(Mark 8:31)

Peter misunderstands and rebukes Jesus, who rebukes Peter in return.

"If anyone would come after me, let him deny himself
and take up his cross and follow me.
For whoever would save his life will lose it,
but whoever loses his life for my sake and the gospel's will save it."
(Mark 8:34-35)

Second Passion Prediction

Six days later, Jesus took Peter, James, and John to the top of a mountain, where Jesus was transfigured in radiance. They saw Elijah and Moses, and a voice from the sky identified Jesus, saying *"This is my beloved son; listen to him"* (Mark 9:7). The disciples were amazed, but Jesus commanded them to not speak of it until after he had risen. This is an important moment because it shows direct divine approval of Jesus for a second time.

When they came down the mountain, there was a great crowd with the other disciples. A man came to Jesus and asked him to throw an unclean spirit out of his son, though the disciples had already tried and failed. Jesus rebuked the man for his wavering faith, and he cast the spirit out of the boy. As they traveled through Galilee, Jesus once again foretold his death.

"The Son of Man is going to be delivered into the hands of men, and they will kill him. And when he is killed, after three days he will rise."
(Mark 9:31)

The disciples misunderstand, arguing who among them was the greatest. Jesus teaches: *"If anyone would be first, he must be last of all and servant of all."* (Mark 9:35)

Third Passion Prediction

As Jesus and his disciples traveled, Jesus continued to teach. When they were walking to Jerusalem, Jesus predicted his fate a third time.

"See, we are going up to Jerusalem,
and the Son of Man will be delivered over to the chief priests and the scribes, and they will condemn him to death and deliver him over to the Gentiles.
And they will mock him and spit on him, and flog him and kill him. And after three days he will rise."
(Mark 10:33-34)

James and John misunderstood and asked for seats of honor when Jesus is in glory. Jesus teaches:

"But it shall not be so among you.
But whoever would be great among you must be your servant,
and whoever would be first among you must be slave of all.
For even the Son of Man came not to be served but to serve,
and to give his life as a ransom for many."
(Mark 10:43-44)

The Suffering Messiah

When Jesus and his disciples got close to Jerusalem, Jesus sent two of his disciples to fetch a colt. They brought Jesus the young donkey, on which no one had ever ridden, and they threw their cloaks over its back and on the road. As Jesus rode the colt into Jerusalem, those who saw him spread their cloaks and large leaves on the ground before him, shouting *"Hosanna! Blessed is he who comes in the name of the Lord! Blessed is the coming kingdom of our father David! Hosanna in the highest!"* (Mark 11:9-10). The coming of the Messiah to his temple is marked with a triumphal entry and joyful acceptance.

Later, Jesus inspects a fig tree, symbolic of the temple. He expects fruit and finds nothing but leaves. He condemns the fig tree, and later he condemns the temple, which was turned from a house of prayer into a den of robbers. He threw out all the money changers and pigeon sellers, rebuking them as they ran. While the people were astonished at Jesus' teaching, the religious leaders resolved to destroy him.

As the conflict with the religious leaders intensified, they sought to trap Jesus with difficult questions about the issues of the day—whether to pay taxes, theological debates on the resurrection, and the Law of Moses.

The tables turned when they realized that Jesus not only answered their questions well, but also had a good question of his own.

"And as Jesus taught in the temple, he said,
'How can the scribes say that the Christ is the son of David?
David himself, in the Holy Spirit, declared,
"The Lord said to my Lord,
Sit at my right hand, until I put your enemies under your feet."
David himself calls him Lord. So how is he his son?'
And the great throng heard him gladly."
(Mark 12:35-37)

The royal riddle concerning David is at the heart of Mark's Gospel—Jesus is both the messianic human king and God! This is precisely the conclusion of Peter's first sermon on Pentecost:

"Let all the house of Israel therefore know for certain
that God has made him both Lord and Christ,
this Jesus whom you crucified."
(Acts 2:36)

The Judgment of the Temple and the Second Coming

After answering all of the scribes and Pharisee's questions, one of the disciples asked Jesus what would become of the great temple. Jesus told him that the great buildings would be reduced to rubble. As he sat across from the temple on the Mount of Olives with his disciples, he warned them that not only would there be false prophets, but also be wars, earthquakes, and famine. He told them they would be beaten and hated. Understanding the Olivet discourse—Jesus' warning to his followers that they will suffer tribulation and persecution before the ultimate triumph of the Kingdom of God—recognizes that Jesus is speaking about different events. He uses the language of these things for the fall and judgment of Jerusalem. He also uses the same language for the parousia, or second coming where the heavens and earth will be destroyed.

The Last Two Days

The final two days leading to Jesus' crucifixion are dark days. The people who should have embraced Jesus as their Lord seek to arrest and destroy him. But before any of that could happen, a woman in Bethany anointed Jesus with a pure and costly oil. Those who saw her pour it over Jesus' head scolded her for her wastefulness, but Jesus stopped them and thanked the woman, saying *"She has done what she could; she has anointed my body beforehand for burial"* (Mark 14:8). Once again, Jesus alluded to his upcoming suffering and death. Soon after the anointing, Judas Iscariot went to the chief priests and conspired against Jesus. They promised him money, and in return, he promised his betrayal.

On the first day of Passover, Jesus sat around the table with his twelve disciples, and as they ate together, Jesus said one of them would betray him. They started to get upset and questioned themselves, but Jesus gave no more details. Then, taking the bread and blessing it, he broke it and passed it among them, saying *"Take; this is my body"* (Mark 14:22). He took a cup and blessed it, and then they each drank from it. He said to them,

"This is my blood of the covenant, which is poured out for many. Truly, I say to you, I will not drink again of the fruit of the vine until that day when I drink it new in the kingdom of God."
(Mark 14:24-25).

The chapter's focus is Jesus' association of his own death with the Passover. His body and blood would be the covenant that would satisfy God's judgment and cover with forgiveness the sins of a sinful people. Though Jesus warned the disciples they would fall away in the days to come, Peter remained steadfast in his belief that he would stay strong with Jesus. But Jesus predicted that Peter would deny him three times before the second cock crowed. They all went to the Garden of Gethsemane to pray, and Jesus asked the disciples to stay awake with him. But one by one, they drifted off to slumber. It's then that Jesus asks if God can spare his fate:

"Abba, Father, all things are possible for you.
Remove this cup from me.
Yet not what I will, but what you will."
(Mark 14:36)

The need for Jesus to drink the cup is seen in the sin and failings of everyone in the chapter—the Jewish leaders, the soldiers, Judas, and the disciples. When Jesus returned to the group and found them all asleep, he rebuked them, but then Judas walked into the clearing. Jesus knew it was time for his betrayal, suffering, and death, and he went with the soldiers to carry out his fate.

THE TRIALS: Jewish and Gentile

The failure of the Jewish leadership is sandwiched between the accounts of Peter's failure in his denials. It is easy to wonder whether Peter saw his own denials as equivalent to the failures of the Jewish Sanhedrin.

The Sanhedrin high court of justice trial involved bearing witness or offering testimony. False witnesses and testimony were brought against Jesus, but he would not answer their accusations. He stood and listened as the high priest became more and more agitated. Yet when asked directly whether he was the Messiah, he affirmed it with clarity:

"I am, and you will see the Son of Man seated at the right hand of Power, and coming with the clouds of heaven."
(Mark 14:62)

The high priest jumped up in his chair and demanded the council charge Jesus with blasphemy and condemn him to death, which they did. Jesus was rejected not on the basis of false testimony but on the basis of his own true testimony about himself. As the guards beat Jesus and the crowds spat on him, Peter denied him three times in the square outside, just as Jesus predicted. The Romans and the crowds exchanged the murderer Bar-Abba (Hebrew: father's son) for Jesus. Ironically, the King of the Jews is the Bar-Abba, the Son of God. With the substitution, the ransom is exchanged, a son for a son. The King of the Jews will die in the place of his people.

The Crucifixion, Death and Burial of Jesus

The central theme of Jesus' crucifixion is salvation, although the passers-by derided him (Greek: blasphemed) saying:

"You who would destroy the temple and rebuild it in three days, save yourself, and come down from the cross!
So also the chief priests with the scribes mocked him to one another, saying, 'He saved others; he cannot save himself. Let the Christ, the King of Israel, come down now from the cross that we may see and believe.'
Those who were crucified with him also reviled him."
(Mark 15:28-32)

Again, with tremendous irony to the believing reader, the priests and scribes suggest they will only see and believe if Jesus comes down from the cross. However, as the Gospel has been teaching, it is in dying and picking up the cross that salvation comes to the world.

Jesus will not save himself because he chooses to save us! He first was offered sweet wine mixed with myrrh, designed to dull pain and consciousness. Jesus refused this offering. The second offering was sour wine, designed to prolong pain and consciousness. Jesus accepted this offering. He would take no shortcuts to redemption.

Jesus' body takes the place of Jerusalem, the temple, and all its sacrifices. Mark structures his account of the cross to mirror the lament of the destruction of Jerusalem. *"And the curtain of the temple was torn in two, from top to bottom."* (Mark 15:38)

In being completely forsaken by God and by giving up his life as a ransom for many, Jesus secured salvation and blessing for all who truly see and believe in him. The truth is seeing and believing in a crucified King of the Jews and a crucified Son of God.

Where the passers-by, the chief priests and scribes, and those crucified with him completely stumbled over the cross and failed to see and believe, the Roman centurion saw the way Jesus breathed his last and confessed true belief: *"Truly this man was the Son of God!"* (Mark 15:39)

Fig. 14. *The Confession of Saint Longinus,* illustration from 'The Life of Our Lord Jesus Christ', 1886-94 (w/c over graphite on paper), Tissot, James Jacques Joseph (1836-1902) / Brooklyn Museum of Art, New York, USA / Purchased by Public Subscription / Bridgeman Images.

The call to the reader of Mark is to see and believe in the true salvation that comes through the sacrifice and offering of himself by the Son of God.

Jesus' Burial

The burial story provides confirmation of Jesus' death. Joseph of Arimathea is among the first believing witnesses to Jesus' death and burial. When he asked for Jesus' body, Pilate was surprised that Jesus had already died. He summoned a centurion to confirm it. This makes them unbelieving witnesses to Jesus' death. Joseph took the body of Christ, and after wrapping it in linen, he lay the body in a tomb.

Joseph is the first courageous believer to take Jesus' body as Jesus himself commanded at the Last Supper: He is the one who asks for and is granted the body of Jesus. Joseph was looking for the Kingdom of God.

The Resurrection

When the Sabbath was over, Mary and Mary Magdalene went to the tomb to anoint Jesus' body. But when they arrived, they found that the tomb had been opened. They fearfully approached the entrance, afraid of what might have happened. An angel of the Lord stood inside, and he told them that Jesus had risen. The women's worldly concerns of burial preparations transfigured into wonderment at the unfathomable angelic announcement:

"And he said to them, 'Do not be alarmed.
You seek Jesus of Nazareth, who was crucified.
He has risen; he is not here.
See the place where they laid him.
But go, tell his disciples and Peter that he is going before
you to Galilee. There you will see him, just as he told you.'"
(Mark 16:6-7)

They ran still trembling and amazed by what they had seen. The emphasis in Mark is on Jesus' absence from the tomb. If the burial story emphasizes the courage of Joseph of Arimathea in asking Pilate for the body of Jesus, the empty tomb story emphasizes the fear of the women at the resurrection.

Mark leaves the reader of his Gospel to speculate with the same trembling, astonishment, and fear. After Jesus appears to Mary Magdalene and two disciples, he finally appears to the 11. Throughout the Gospel, Jesus commands people to be silent and not speak; yet in their excitement they cannot help doing so. But after the resurrection he commands his disciples to speak, to go, to tell, saying:

"Go into all the world and proclaim the gospel to the whole creation. Whoever believes and is baptized will be saved,
But whoever does not believe will be condemned.'"
(Mark 16:15-16)

With that, Jesus ascended into heaven, and the disciples went out and preached just as the Son of God had instructed.

CHAPTER 1 NOTES:

CHAPTER 2
The Story of the Early Church

OBJECTIVE: The maturing Christian will understand the cosmic shift in power caused by the advent of the Messiah and the outpouring of his Holy Spirit.

PENTECOST TO PAUL: Acts 1-9

The beginning of the church as described in the Book of Acts starts with the Ascension and moves to Pentecost, the stoning of Stephen, and the conversion of Paul.
Jesus' Ascension and the outpouring of the Holy Spirit on Pentecost mark the beginning of the dramatic revolution of the powers of this world.

"But you will receive power when the Holy Spirit has come upon you, and you will be my witnesses in Jerusalem and in all Judea and Samaria, and to the end of the earth."
(Acts 1:8-9)

It is the moment when Jesus Christ's kingdom is brought forward in tremendous power as foretold by the prophets. Acts tells the story of how the inciting moment of spiritual empowerment rippled out from Jerusalem into the greater areas. It follows the apostles as they carried the Word out into a world that persecuted them. And it shows the humble and diverse community of believers that Jesus inspired. There are three major themes in Acts: inspiration through Jesus Christ; spiritual boldness; and the persecution of the Christian community.

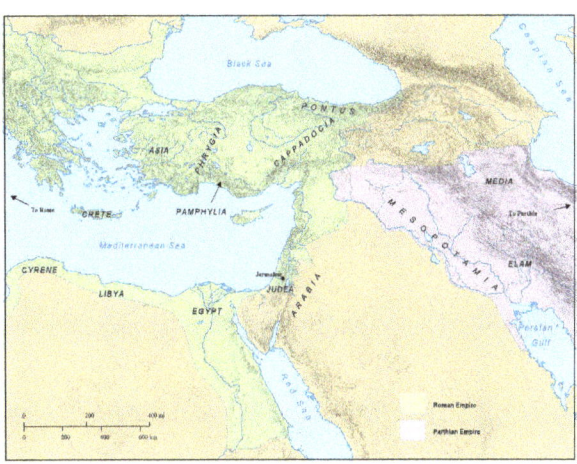

Map 1. *World at the Time of Pentecost* / www.biblemapper.com / Used with Permission.

Geography

The church began in Jerusalem, the then-capital of the nation of

Israel. It expanded to Judea and Samaria, shorthand for the Northern Kingdom and the Southern Kingdom, and then to the ends of the Earth. Paul's goal was to preach the Gospel to the entirety of the Mediterranean, eventually reaching Spain.

The books of the New Testament bear the names of these cities and regions: Galatia (Galatians), Rome (Romans) and Ephesus (Ephesians).

Christianity vs. Political Authority

During the time of Acts 1-9, around 30-37 A.D., the Roman emperor Tiberius reached the end of his reign. In his later years, he had become increasingly paranoid about treason, and so he frequently tried, persecuted, and executed political prisoners. Roman entertainment at the time was frequently violent and featured the elaborate torture and deaths of slaves and political prisoners. Because Roman rule was extremely bureaucratic, Tiberius' strict and bloodthirsty policies trickled down to the lower-level authorities in Rome's outlying territories such as Judea. Roman authorities all over the empire looked to quash any kind of rebellion before it began because if they allowed a rebellion or treasonous movement to flourish, they might be punished or demoted by their superiors.

Judaism was a state-sanctioned religion while the rest of the empire was predominately pagan. This permission meant that the Romans did not require the Jewish population to assimilate, and in parts of the Empire, Jewish people flourished. However, with the birth of Jesus, there was a shift. Though many followers of Christ were Jewish and therefore a semi-protected population, they did not practice Judaism the same way as the traditional Jews. These followers of Christ were called Nazarenes until the label "Christian" became the official name (Acts 11:26, at Antioch).

After Pentecost, the authorities of the area, especially the Jewish Sanhedrin, began to pay more attention to the growing group of Christians. As Christians set themselves apart more and more from Judaism, and garnered more criticism from the Jewish authorities, they became more vulnerable to attack from the political powers.

The confession that early Christians made—Jesus Christ is the Lord—is the same confession that a Roman citizen would have to make about the emperor—Caesar is the Lord. It was a fairly common practice for the despot to assert not only a political authority, but a divine spiritual authority as well. This enabled emperors such as Augustus and Tiberius to assert their dominance over all their citizens in a power play. If they were required to pledge their allegiance to the emperor, they would have to be loyal to him as well. But Jesus taught his followers that God is the only authority, and he instructed people to repent and only be loyal to God.

The announcement of Jesus' lordship was an inherently subversive act because deciding to follow Jesus meant disavowing all authorities except Jesus. This was unacceptable to the Roman leaders as well as the Jewish leaders. People flocked to Jesus to be liberated from sin and oppressive political regimes, but the political regimes noticed the power slipping from them and sought to discourage and end Christianity by any means necessary. They persecuted Christians, especially those who preached the Gospel openly. The Book of Acts heavily features Christian persecution because it was the terrifying reality of being a Christian in those days and an integral part of the formation of the early church.

The Ascension

The season between Easter and Pentecost is called the Great Fifty Days. Forty days after Jesus rose from the dead, the Ascension took place. Ten days after Ascension is Pentecost, which is the outpouring of the Holy Spirit upon the church and those gathered in Jerusalem.

Over the span of the forty days following Jesus' resurrection, he appeared to the disciples and taught them about the kingdom of God. On the last day, the disciples gathered together, and they asked Jesus the question that had been on their minds:

"'Lord, will you at this time restore the kingdom to Israel?' He said to them, 'It is not for you to know times or seasons that the Father has fixed by his own authority. But you will receive power when the Holy Spirit has come upon you, and you will be my witnesses in Jerusalem and in all Judea and Samaria, and to the end of the earth.'"
(Acts 1:6-7)

This particular commissioning of the disciples is, in a sense, not unlike the Great Commission.

"All authority in heaven and on earth has been given to me. Go therefore and make disciples of all nations, baptizing them in the name of the Father and of the Son and of the Holy Spirit,

Fig. 1. *The Ascension,* 1721 (oil on canvas), Troy, Jean Francois de (1679-1752) / Musee des Beaux-Arts, Rouen, France / Bridgeman Images.

teaching them to observe all that I have commanded you. And behold, I am with you always, to the end of the age."
(Matthew 28: 18-20)

The Lord commissioned his disciples, so they would create a community of believers. He made it clear that he wanted them in the world preaching the Gospel. Leaving his disciples to spread the Gospel, a cloud lifted Jesus into the heavens. The disciples watched, mouths agape with awe and wonder, as Jesus ascended to the kingdom of God. As they were gazing into heaven, two men stood by them in white robes saying,

"Men of Galilee, why do you stand looking into heaven?
This Jesus, who was taken up from you into heaven,
will come in the same way as you saw him go into heaven."
(Acts 1:11)

This is the enthronement moment, when Jesus takes his rightful place on the throne of heaven. This moment was foretold by many prophets, but Daniel's prophecy is the most detailed.

Prophesy of Daniel

The Book of Daniel illustrates the Ascension in a strange vision. King Belshazzar had thrown Daniel in prison for his faith, but while Daniel sat in bondage, he received a vision that Belshazzar is not the king of the universe or the world; there is a greater, higher king. Daniel sees four evil beasts representing four evil empires, two of which had yet to exist. As the snarling beasts fought for dominance, he saw a fifth figure.

"I saw in the night visions, and behold, with the clouds of heaven there came one like a son of man, and he came to the Ancient of Days and was presented before him. And to him was given dominion and glory and a kingdom, that all peoples, nations, and languages should serve him; his dominion is an everlasting dominion, which shall not pass away, and his kingdom one that shall not be destroyed."
(Daniel 7:13-14)

The term Son of Man is used to refer to Jesus throughout the Bible, so this fifth figure must be Jesus. His vision confirmed that the kingdom of God prevails over all, while also affirming the Ascension of

Jesus. Daniel describes Jesus' Ascension from above, giving the event its significance, understanding, and theological meaning.

"As for me, Daniel, my spirit within me was anxious, and the visions of my head alarmed me. I approached one of those who stood there and asked him the truth concerning all this. So he told me and made known to me the interpretation of the things. 'These four great beasts are four kings who shall arise out of the earth. But the saints of the Most High shall receive the kingdom and possess the kingdom forever, forever and ever.'"
(Daniel 7:15-18)

In the Book of Acts, the Ascension is described from below as the disciples watch Jesus rise into the heavenly realms—it is a fulfillment of Daniel's prophetic vision. Followers of Christ are the saints who will receive the kingdom of God. The Book of Acts is about the ascent of Jesus, and the opposition to his lordship from the powers, principalities, and authorities of the world, just as Daniel saw in his vision.

Witness in Jerusalem

Pentecost marks the beginning of the early church because it is when the disciples received Jesus' promise of the Holy Spirit. The disciples were gathered in a room when they heard a great rush of wind. As they looked around, Holy Spirit fell upon them with power as promised, in great tongues of flames. They began to speak in other languages, full of the Holy Spirit. Receiving the power of the Holy Spirit meant they were ready to spread the Gospel.

Fig. 2. *Pentecost,* 1732 (oil on canvas), Restout, Jean II (1692-1768) / Louvre, Paris, France / Bridgeman Images.

At this time, all kinds of people were in Jerusalem for the Feast of Weeks, a harvest festival celebrating the first fruits of the season. Although they were all Jewish, or God-fearers, they were from different places and spoke different languages. They heard the disciples speaking and proclaiming praises and gathered together to listen. They were astonished, as each of them heard the disciples preaching in their own language though they were speaking in tongues. Some thought they were drunk, but Peter quoted the Book of Joel, pointing out that this was the fulfillment of what God had been planning. It was a miracle of hearing as much as speaking.

"And it shall come to pass afterward, that I will pour out my Spirit on all flesh; your sons and your daughters shall prophesy, your old men shall dream dreams, and your young men shall see visions. Even on the male and female servants in those days I will pour out my Spirit."
(Joel 2:28-29)

Peter began to testify to the great works of Jesus, boldly bearing witness to the divinity of Jesus Christ. And each person heard it in their language, and the words sank into their hearts. They asked Peter,

"'Brothers, what shall we do?' And Peter said to them, 'Repent and be baptized every one of you in the name of Jesus Christ for the forgiveness of your sins, and you will receive the gift of the Holy Spirit. For the promise is for you and your children and for all who are far off, everyone whom the Lord our God calls to himself.'"
(Acts 2:37-39)

Three thousand people were baptized in the name of Jesus that day. The massive flood of Holy Spirit was the catalyst that began the early church, and from that day, more and more people received the Holy Spirit. The Pentecostal unfolding was the first major outpouring of Jesus once he had taken the throne, and the events of Pentecost illustrate the effect of following Jesus.

The fact that everyone heard each other speak in their own language shows the unity possible through Jesus—it was a reversal of Babylon, when humanity divided in language as a punishment for its sinfulness. God confused human languages and scattered them to the ends of the Earth. The Lord created many languages to prevent humans from being secular and selfish in philosophy; we should be theocentric and God-glorifying, united in worship. The reverse happened at Pentecost, revealing the unfolding purposes of his plan. God's design is that we only can become united under him. Now that Jesus reigned, salvation would overcome all divisions.

Pentecost in Jerusalem is the epicenter, Ground Zero, for the fulfillment of Jewish prophecy. It exploded from there.

"And it shall come to pass that everyone who calls on the name of the Lord shall be saved."
(Joel 2:32)

The outpouring of the Holy Spirit signaled the moment had arrived when the spirit of God was poured out on all people who call on the name of the Lord. The announcement of the lordship of Jesus Christ calls for a response, a submission of will. The word 'repent' literally means 'to turn.' The people who witnessed Peter's sermon were filled with the Holy Spirit, and they turned away from the oppression of sin and toward the liberation of Christ.

This moment of holy reception also signified a change in the spiritual arena. The Holy Spirit followed the disciples as they preached, and it cast the demons out of every city, claiming that place for the Lord. The battle between the Holy Spirit and demonic entities waged in the background of the ministry—the Holy Spirit brought spiritual liberation and unseated demonic power in a manifestation of the disciples' work. It is by the Holy Spirit that converts were saved from the sinful slavery of demonic influence and brought into God's pure love.

The New Fellowship

In a culture and city plagued by greed and selfishness, the early church defied convention. The earliest days of the church were marked with sharing and unity in the spirit of God. They devoted themselves to the apostles' teaching, fellowship, breaking of bread and prayer, finding solace and comfort in the community they built for each other. The Lord continued to show signs and miracles through the disciples, and they had generous and glad hearts, praising God and finding favor with everyone. They held everything in common and took care of the needy. Essentially, these early Christians did their best to follow the teachings of Jesus, and the result was the rapid expansion of the church, with thousands and thousands of people coming to the Lord.

Healing at the Temple

One day, as Peter and John walked into the temple, they heard a lame beggar asking for alms. They looked at the man, and Peter said, *"'I have no silver or gold, but what I do have I give to you. In the name of Jesus Christ of Nazareth, rise up and walk!'"* (Acts 3:6) Peter pulled the man to his feet, and the beggar began to walk. He walked into the temple with them, proclaiming the glory of God. The people of the temple recognized him as the beggar, and they were astonished and amazed by the miracle. Peter admonished the gawking crowd and preached about Jesus to them, so they might know how the man was healed.

The priests, captains of the temple, and Sadducees seized Peter and

Fig. 3. *St. Peter and St. John Healing the Paralytic*, 1783 (oil on canvas), Ramos y Albertos, Francisco Javier (1744-1817) / Private Collection / Photo © Christie's Images / Bridgeman Images.

John for proclaiming Jesus, and they kept them in custody until the next day. The Sanhedrin was the Jewish high court comprised of 71 men and led by the high priest. It convened in Herod's temple. The council could decide the fate of its people, with the exception of the death penalty, which was determined by the Romans. The next day, they appeared before the court of high priests, rulers, elders, and scribes.

"And when they had set them in the midst, they inquired,
'By what power or by what name did you do this?'
Then Peter, filled with the Holy Spirit, said to them,
'Rulers of the people and elders,
if we are being examined today concerning a good deed done to a crippled man,
by what means this man has been healed,
let it be known to all of you and to all the people of Israel
that by the name of Jesus Christ of Nazareth,
whom you crucified, whom God raised from the dead—
by him this man is standing before you well.
This Jesus is the stone that was rejected by you, the builders,
which has become the cornerstone.
And there is salvation in no one else,
for there is no other name under heaven given among men
by which we must be saved.'"
(Acts 4:7-12)

The passage about the rejected stone becoming the cornerstone is quoted six times in the New Testament and refers to an Old Testament passage. Peter adds Jesus' name: "This Jesus is the stone that was rejected by you." He makes clear that Jesus is the cornerstone of the kingdom of God, and there is salvation in no one else.

The authorities recognized Peter and John as Jesus' disciples, but they could not do much to punish them because so many people already had seen and heard about the healing. If they punished the men, they might find themselves with a rebellion, but they needed to assert their authority. They decided to release Peter and John but commanded them to stop preaching in Jesus' name.

"'What shall we do with these men? For that a notable sign has been performed through them is evident to all the inhabitants of Jerusalem, and we cannot deny it. But in order that it may spread no

further among the people, let us warn them to speak no more to anyone in this name.' So they called them and charged them not to speak or teach at all in the name of Jesus."
(Acts 4:16-18)

Peter and John answered, "Whether it is right in the sight of God to listen to you rather than to God, you must judge, for we cannot but speak of what we have seen and heard" (Acts 4:19-20). The disciples continued to defy the earthly authorities in favor of the authority of God, and tensions between the Jewish authorities and Christians solidified.

A Revolutionary Community

United in their love of Christ, the early Christian church shared everything with each other. Those who had properties sold them and brought the proceeds to the apostles, who then distributed the proceeds among the group. No one experienced need. They didn't even claim any possession as their own— everything belonged to the community. This radical generosity did not come without radical discipline, though. When a man named Ananias and his wife Sapphira sold a piece of property, they kept some of the profits and took the rest to Peter. But Peter perceived Ananias' dishonesty through the Holy Spirit, and after asking he had done this, he said, *"'You have not lied to man, but to God'"* (Acts 5:4). Upon hearing Peter's words, Ananias dropped dead. Three hours later, Peter confronted Sapphira, who did not yet know what happened to her husband. When she also lied to Peter about the selling price of their land, he said, *"'How is it that you have agreed together to test the Spirit of the Lord? Behold, the feet of those who buried your husband are at the door, and they will carry you out'"* (Acts 5:9). Then she, too, collapsed and died. When the congregation heard about this, they were struck with fear.

Continued Persecution

Despite the warnings of the Sadducees and other officials, the apostles continued to preach in the temple. Their sermons about Jesus became wildly popular, and people would take their sick into the streets so that Peter's shadow would fall on them as the apostles walked into the temple.

The Gospel was spreading through Jerusalem and outside of the city, and the authorities became angrier every day, as their power slipped through their fingers one convert at a time. One day, as the apostles preached, the Sadducees showed up and arrested them. They

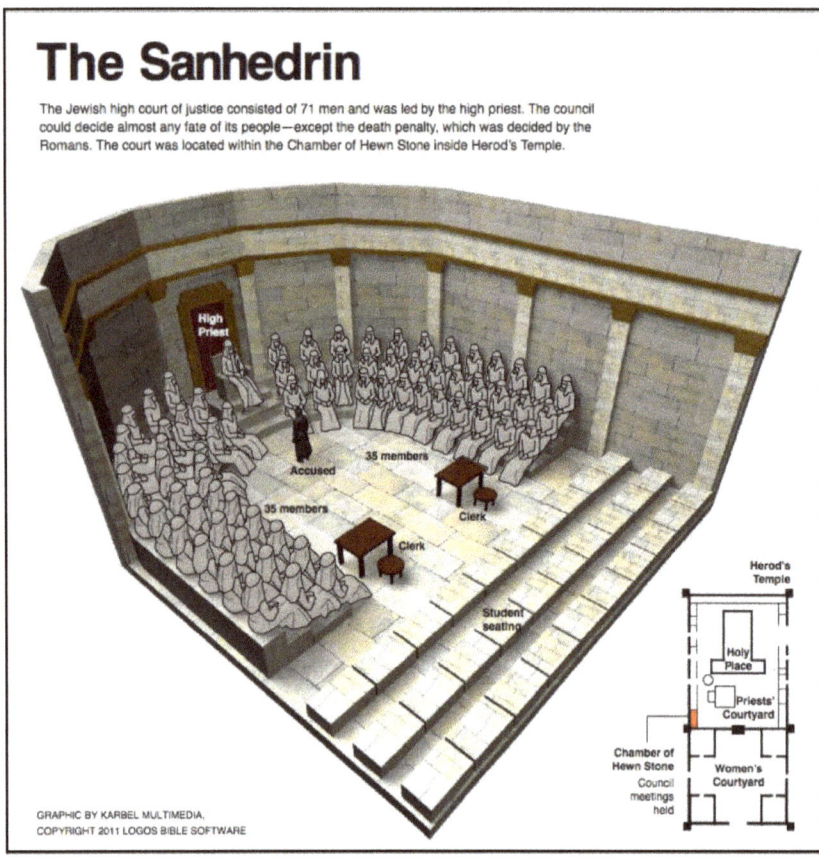

Fig. 4. *Graphic by Karbel Multimedia,* Copyright 2011, Logos Bible Software.

hauled them to the prison, intending to punish them the next day. But during the night, an angel of the Lord opened the lock and led them out to freedom. The angel instructed the disciples to continue to teach about Jesus in the temple, so they went immediately at daybreak and taught as the sun rose.

When the high priest and council gathered that morning, they sent for their prisoners. A guard unlocked their cell, only to discover that the disciples had somehow escaped, and everyone was confused. How could they have gotten out of the locked cell, especially since the guards had remained there all night? But someone came to them and told the council that the men they'd arrested were preaching in the temple. Officers went and brought them to the court, but they did so without force because they worried the people might stone them.

Again, the high priest questioned the apostles and chastised them for continuing to speak of Jesus. But Peter replied, *"'We must obey God rather than men. The God of our fathers raised Jesus, whom you killed by hanging on a tree. God exalted him at his right hand as Leader and Savior, to give repentance to Israel and forgiveness of sins. And we are witnesses to these things, and so is the Holy Spirit, whom God has given to those who obey him'"* (Acts 5:29-32). This enraged the council, and they began to call for their deaths. But an honorable Pharisee stood and addressed the rest of the leaders. He argued that they should leave the apostles alone: if they were falsely speaking in the name of the Lord, their following soon would disperse, but if they were truly of God, no government would be able to stop them. Afraid to oppose the will of God, they resolved to release them. But first, they beat the apostles and charged them to stop preaching about Jesus.

The apostles rejoiced in their persecution in the name of the Lord, and they did not stop teaching the Gospel. The Holy Spirit and their devotion to Christ gave them the courage to continue spreading the Word despite the consequences.

The Witness of Stephen

As the church grew, the community required more from the apostles than they were able to humanly supply, and so the 12 gathered everyone together and requested that they choose seven men to serve as deacons. One of the men they chose and prayed over was called Stephen. He was full of the Holy Spirit, and through the power of the Lord, he performed great wonders and signs.

Stephen preached to the synagogues, and many people argued with him. But when Stephen answered their arguments, they saw the truth and wisdom of the Spirit in his answers. However, a few men gathered against Stephen and spread the rumor that he had blasphemed against God and Moses. This would have been an egregious offense— it was one thing to declare Jesus the Son of God, but it was another to speak directly against God and Moses. The rumors spread like wildfire, and the officials seized Stephen and brought him before the court, where the men had set up false witnesses who testified to Stephen's blasphemy. When the council asked Stephen if the witnesses were true, they saw that his face was full of peace and righteousness.

Stephen recounted the story of Moses to the court in great detail, highlighting how authorities rejected Moses as a prophet. He closed his speech by directly addressing the council, saying:

"'You stiff-necked people, uncircumcised in heart and ears, you always resist the Holy Spirit. As you fathers did, so do you. Which of the prophets did your fathers not persecute? And they killed those who announced beforehand the coming of the Righteous One, whom you have now betrayed and murdered, you who received the law as delivered by angels and did not keep it.'"
(Acts 7:51-53)

This infuriated the council, and they vowed to kill him. But Stephen, full of the Holy Spirit, had a vision of Jesus standing at the right hand of God, and he said it aloud to the council. But they plugged their ears and crowded around him, and they cast him out of the city and stoned him. As rock after rock hit Stephen, he cried out, *"'Lord Jesus, receive my spirit!'"* and with his last breath, he said, *"Lord, do not hold this sin against them'"* (Acts 7:59-60). And then Stephen died.

Stephen became the first martyr for Jesus, the first to die for the cause. The word martyr comes from the Greek word martur, meaning witness. Stephen bore witness to the truth and salvation of Jesus Christ, and by doing so, he became a martyr. This act of violence against a Christian spreading the Gospel began a spree of Christian persecution all across the area. However, rather than acting in fear, the apostles and followers of Jesus embraced their persecution and worshipped more fervently than ever.

Witness in Judea and Samaria

The witnesses of the stoning of Stephen laid their garments at the feet of a young man named Saul, who had approved Stephen's execution. The day Stephen died, authorities chased Christians out of their places of worship, and they fled all throughout Judea and Samaria. Only the apostles stayed in Jerusalem. As the devout mourned Stephen, Saul broke open house after house and dragged men and women to prison for their faith. Jerusalem was a dangerous place for a Christian, but even still, the apostles spread the Gospel courageously in Jerusalem and elsewhere.

Fig. 5. *The Stoning of St. Stephen,* 1625 (oil on panel), Rembrandt Harmensz. van Rijn (1606-69) / Musee des Beaux-Arts, Lyon, France / Bridgeman Images.

The deacon Philip was one of the displaced Christians who left Jerusalem, and so he went to Samaria and began to teach about Jesus. He cast out unclean spirits, and he healed those who suffered from paralysis. Wherever the word of Jesus took hold, the demons and unclean spirits fled, leaving the people liberated in the presence of the Holy Spirit. But the Holy Spirit had not yet fallen on Samaria despite the baptisms of many citizens, so Peter and John came to help Philip pray for the city.

A man called Simon witnessed the apostles praying and laying their hands on the newly baptized. He saw that they received the Holy Spirit. Now, before the arrival of the Gospel, Simon had practiced magic. He amazed and bamboozled the people of Samaria with his tricks, and many believed he received his power from God. But when Simon saw Philip performing signs and miracles, he was amazed. He ran to Peter, John, and Philip as they were laying hands, and he held out a sack of gold, saying,

"'Give me this power also, so that anyone on whom I lay my hands may receive the Holy Spirit!' But Peter said to him, 'May your silver perish with you, because you thought you could obtain the gift of God with money! You have neither part nor lot in this matter, for your heart is not right before God. Repent, therefore, of this wickedness of yours, and pray to the Lord that, if possible, the intent of your heart may be forgiven you.'"
(Acts 8:19-22)

Simon asked them to pray for him, and then he hurried away. The early church utterly rejected materialism, which was another way they stood against authority. Corruption was rife among Jewish and Roman officials, and by rejecting money, property, and other goods, the early Christians were truly committed to the kingdom of God. When the apostles had testified and spread the Gospel, they returned to Jerusalem.

But an angel of the Lord told Philip to go south to Gaza. As Philip started down the dusty, hot road toward the desert, he met an Ethiopian eunuch who served on the royal court of Queen Candace of Ethiopia. The eunuch, on his way back from worshiping in Jerusalem, sat in his chariot reading Isaiah. The Spirit told Philip to go to this man, so Philip ran up and asked him if he understood what he was reading. The eunuch invited Philip to sit with him, and they began to discuss the scripture.

When Philip told the eunuch about the Gospel of Jesus, his heart was full of joy, and coming upon some water, he asked Philip to baptize him. Philip baptized the eunuch, but when they came out of the water, the Holy Spirit whisked him away, and Philip found himself in Azotus, where he continued to travel and minister. The conversion of this Gentile is significant because the majority of converts prior to this point would have been Jewish. This is symbolic of the fact that Jesus came to save all people, not just the Jewish population. The Gentile conversion narrative continues in Acts 10 with the story of Cornelius.

The Conversion of Saul

Meanwhile, Saul continued to persecute Christians. As one of the most outspoken opponents of the early church, Saul went to the high priest and asked for letters that would allow him to detain any Christians he encountered in Damascus and bring them to Jerusalem for punishment. He received them because the Jewish elders were intent on quashing any challenge to their authority, and Saul was a main instrument of this persecution.

But on his journey to Damascus, Saul experienced a transformation. He saw a flash of light, and he fell to the ground. A voice said, *"'Saul, Saul, why are you persecuting me?' And he said, 'Who are you, Lord?' And he said, 'I am Jesus, whom you are persecuting. But rise and enter the city, and you will be told what to do'"* (Acts 9:4-7). Saul stood, but the world around him appeared dark, and he realized he had been

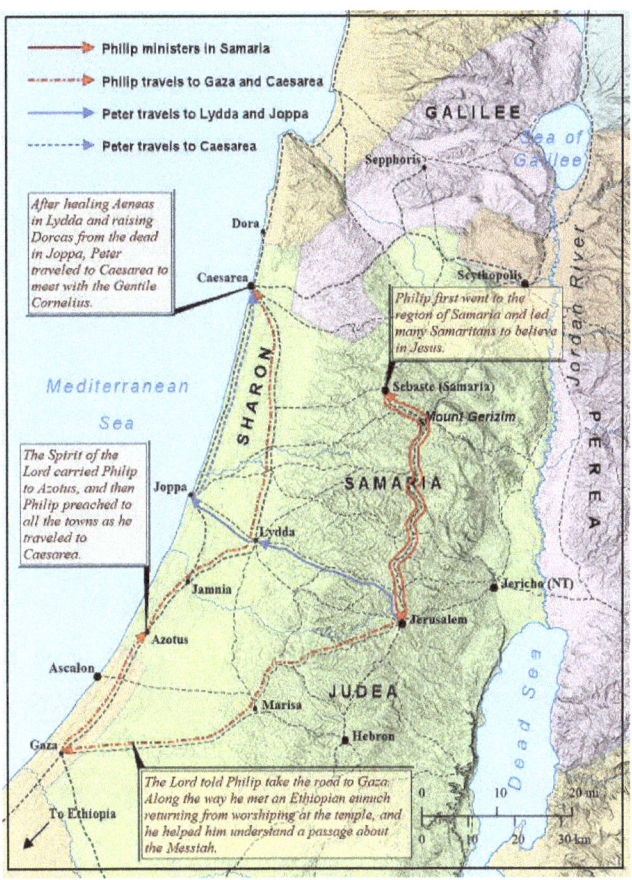

Map 2. *Ministry of Philip and Peter* / www.biblemapper.com / Used with Permission.

struck blind by the Lord. His companions led him by the hand into Damascus, and for three days he did not eat or drink.

The Lord appeared to one of his disciples who lived in Damascus, a man named Ananias. He directed Ananias to go to Saul and lay hands on him, but Ananias knew of Saul's deeds and felt afraid. But the Lord insisted that Ananias go, so he left his house and went to heal Saul. When Ananias placed his hands on Saul and declared Jesus' name, the scales fell from Saul's eyes, and he could see. Ananias baptized him, and Saul became a part of the group he had persecuted. Saul the persecutor became Paul the Christian.

Paul spent time with the disciples at Damascus, and he began to proclaim Jesus in the synagogues, much to the surprise of people who recognized him. The more Paul preached, the stronger he became, much to the dismay of the Jewish authorities. They plotted to kill Paul for his conversion, but the disciples hid him, and Paul escaped to Jerusalem.

When Paul arrived in Jerusalem, the disciples were afraid of him and

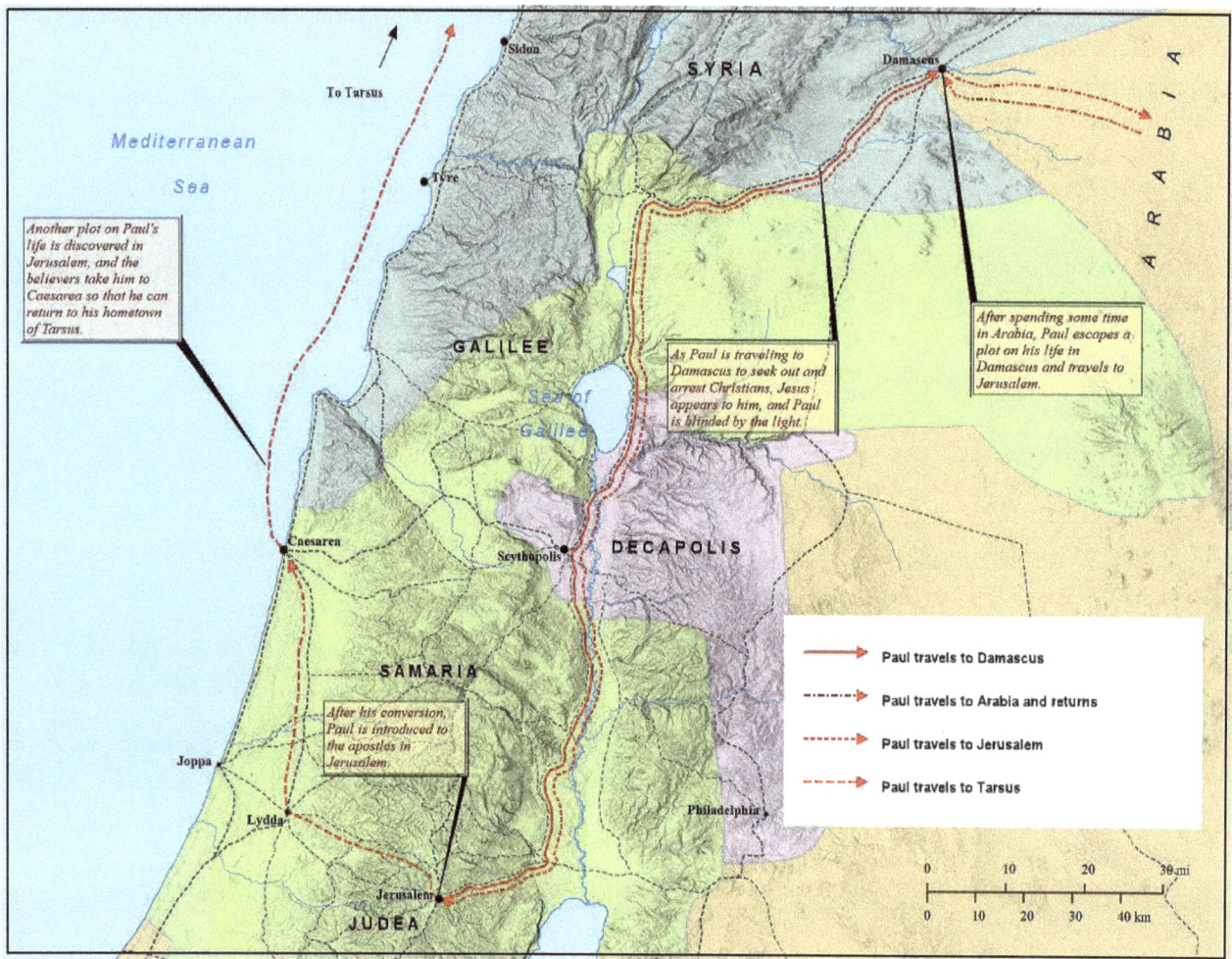

Map 3. *The Conversion of Paul and Paul's Early Journey* / www.biblemapper.com / Used with Permission.

56　New Covenant and the Early Church

did not believe that he was truly one of them. But Barnabas told them the amazing story of Paul's experience on the road to Damascus and his ensuing baptism, and they accepted him. Some believe that Paul is the true twelfth disciple because of his impact on early Christianity. After Jesus left them, the 11 disciples cast lots to decide who should join them. This was a common method for decision making, as they considered it fair and unbiased. They chose Matthias to join their ranks as the twelfth disciple, but because men appointed Matthias via lot rather than by God, some feel his discipleship is illegitimate. Those who believe this argue that because the Lord appointed Paul, he is the true twelfth apostle.

Paul preached boldly in the name of the Lord and argued with the Hellenists, the Jewish people who spoke Greek. He tried to smooth the clash between the Jews and Gentiles. Still, people plotted murder against Paul, so the disciples moved him to Caesarea. Paul's conversion demonstrated the complete power of Jesus' forgiveness. Though Paul had persecuted Christians with hate in his heart, Jesus made him clean and gave him the Holy Spirit. Paul went on to write many sermons and worked to facilitate the spread of Christianity all over the known world.

Fig. 6. *The Conversion of St. Paul,* 1601 (oil on canvas), Caravaggio, Michelangelo Merisi da (1571-1610) / Santa Maria del Popolo, Rome, Italy / Bridgeman Images.

Miracles of Peter

At this point, Acts focuses in on Peter's works as a disciple. Peter traveled all over the area spreading the Gospel and performing good works. While he was in Lydda, he met a man named Aeneas who had suffered paralysis for eight years. Peter healed Aeneas in the name of Jesus Christ, and all the residents of Lydda and Sharon turned to the Lord when they saw Aeneas healed.

A disciple named Tabitha worked in nearby Joppa, performing good deeds and acts of charity. She became sick and died, and those close to her prepared her body for funeral rites, laying her body in an upper room. The disciples in the area called Peter, and when he arrived in Joppa, they took him to her body. The widows stood near her, and they watched in awe as Peter knelt and prayed. He turned to the body and commanded her to arise, and she came back to life. He called everyone together and presented Tabitha alive, and a sense of amazement swept over the crowd. Jesus' power through Peter showed the early church the full extent of their salvation: just as Jesus could call someone back from death, he could give them eternal life in heaven.

The Reign of the Lord's Anointed

The day of Pentecost sent shockwaves through the socio-political and spiritual arenas of the early age. The events of Acts 1-9—the Ascension, stoning of Stephen, and the conversion of Paul—set the stage for the next phase of the spread of the Gospel. Word of Jesus and his great miracles, compounded with the good works of the apostles and disciples, spread like wildfire from Jerusalem and into the surrounding areas. This powerful narrative inspired nearly all who heard it to follow Jesus, and the movement grew larger every day. But as the early church grew, the Roman Empire began to lose traction with a series of unpredictable emperors and a revolving door of regional and local authorities. This heightened the political persecution of Christians, but only strengthened the convictions of the early church members. They continued to rejoice and spread the Gospel, despite the dangerous circumstances.

"Why do the nations rage and the peoples plot in vain?
The kings of the earth set themselves, and the
rulers take counsel together,
against the Lord and against his Anointed, saying,
'Let us burst their bonds apart and cast away their cords from us.'

He who sits in the heavens laughs; the Lord holds them in derision.
Then he will speak to them in his wrath, and terrify
them in his fury, saying,
'As for me, I have set my King on Zion, my holy hill.'

I will tell of the decree: The Lord said to me,
'You are my Son; today I have begotten you.
Ask of me, and I will make the nations your heritage,
and the ends of the earth your possession.
You shall break them with a rod of iron and dash them in pieces
like a potter's vessel.'

Now therefore, O kings, be wise; be warned, O rulers of the earth.
Serve the Lord with fear, and rejoice with trembling.
Kiss the Son, lest he be angry, and you perish in the way, for
his wrath is quickly kindled.
Blessed are all who take refuge in him."
(Psalm 2:1-12)

CHAPTER 2 NOTES:

CHAPTER 3
The Jerusalem Council

OBJECTIVE: The maturing Christian will understand the tensions experienced in the Early Church between grace and law, faith and obedience, and how the Church addressed these tensions in Council and through Apostolic letters.

INTRODUCTION

Acts 11-15 and the epistles from Paul to the Galatians and from James to the wider church show the early church experiencing its first major growing pains. The epistle from James could very well be offering counter balance to Paul's emphasis on grace in his letter to the Galatians and offers theological advice to the early church. While Paul and Barnabas traveled across the Mediterranean to fulfill their charge of spreading the gospel to the ends of the earth, they encountered persecution at the hands of both Jew and Gentile populations even as they won converts of all creeds.

As the early church gained more Gentile converts, the debate began regarding the moral standards of these new Christians. Should they be forced to follow the Jewish laws and undergo circumcision, and what is the alternative moral code if not? Conflicts arose among church leaders, and tensions among the various religious populations spiked. The first Jerusalem Council convened to discuss and reconcile the debate and thus began the tradition of the Council.

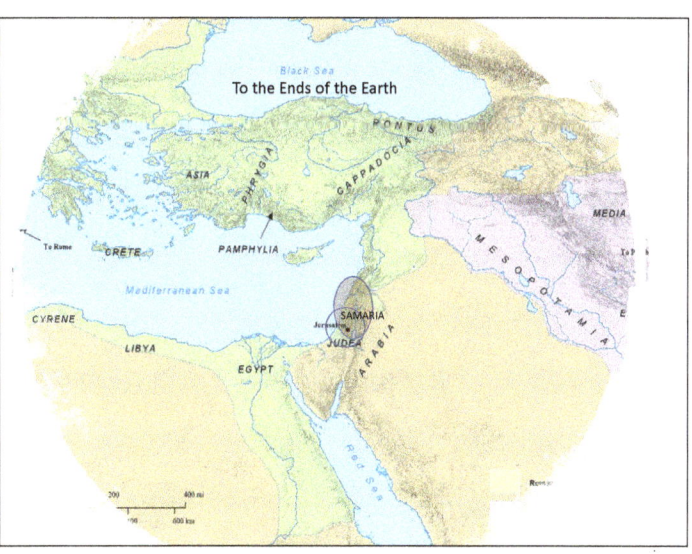

Map 1. *To the Ends of the Earth* / Bible Mapper.com. Used with permission.

"The report of this came to the ears of the church in Jerusalem, and they sent Barnabas to Antioch. When he came and saw the grace of God, he was glad, and he exhorted them all to remain faithful

to the Lord with steadfast purpose, for he was a good man, full of the Holy Spirit and of faith. And a great many people were added to the Lord. So Barnabas went to Tarsus to look for Saul, and when he had found him, he brought him to Antioch. For a whole year they met with the church and taught a great many people. And in Antioch the disciples were first called Christians."
(Acts 11:22-26)

HISTORICAL CONTEXT: 38-48 A.D.

To understand the tensions between the Gentile and Jewish populations, it is essential to examine the politics of the ruling parties. From 38-48 A.D., the Roman Empire had several different emperors with varying degrees of control over Europe and the Mediterranean. In 37 A.D., the Roman emperor Tiberius died, leaving the throne to Caligula. His rule was rife with conflict as Caligula lived up to his nickname: Caligula The Mad. Amid rumors of incest, conspiracies, and bloodthirsty behavior, Caligula expanded the imperial cult. Obsessed with himself and his absolute power, he erected statues to himself and deified his sister after her death. In 40 A.D., he ordered that altars made in his image be placed all over the empire, especially in the temple in Jerusalem. The people met this decree with civil disorder and protest, and these attempts to install statues in temples only furthered the dissatisfaction and tension in the provinces overseen by Rome. Following an increase in taxes to finance military campaigns, Caligula was assassinated in 41 A.D., and Emperor Claudius came into power.[1]

Fig. 1. *St. Barnabas,* 1494 (wall painting), Goul, Philippos (fl.1494) / Church of Timios Stavros (Holy Cross) tou Agiasmati, Platanistasa, Cyprus / Sonia Halliday Photographs / Bridgeman Images.

Claudius appointed King Herod Agrippa to rule over Judea in 41 A.D., which previously had been under the supervision of the Roman prefect, Pontius Pilate. This calmed some of the unrest among the Jewish people as King Herod mostly upheld the Jewish traditions. However, after his death in 44 A.D., the region was officially annexed by the Roman Empire, and the region fell under the rule of the Roman Procurators for 20 years.[2]

---

[1] https://www.unrv.com/early-empire/caligula-mad.php
[2] https://www.unrv.com/provinces/judaea.php

Tension Between Jews and Gentiles

While the Jews were allowed to settle some disputes among themselves, this independence did not ease tensions between the monotheistic faith they practiced and the polytheistic pagan religions of the Gentiles. Judaism was the only monotheistic religion in the region, and the pagan religions all featured pantheons of gods and goddesses representing various natural aspects and features. The Roman pagans also deified their emperors and members of the ruling family. They had temples and rituals dedicated to their gods, and their lifestyles were extremely different from the Jewish peoples. Animals sacrificed to the idols in their temples became food for their villages, and they often communed with their gods through sexually immoral practices. While some of the Gentiles were "god-fearers" and learned in the Jewish temples, many were not. The Jewish people saw the pagan Gentiles as dirty and especially immoral, and they had great disdain for the group as a whole.

The Law of Moses set the Jewish people apart in more ways than just cleanliness and morality. It also required that any man born into or converting to the Jewish faith undergo circumcision. This physical alteration furthered the cultural divide between Jews and Gentiles. Judaism's rigorous religious standards and insular community meant that the line between religion and culture blurred.

To practice the Law of Moses was paramount to Judaism, but these choices were also traditional and therefore cultural. Because Jesus was Jewish, some incorrectly considered Christianity a sect of Judaism. After all, Jesus fulfilled the prophesies in the Old Testament. Those who saw it as a sect of Judaism believed that any convert to Christianity also should follow the laws of Moses. During the period when the Gospel spread only among Jews, this was not a problem. However, as soon as Gentiles began to convert, the debate about circumcision and the other laws of Moses began.

It did not help that if Christianity was indeed a sect of Judaism, believers would be protected by the state because of the independent status of Judaism. However, Christianity is not a sect of Judaism, but a New Covenant created by the one true God, and thus believers garnered persecution and discrimination. Converts could expect excommunication from their families and communities in addition to political persecution. Heretics in the Jewish faith and outsiders in the Gentile pagan communities, the early church leaders traveled quickly because they were chased or threatened out of almost every town.

The divisions among the Roman ruling classes, the large pagan communities, and the smaller, self-ruling Jewish population created friction in nearly every aspect of life during this time. The belief in the

The Gospel Setting

Early Christians wrestle with their vocation in light of these questions:

- *How should converted Jews live in light of the Messiah?*

- *How should converted Gentiles live in light of the Messiah?*

- *How should converted Jews and Gentiles relate to one another?*

- *How should converted relate to the unconverted Jew and Gentile?*

erasure of divisions through Christ is one of the most subversive and radical concepts of the faith.

Converting Gentiles

Acts 11-15 describes the ongoing journey of the disciples. As they began to preach, the disciples and deacons focused on spreading the Gospel to the Jewish people. They preached in synagogues and converted many Jews. After all, the Old Testament identified the Jewish people as the *"chosen people,"* and Jesus was a Jew. It made sense for them to first communicate within their societal group, especially in such a highly divided society. But once Peter had the vision of the animals where the Holy Spirit told him, *"What God has made clean, do not call common"* (Acts 11:9). Peter understood that the Gospel was meant for all people, not just the Jews. So, he went to Cornelius as the Lord commanded, and he shared the good news of Jesus Christ with all the Gentiles there. The Holy Spirit entered them all, and Cornelius and his friends became some of the first Gentile converts.

Upon arriving back in Judea, the circumcised believers challenged Peter's actions. They felt angry that Peter had broken the rules of cleanliness by staying and eating with gentiles, but Peter remained calm and told them about his heavenly vision and the outpouring of the Holy Spirit on the Gentiles. Once Peter explained, those who criticized him praised the Lord, saying, *"Then to the Gentiles also has God granted repentance that leads to life"* (Acts 11:18).

The stoning of Stephen and ensuing persecution of Christians had caused many believers to scatter from Jerusalem into the surrounding cities and provinces. The majority of the displaced believers only shared the Gospel with fellow Jews, but some traveled from Cyprus and Cyrene to Antioch to preach to the Greeks. *"And the hand of the Lord was with them, and a great number who believed turned to the Lord"* (Acts 11:21). The Gospel was so successful in Galatian Antioch that the church in Jerusalem sent Barnabas to encourage the fledgling Christian community. Barnabas facilitated more conversions, but he knew that he could accomplish more with a partner. So, Barnabas traveled to Tarsus to find Paul. The two returned to Antioch, and together they met with the church there and taught. It was in Antioch that the disciples were first called Christians.

Peter's Imprisonment

Though the Word was gaining traction outside of Jerusalem, King Herod remained steadfast in his persecution of the Christians. He saw the approval of the Jews after he put James to death, and he realized that if he continued to kill the Christian leaders, he would stay popular among Jews. He needed this public approval to maintain his position, and the Roman overseers expected him to quash rebellion quickly and effectively. So, he seized Peter, arrested him, and threw him in prison. Herod remembered that the Christians had a knack for slipping out of imprisonment, so he ordered 16 soldiers to guard him. Because Herod arrested Peter during Passover, he had to wait until after the holiday passed to bring Peter to a public trial.

The church members prayed fervently to God on behalf of Peter, and the night before Peter's trial, a miracle occurred. As Peter slept bound by chains to two guards, an angel of the Lord appeared and shone a light in the dark cell. Striking Peter on the side to wake him, the angel commanded Peter to get up, and the chains released their grip on his wrists. Peter thought he was dreaming or seeing a vision. The angel told him to put on his clothes, cloak, and sandals, and Peter complied. He followed the angel past the first and second guards and through the iron gate as though they were invisible. Peter started down the street and turned to look for the angel, but he had already left him.

He realized that he had not seen a vision at all, and he said to himself, *"Now I am sure that the Lord has sent his angel and rescued me from the hand of Herod and from all that the Jewish people were expecting"* (Acts 12:11). He hurried down the empty streets to the house of Mary, the mother of John. A number of people from the church were gathered there praying for his safety, and they did not believe it when a servant said Peter knocked on the door. They told her she was seeing his angel, but when the knocking persisted, they were astonished to find Peter in the flesh. Instead of staying in safety, he told those gathered at Mary's house to spread the word of his miraculous release, and he left.

When the sun rose and revealed Peter's absence, the guards scrambled to find him. They couldn't figure out how he had escaped, and Herod executed the two guards who had presumably let him go.

Herod then traveled from Judea to Caesarea to settle disputes with the people of Tyre and Sidon. They petitioned him for peace between their areas because they depended on the crops of Judea. On the day of the audience, Herod dressed in his royal robes and took his place on the throne before the people. He delivered such a rousing speech that the pagan people thought Herod was a god, and they shouted at him, *"The voice of a god, not a man!"* (Acts 12:22). Herod took the praise as his own. He did not correct the people or give glory to the Lord, so immediately an angel struck him, and Herod died and was *"eaten by worms"* (Acts 12:23). The historical record lists Herod's death as occurring in 44 A.D.

To the Ends of the Earth

Meanwhile, the church in Galatian Antioch flourished. Prophets and teachers flocked to the church to teach and share the connection of Christ. The Holy Spirit came to Barnabas and Paul as they worshipped and told them it was time for them to fulfill their calling. The two traveled from Antioch to Seleucia and took a boat to Cyprus. They had to keep moving because they stirred up communities wherever they went with their proclamations of Jesus. When they arrived in the synagogues in Salamis, John served as their Greek translator. They traveled the island preaching until they came to Paphos. The Roman proconsul, Sergius Paulus, sent for Barnabas and Paul because he had heard about their works and wanted to know more.

However, Sergius had a trickster advisor called Elymas. Elymas practiced sorcery and sought to keep his superior away from the faith. When Paul saw him, he looked deep into his eyes, and full of the Holy Spirit, he condemned Elymas as a child of the devil and an enemy of the Lord, striking him blind. Elymas fell, lost in darkness, and the proconsul, amazed by what he had seen, believed in the Lord Jesus. The conversion of a such a powerful Roman meant that Christianity could flourish in Paphos.

Paul and Barnabas resumed their travels, sailing from Paphos to Perga, from Perga to Pisidian Antioch. They attended a Sabbath service at the local synagogue, and after reading from the Law and the Prophets, the leaders asked if the two had any words of encouragement for the congregation.

Fig. 2. *The Deliverance of St. Paul and St. Barnabas* (oil on canvas), Halle, Claude-Guy (1652-1736) / Musee de la Ville de Paris, Musee Carnavalet, Paris, France / Bridgeman Images.

Paul recounted the journey of the people of Israel, the story of Samuel the prophet, and the appointment of King David. He reminded the people of how Jesus fulfilled the prophecies of the Old Testament, and he said, *"Let it be known to you therefore, brothers, that through this man forgiveness of sins is proclaimed to you, and by him everyone who believes is freed from everything from which you could not be freed by the Law of Moses"* (Acts 13:38-39). The crowd and synagogue leaders were so moved by Paul's words that they invited them to speak again the next Sabbath. The next week, nearly the entire city came out to hear the word of God. But the Jewish people were jealous of the large crowd, and they contradicted Paul and spoke ill of him. Not ones to shy away from confrontation, Paul and Barnabas addressed the jealous people, saying, *"It was necessary that the word of God be spoken first to you. Since you thrust it aside and judge yourselves unworthy of eternal life, behold, we are turning to the Gentiles. For so the Lord has commanded us, saying, 'I have made you a light for the Gentiles, that you may bring salvation to the ends of the earth'"* (Acts 13:46-47). The Gentiles who witnessed the disciple's response were filled with joy, but the Jewish leaders incited their community to action. They organized a group of wealthy and powerful Jews, and they threw Paul and Barnabas out of the city. Paul and Barnabas, full of joy and the Holy Spirit, shook the dust from their clothes and started their journey to Iconium.

In Iconium, the two apostles continued preaching the Gospel and converting many Greek and Jewish people to Christianity. However, as in nearly every place they spoke, the group of dissenting Jews spread false rumors and sought to poison the minds of the community against Christ. The Holy Spirit worked through Paul and Barnabas, and they performed signs and miracles that endeared many to the Lord but further infuriated the non-believers. The dissenters, both Jew and Gentile, took advantage of the divided city, for only half of the people had converted so far, and they hatched a plot to stone Paul and Barnabas. But the Holy Spirit was with the apostles, and so they fled to Lystra and Derbe before any harm could befall them.

Lystra put Paul and Barnabas in a difficult position. After Paul healed a lame man in front of a crowd, the crowd began to shout and proclaim, *"The gods have come down to us in the likeness of men!' Barnabas they called Zeus, and Paul, Hermes, because he was the chief speaker"* (Acts 14:11-12). In Greek mythology, Zeus was the king and father of the pantheon of gods, and Hermes was the herald and messenger for Zeus. It was common in the Greek myths for their gods to assume human form and walk among them, so upon hearing of the miracle, the priest of Zeus brought bulls and wreaths to the city gates to perform sacrifices. In the eyes of the pagans, if the priest did not perform the proper sacrifices, they risked spurning that deity and inciting his wrath. When Paul and Barnabas realized what the people were saying, they tore their clothes and rushed to correct them. Paul addressed the crowd:

"Men, why are you doing these things? We also are men, of like nature with you, and we bring you good news, that you should turn from these vain things to a living God, who made the heaven and the earth and the sea and that is in them. In past generations he allowed all nations to walk in their own ways. Yet he did not leave himself without witness, for he did good by giving you rains from heaven and fruitful seasons, satisfying your hearts with food and gladness."
(Acts 14:15-17)

Map 2. *Paul's First Missionary Journey* / Bible Mapper.com. Used with permission.

Fig. 3. *Ruins of the Church of St. Paul and the town of Pisidia Antioch.*

Despite the apostles' protests and corrections, some of the crowd still wanted to sacrifice to them. After all, their beliefs were pervasive, and they were afraid what might happen if they angered their gods. Just as things were spiraling out of control, a group of non-believing Jews came into Lystra from Pisidian Antioch and turned the crowd against them. They dragged Paul past the city gates and lobbed stone after stone at him until he lay still on the ground. The angry crowd left him for dead, but Paul survived. The next day, he and Barnabas traveled to Derbe.

Fig. 4. *The Sacrifice at Lystra* (cartoon for the Sistine Chapel) (PRE-RESTORATION), Raphael (Raffaello Sanzio of Urbino) (1483-1520) / Victoria & Albert Museum, London/ Bridgeman Images.

In Derbe, they avoided persecution and converted a large number of people. Then they traveled back through Lystra, Iconium, and Pisidian Antioch, encouraging and strengthening the churches they had established there. In each church, they chose or elected elders and prayed and fasted with them to commit them to the Lord. They continued to travel from Pisidia to Pamphylia, Perga, Attalia, and finally, back to Galatian Antioch, which had become a hub for the faith. They stayed with the church in Antioch and told them of the good works the Spirit had done through them, especially for the Gentiles.

The Jerusalem Council

While Paul and Barnabas were teaching in Antioch, some other believers arrived from Judea, but their message contradicted what Paul and Barnabas had taught. These people taught the Gentile believers that in order to reach salvation, they needed to be circumcised according to the laws of Moses. Paul and Barnabas fiercely disagreed with this philosophy, but it was such a pervasive idea that they journeyed to Jerusalem to ask the apostles and elders. When they reached Jerusalem, they told the church all they had done and about the great number of Gentiles they had converted. However, the Pharisee believers declared that the converted Gentiles must follow the Laws of Moses and be circumcised. They did not understand that the coming of Jesus had nullified the Old Covenant and that the New Covenant of Jesus had new criteria for salvation. The council of apostles and elders convened, and Peter addressed them after much discussion:

Fig. 5. This modern icon represents the Church of the *"Council of Jerusalem"* described in the Acts of the Apostles, designed by Sister Maddalena, 2013, Jerusalem.

"'Brothers, you know that in the early days God made a choice among you that by my mouth the Gentiles should hear the word of the gospel and believe. And God, who knows the heart, bore witness to them, by giving them the Holy Spirit just as he did to us, and he made no distinction between us and them, having cleansed their hearts by faith. Now, therefore, why are you putting God to the test by placing a yoke on the neck of the disciples that neither our fathers nor we have been able to bear? But we believe that we will be saved through the grace of the Lord Jesus, just as they will.'"

(Acts 15:7-11)

The group fell silent and thoughtful, and then they agreed that instead of demanding that the Gentile converts follow the Law of Moses, they should instead *"abstain from the things polluted by idols, and from sexual immorality, and from what has been strangled, and from blood"* (Acts 15:20). Then the council penned a letter describing their agreement on the matter and prescribing the actions the Gentiles should take. They chose Judas and Silas to travel to Antioch with Paul and Barnabas, and the Antioch church rejoiced in their encouragement. After Judas and Silas left, Paul and Barnabas had a disagreement. They had decided to go back to visit the churches they had helped set up, but Barnabas wanted to take Mark with them. Paul disagreed with his choice of companion because Mark had deserted them in Pamphylia, and because they could not reconcile their disagreement, they parted ways—Barnabas and Mark went to Cyprus, and Paul and Silas went to Syria.

GALATIANS: False Teachings and True Good News

Upon pondering the debate about the relationship between the Laws of Moses and New Covenant of Jesus, the Apostle Paul wrote this letter to the Christian Church located in Galatian Antioch. As with all of the epistolary books of the Bible, it is meant to reconcile theological conflicts in the early church. Paul had been informed that the Galatian Christians were *"turning to a different gospel—not that there is another one"* (Galatians 1:6-7) which was being taught by false teachers who were distorting the message. This letter likely was written prior to the Jerusalem Council described in Acts 15—sometime around 46-47 A.D. That timeline makes it one of Paul's earliest letters. The later letter to the Romans more fully develops the theology behind Paul's argument with the Galatians.

What was this "different gospel?" One of the first challenges faced by early Christians was how to address and apply the laws of Moses in light of the coming of the Messiah, Jesus Christ. The first Christian council of Jerusalem was convened to address this very question.

"But some men came down from Judea and were teaching the brothers, 'Unless you are circumcised according to the custom of Moses, you cannot be saved.' And after Paul and Barnabas had no small dissension and debate with them, Paul and Barnabas and some of the others were appointed to go up to Jerusalem to the apostles and the elders about this question."
(Acts 15:1-2)

Because the Gentile converts previously had lived pagan lifestyles, they did not know how to live a moral life. Some ate idolatrous food and engaged in sexually immoral practices despite their conversion, and the Jewish Christians sought to correct this behavior. However, some of the Jewish Christians tried to persuade and teach Gentile converts that they must adhere to Jewish laws related to circumcision, diet, Sabbath and the like. They equated the Jewish laws with absolute morality and did not understand that the New Covenant had new laws. These false teachers are sometimes called *"Judaizers"* because they insisted Gentile Christian converts follow the old ways.

"But when I saw that their conduct was not in step with the truth of the gospel, I said to Cephas before them all, 'If you, though a Jew, live like a Gentile and not like a Jew, how can you force the Gentiles to live like Jews?'"
(Galatians 2:14)

Clearly, something new had come about with the advent of the Messiah and the outpouring of the Spirit at Pentecost: namely, the New Covenant. But how does the New Covenant relate to the covenants made by God with Abraham and Moses? The early Christian leaders struggled to communicate this relationship, and this is the question that lies at the heart of the Book of Galatians.

Paul taught the church that in the Good News through Jesus Christ, God now has brought an end to the slavery, curse, and condemnation brought about by the Law of Moses. Moreover, God is now, through the Gospel of Jesus Christ, fulfilling the incredible covenant promises that were originally given to Abraham concerning the nations of the world. (See Genesis 12:1-3)

The Structure of the Letter to the Galatians

Paul crafted his letter to provide personal and theological backing to the Galatian Christians to empower them to resist the burdensome teaching of the Judaizers and stand fast in their freedom in Christ. He uses emotional, logical, and ethical rhetoric to convey his points.

The Letter to the Galations: Chapters 1-6

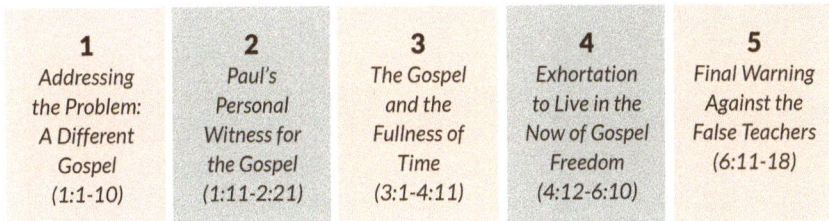

1	2	3	4	5
Addressing the Problem: A Different Gospel (1:1-10)	Paul's Personal Witness for the Gospel (1:11-2:21)	The Gospel and the Fullness of Time (3:1-4:11)	Exhortation to Live in the Now of Gospel Freedom (4:12-6:10)	Final Warning Against the False Teachers (6:11-18)

Paul opens his letter rather abruptly in order to get right to his concern for the Galatians. He shares his own personal struggle with the issue with which they are facing (Galatians 1:11-2:21). He then provides the theological and historic understanding for the Gospel which explains why the Judaizers are so deeply incorrect in their assertions (Galatians 3:1-4:11). Next, he exhorts the Galatians to stand firm in their true identity and freedom in Jesus Christ (Galatians 4:12-6:10). He closes with a final warning against the false teachers (Galatians 6:11-18).

ADDRESSING THE PROBLEM: A Different Gospel

Out of all of Paul's letters, his opening to the Galatians is the most succinct. Typically, before launching into his main points, Paul offers encouragement and prayerful thanksgivings for the church or individual to whom he is writing. In this letter, he launches directly into his concerns.

"I am astonished that you are so quickly deserting him who called you in the grace of Christ and are turning to a different gospel— not that there is another one, but there are some who trouble you and want to distort the gospel of Christ."
(Galatians 1:6-7)

Paul perceived that the Galatian Christians were adopting a false belief, and that would have dramatic implications for them if they accepted those false teachings. It was absolutely critical that they understand the serious nature of false teaching and the consequences facing those who teach falsely: *"Let him be accursed"* (Galatians 1:9).

Paul engenders them to follow his example in seeking to be God-pleasers rather than people-pleasers. The young Gentile Christians were allowing themselves to be influenced and controlled by people who did not have their freedom in Christ at heart. They needed to be made of stronger stuff. The approval of God is all that matters for the Christian, even if it means certain *"important"* people disapprove. Paul's own witness for the Gospel bears this out.

Fig 6. *St. Paul the Apostle* (oil on canvas), Vignon, Claude (1593-1670) / Galleria Sabauda, Turin, Piedmont, Italy / Bridgeman Images.

Paul's Personal Witness for the Gospel

As he does in his other letters, Paul uses his own story and witness as an example for others to follow. The Galatians needed to be strong and personally secure to resist the peer pressure from those who would Judaize them. Paul wanted them to know that he had to fight the battle against Jewish zeal for the law in his own life personally and in the relationships with fellow leaders in the church.

Paul was himself a zealous advocate for Judaism— to the point of violently persecuting the church and seeking to destroy it. (Galatians 1:13) Yet God in his grace would not allow him to persist in that posture toward the church (Galatians 16). God called him to a new revelation in light of the Good News of Jesus Christ for the nations of the world. Paul consulted with the apostles concerning the Gospel. He and the message that he was given to proclaim was confirmed by the other apostles (Galatians 2:1-10).

But even the Apostles gave into the pressure of those who continued to assert the Jewish law—the Apostle Peter (Cephas) being one of them!

"But when Cephas came to Antioch, I opposed him to his face, because he stood condemned. For before certain men came from James, he was eating with the Gentiles; but when they came he drew back and separated himself, fearing the circumcision party."
(Galatians 2:11-12)

Just as he is asking the Galatians to do, Paul had to stand up to powerful people and argue for the truth of his message. Paul recounts the words he used to stand up to Peter and the other Christians, to point out the inconsistency between their own beliefs and actions. (Galatians 2:14-21). They were being hypocrites by placing expectations on others that they themselves were not able to keep, expectations that were inconsistent with their own understandings of the law and the cross. The crux of his argument is that no one will be justified *"by the works of the law,"* but rather by faith in Christ. The requirements of the law are met on the cross by Christ, so with Christ we *"die to the law"* in order to live to God. (Galatians 2:19) The key to righteousness for both Jew and Gentile alike is union with Christ through faith in him and his work—not by keeping the Torah.

Fig. 7. *Saints Peter and Paul,* oil on canvas. 1619. Jusepe de Ribera/Wikicommons.

"I have been crucified with Christ. It is no longer I who live, but Christ who lives in me. And the life I now live in the flesh I live by faith in the Son of God, who loved me and gave himself for me. I do not nullify the grace of God, for if righteousness were through the law, then Christ died for no purpose."
(Galatians 2:20-21)

The Gospel and the Fullness of Time (Galatians 3:1-4:11)

Paul then turns from his own witness to *"...the truth of the Gospel"* (Galatians 2:14), calling the Galatians to come out from under the spell of those who would lead them back into bondage under the Law of Moses. Paul gives three things to help them to correct their behavior.

> "In you shall all the nations be blessed."
> *Galations 3:8*

First, he charges them to place the prominence of Christ crucified in the center of their vision. If righteousness could be attained by the works of the law, then the cross was pointless (Galatians 2:21).

Second, he recounts their experience with the gift of the indwelling Holy Spirit of God. This is the gift of the New Covenant. Why would they want to go back to the old ways of bondage and struggle under the law and the flesh? Paul will return to and expand on this second point in Galatians 4:12-6:10.

Third, he explains that the Gospel is the long-awaited fulfillment of the covenant given to the patriarch Abraham. The plan of God always was to bring the blessings of God's covenant to the nations of the world (Genesis 12:3). Abraham's offspring was given an incredible promise of blessing that is inherited in due time.

Finally, Paul argues that the promise was made to a singular offspring: Jesus Christ. This child of Abraham would bear the curse of sin and the condemnation of the law on his person *"…by becoming a curse for us"* (Galatians 3:13).

The question then is raised: what is the purpose of the Law of Moses? (Galatians 3:19) The law serves a temporary purpose to restrain sin—not unlike a parental guardian restrains unruly children until they reach an age of personal responsibility and self-control (Galatians 3:24-25). But ever since the coming of Christ and the baptism into him, there is no longer the need for the guardian (Galatians 3:25).

Fig. 8. *Christ on the Cross*, c.1630 (oil on canvas), Velazquez, Diego Rodriguez de Silva y (1599-1660) / Prado, Madrid, Spain / Bridgeman Images.

"…for in Christ Jesus you are all sons of God, through faith. For as many of you as were baptized into Christ have put on Christ. There is neither Jew nor Greek, there is neither slave nor free, there is no male and female, for you are all one in Christ Jesus. And if you are Christ's, then you are Abraham's offspring, heirs according to promise."
(Galatians 3:26-29)

The implication is that those in Christ find their identity and righteousness completely in him alone and not in the *"works of the law."* Indeed, in him there is no other identity than heirs of the promise.

Paul asks, if we are indeed mature adult heirs of the promise, why would we want to go back under the bondage of the parental-guardianship of the law? We have been redeemed by Christ from that slavery to receive the full adoption as sons! (Galatians 4:5) With the privilege of adoption comes the outpouring of the Holy Spirit. Paul now turns to the call to live in the freedom of the Spirit of Adoption.

Exhortation to Live in the Now of Gospel Freedom (Galatians 4:12-6:10)

Having recalled to their minds three arguments for the truth of the Gospel, Paul exhorts them to live in the freedom they once enjoyed when they had first received the Gospel. Paul desperately wants to see them live into their true identity in Christ through his Holy Spirit. He describes his heart for them as *"laboring in the pains of childbirth"* (Galatians 4:19). His words for them are painful to write—but profoundly worth the hard labor if they will receive and live the life of Christ (Galatians 4:19).

Using an allegory, Paul compares those who would remain under the slavery of the law and the covenant of Mount Sinai to Abraham's wife Hagar. Yes, she bore children, but they were children for slavery. The other woman is Sarai, who bore Isaac and the children of the promise, children of freedom (Galatians 4:21-31). He challenges the Galatians to find their identity as children of freedom! (Galatians 4:31)

Fig. 9. Molnar, Jozsef. *Abraham's Journey from Ur to Canaan.* 1850. Oil on canvas. Hungarian National Gallery, Budapest / Bridgeman Images.

"For freedom Christ has set us free; stand firm therefore, and do not submit again to a yoke of slavery."
(Galatians 5:1)

The Galatians were doing well in their understanding of their freedom in Christ. But Paul has harsh words for those leaders who have misled them back to the law of circumcision—that they would go the whole way with the knife. Paul argues that if you accept circumcision, then you have to come completely back under the slavery of the entire law. The implications are dire. The law severs people from Christ and forfeits his grace.

The life of the Spirit will accomplish its work of sanctification apart from the burden of the law, if they will keep in step with the Spirit (5:16). Paul describes the works of the flesh, and the fruits of the Spirit. (5:16-26)

"But the fruit of the Spirit is love, joy, peace, patience, kindness, goodness, faithfulness, gentleness, self-control; against such things there is no law. And those who belong to Christ Jesus have

Fig. 10. *The Outpouring of the Holy Ghost*, Tristan de Escamilla, Luis (1586-1624) / National Museum of Art of Romania, Bucharest, Romania / Cameraphoto Arte Venezia / Bridgeman Images.

crucified the flesh with its passions and desires."
(Galatians 5:22-24)

Paul concludes his letter with final encouragements about the practical day-to-day life walking in the fruits of the Spirit and calls them to resist the peer pressure of the Judaizers, who care more about the *"good show"* in the flesh, than the inward *"new creation"* that comes from the cross of Christ and the Spirit of God.

After Paul wrote the letter to the Galatians, the Jerusalem Council convened to create moral guidelines separate from the laws of Moses, in order that the Gentile converts would understand how to live under Christ and the Jewish converts would understand their freedom from the Torah. Though conflicts raged on across the Middle East, the early church took a large step toward peace in their community and continued to seek truth in the Holy Spirit.

PURE RELIGION: The Book of James

While Paul sought to clarify the issue of circumcision and protect the Galatians from false teachers by emphasizing the importance of faith, James took the theology a step further. Once the argument over circumcision and Christianity's relationship to the Law of Moses had been settled, the focus changed from conversion philosophy to liturgical and practical philosophy. In his letter, James outlines the reality of being an authentic Christian. James argues that faith alone is not enough—you must practice what is preached to truly experience the grace of God. There is no way to know with any certainty whether Paul's letter to the Galatians came before or after James' letter. But Paul seems to have laid the foundation for James in Galatians by explaining how to be justified by grace thorough faith in Jesus, and James wrote about how to practice and manifest this faith in authenticity.

James' letter is his only work included in the New Testament. There are three James mentioned in the New Testament: James the brother of John, Son of Zebedee and one of the twelve disciples (Luke 6:14), James the son of Alphaeus, and one of the twelve (Luke 6:15), and James the Just, brother of Jesus and the first Bishop of the Church of Jerusalem. The church has traditionally held the author of this letter to be James the Just, the brother of Jesus and first Bishop of Jerusalem. We read about him in Acts 15 where he presided over the first council of the Church in Jerusalem (see also Acts 21; Galatians 1:19, 2:9, 12; and Jude 1:1).

James' letter is addressed broadly to *"the twelve tribes in the Dispersion"* (James 1:1). Before the new covenant, this phrase would have specifically applied to the natural born descendants of Abraham, Isaac, and Jacob who had been exiled outside of the physical geographic boundaries of Israel, the Promised Land. In light of the coming of the Messiah and the New Covenant, the writers of the New Testament applied this language to the spiritual children of Abraham, Isaac and Jacob, Jew and Gentile alike. For example, Peter uses the same terminology as he writes to the churches in Asia Minor when he calls them *"elect exiles of the dispersion."* In this letter, James addresses the entire Church of Jesus Christ.

His primary concern in the letter is for the manifestation of authentic Christianity. There is no way for one human being to perceive the true spiritual state of another person's soul: only God perceives the heart. What we do see are external religious piety and expressions of faith. James is primarily concerned about those who would be tested by the trials of this world and prove to be authentic or inauthentic on the Day of the Lord. It is not those who merely claim to be *"religious"* or say *"I have faith"* that are the true people of God. The authentic Christian will bear the marks of spiritual authenticity in his speech and in his good works. Religion is the external manifestation of the inward heart orientation toward God and others. James writes:

> "If anyone thinks he is religious and does not bridle his tongue but deceives his heart, this person's religion is worthless. Religion that is pure and undefiled before God the Father, is this: to visit orphans and widows in their affliction, and to keep oneself unstained from the world."
> (James 1:26-27)

To James, religion is worthless unless it is pure and undefiled before God. The test and the difference is in the speech and actions of the *"religious"* person. A person who shows forth pure religion will manifest a bridled tongue, generous actions toward the needy, and a holiness of life.

James asserts that the period of trial, suffering, and waiting in which the exiled people completed, produced steadfastness. (James 1:2-4). In the years after Galatians, Christian persecution picked up speed, so James is reconciling the political atmosphere with Christian philosophy. There would have been enormous pressure to leave the church— a true test of faith. He describes four essential disciplines for the believers in the midst of the test of faith. Through believing in prayer for wisdom (James 1:5-8), practicing lowliness with respect to wealth (James 1:9-11), remaining steadfast in the face of temptation (James 1:12-15), and listening and responding to God's word (James 1:16-25), the full manifestation of the fruits of faith will show forth in the speech, actions, and character of those who truly have pure religion.

Fig. 11. *Martyrdom of St James,* by Giovanni Battista Piazzetta, 1722-1723, oil on canvas, 1682-1754, 165x138 cm / San Stae (San Eustachio), Venice, Italy / De Agostini Picture Library / F. Ferruzzi / Bridgeman Images.

The opening and closing chapters of the letter provide an eschatological context for perspective on the realities of the people of God. Until the "coming of the Lord" (James 5:7) the exiled people of God (James 1:1) are going through a period of trial and suffering. In this period, the godly are downtrodden, the wicked are wealthy, temptation and sin abound.

"Count it all joy, my brothers, when you meet trials of various kinds, for you know that the testing of your faith produces steadfastness. And let steadfastness have its full effect, that you may be perfect and complete, lacking in nothing."
(James 1:2-4)

The next three sections will focus on three main areas where the *"religion"* or *"faith"* of the professed Christian will be *"perfected and completed"* or proven to be *"religion that is worthless"* (James 1:26).

The Letter of James: Chapters 1-5

1	2	3	4	5
The Test of Faith: Worthless or Pure Religion (1:1-27)	The Call to Generosity to the Poor: Partiality and Generosity (2:1-26)	Bridling the Tongue (3:1-18)	Keeping Oneself Unstained from the World (4:1-5:6)	Patience, Integrity, Prayer and Mutual Accountability (5:7-20)

THE CALL TO GENEROSITY TO THE POOR: Partiality and Generosity

The first area of fruitfulness for authentic Christian faith is in matters of wealth and poverty. The allure of the wealth of this world is in direct opposition to faith in the Kingdom of God. As Jesus taught, you cannot serve both God and money (Luke 16:13). The first temptation is to show partiality to the rich. James instructs:

"My brothers, show no partiality as you hold the faith in our Lord Jesus Christ, the Lord of glory. For if a man wearing a gold ring and fine clothing comes into your assembly, and a poor man in shabby clothing also comes in, and if you pay attention to the one who wears the fine clothing and say, 'You sit here in a good place,' while you say

to the poor man, 'You stand over there,' or, 'Sit down at my feet,' have you not then made distinctions among yourselves and become judges with evil thoughts?"
(James 2:1-4)

The rich of this world need to be warned of the allure of wealth (See James 4:13-5:6). They are to be very careful that in their wealth they do not sin against the Sovereign Lord and humble poor. On the contrary, those who have been entrusted with earthly wealth should give in "good works" to the poor. Actions of generosity is a key area when faith is tested, completed, and perfected. The heroes commended for their faith in the Scriptures such as Abraham (James 2:21-24) and Rahab (James 2:25) manifest their faith by their actions. Good words of faith unmatched with good deeds of faith indicates a dead faith (James 2:17, 26)

Bridling the Tongue

The speech of the tongue is powerful index of the heart. Jesus warned the Pharisees of the defilement that comes from the mouth (See Matt. 15:10-20). The mouth reveals or betrays the state of the heart, and James warns of the potential for self-deception. When a man says, "I am religious" and at the same time has an "unbridled tongue," he "deceives his heart" (James 1:26). James argues that the tongue should be bridled like a wild horse: that is why teaching the Gospel should be constrained to those who show such self-control (James 3:1). The tongue needs to be controlled. Ships have rudders, and horses respond to the bit and bridle, but humans must use self-control to keep the tongue in check. An out of control tongue can do great harm like a wildfire in a forest (James 2:5-8)

"For every kind of beast and bird, of reptile and sea creature, can be tamed and has been tamed by mankind, but no human being can tame the tongue. It is a restless evil, full of deadly poison. With it we bless our Lord and Father, and with it we curse people who are made in the likeness of God. From the same mouth come blessing and cursing. My brothers, these things ought not to be so. Does a spring pour forth from the same opening both fresh and salt water? Can a fig tree, my brothers, bear olives, or a grapevine produce figs? Neither can a salt pond yield fresh water."
(James 3:7-12)

While no human can tame the tongue, God can! This is why James turns to the four disciplines mentioned in chapter one. Listed first, the prayer for wisdom from above is of primary importance. The good fruit that can come from the tongue is only produced by the *"wisdom from above."* This wisdom is attained by prayer in faith James (1:5-8). The character of this wisdom shows its divine source. *"The wisdom from above is first pure, then peaceable, gentle, open to reason, full of mercy and good fruits, impartial and sincere. And a harvest of righteousness is sown in peace by those who make peace."* (James 3:17-18)

Remaining Unstained by the World

In chapter 4, James turns to his third fruit, the call to personal holiness. Earlier, he had described the holy life of pure and undefiled religion as a call to *"keep oneself unstained from the world"* (James 1:27). The occasion of conflicts and fights in interpersonal relationships actually serve to reveal the *"stain of the world"* within the unperfected and uncompleted heart. James asks,

"What causes quarrels and what causes fights among you? Is it not this, that your passions are at war within you? You desire and do not have, so you murder. You covet and cannot obtain, so you fight and quarrel. You do not have, because you do not ask. You ask and do not receive, because you ask wrongly, to spend it on your passions. You adulterous people! Do you not know that friendship with the world is enmity with God? Therefore, whoever wishes to be a friend of the world makes himself an enemy of God."
(James 4:1-4)

The conflicts are rooted in *"friendship with the world,"* so the pure and undefiled heart cannot be friends with the world. The call to the Christian is to recognize the three forces of evil at play: sin, the world, and Satan. Drawing on the "word of truth," James exhorts:

"Or do you suppose it is to no purpose that the Scripture says, 'He yearns jealously over the spirit that he has made to dwell in us?' But he gives more grace. Therefore it says,'God opposes the proud, but gives grace to the humble.' Submit yourselves therefore to God. Resist the devil, and he will flee from you. Draw near to God, and he will draw near to you. Cleanse your hands, you sinners, and purify your hearts, you double-minded. Be wretched and mourn and weep. Let your laughter be turned to mourning and your joy to gloom. Humble yourselves before the Lord, and he will exalt you. (James 4:5-10)

He again issues a stern warning to be careful in our speech to one another (James 4:11-12) and to avoid the pride of wealth and neglect of the poor (James 4:13-5:6).

Patience, Integrity, Prayer and Mutual Accountability (James 5:7-19)

As James closes his letter, he returns to the themes with which he began. The Christians are living in exile from their true home during a time of trial and testing while they wait for the coming of the Lord: *"the Judge is standing at the Door"* (James 5:9). Therefore, they should be people of patience and steadfastness, like Job (James 5:7-11). They should be a people of integrity who have no need to make vows because their actions always align with their words (James 5:12). They should be people who are persistent in prayer for one another on all occasions (James 5:13-18). And finally, they should hold one anoth-er mutually accountable to not *"wander from the truth"* (James 5:19) but rather to bring the sinner back from his *"wandering"* in order to *"save his soul from death"* (James 5:20). James is a pastor whose heart for the church is authenticity and faithfulness until the Lord returns.

James' letter shows the theological problems the early church faced as they grew, while Paul's letter to the Galatians shows the liturgical problems inherent in a nascent faith. James emphasizes the ideals that Jesus preached in an attempt to remind the entire Christian Church to return to the original authenticity. Christ demands authentic faith paired with genuine actions— performative religion has no place in the Church. Amidst the political pressures and negative social climate of the period, James charged the early church to stay faithful and truthful in all things. In a time of divisions, he reminded them of the loving unity possible through pure communion with Christ and exhorted them to find and maintain their community.

CHAPTER 3 NOTES:

CHAPTER 4
The Day of The Lord

OBJECTIVE: The maturing Christian will understand the practical role that eschatology (the study of the last days) plays in shaping the New Covenant.

INTRODUCTION

Acts 16-18 tracks Paul and Silas as they took the Gospel farther than ever before, all the way to modern-day Greece. As they got closer to the seat of Roman power, they began to encounter more intense opposition to the Word, and citizens in more cities chased them out in anger. Despite their persecution, they won converts and established fledgling churches everywhere they preached. The new converts and communities stood strong under tests of their perseverance, as the social climate grew increasingly resistant to Christian discourse and practice.

Though these churches showed promise, the members had a lot of questions and their lack of knowledge made them vulnerable to false teachers. Paul penned two letters to the church in Thessalonica in an attempt to resolve their questions and encourage them to keep the Christian path. Paul instilled hope in the persecuted Christians by telling them about the Day of the Lord—the return of Jesus Christ.

Map 1. *Paul's Second Missionary Journey/* biblemapper.com.

Tensions Between Romans, Jews, and Christians

By 49 A.D., Roman leadership had begun to notice the upheaval in the Jewish community. While Christianity would have been virtually indistinguishable from Judaism to the Roman leaders, it's likely that Christianity had already arrived in Rome, though not in any strong manner. In 49 A.D., Emperor Claudius issued an edict expelling Jews from Rome despite the productivity and social standing of many Jewish people. In Acts 18, Paul encounters two Jewish people leaving Rome because of Claudius' ban. Because the scripture does not mention Paul converting them, they were probably already Christians. Though Claudius and high-ranking Romans wouldn't have noticed the small but growing Christian movement, the Jewish community did. Claudius took note of the social upheaval in Rome and because of his close relationship with King Herod, he may have heard about the civil disturbances in the cities of Judea. In an effort to maintain the Pax Romana, Claudius banned Judaism in the capital city. But no matter his reasoning, Claudius' edict expelling Jews heightened already tense relations between the Jewish and Gentile communities. The introduction of Christianity in particular divided cities caused explosive reactions.

Three Conversions in Macedonia

After Paul and Barnabas parted ways, Paul journeyed to Derbe and Lystra with Silas. While they were there, the apostles met a young man named Timothy. The church leaders in Lystra and Iconium spoke well of Timothy, and so Paul invited him to join their group and travel with them.

However, Timothy's mother was a Jewish believer, and his father was Greek. Paul knew that Timothy would face criticism from the Jews they sought to convert if he was not circumcised, so Paul had him circumcised despite the lack of biblical necessity. This way, Timothy would be able to preach to Jews and Greeks alike without fear that his audience would deflect his words on the basis of his personal heritage. Paul and Silas continued their travels through the cities with Timothy, strengthening and encouraging the churches along the way.

They passed through Phrygia and Galatia, and they skipped Asia Minor altogether. One night, as everyone else slept, Paul had a vision of a man from Macedonia. The man urged him to go there immediately. In the morning, Paul told the others of what he had seen, and they traveled directly to Macedonia because they knew Paul's vision was a sign from God.

While in Macedonia, Paul made three important conversions. The first occurred in Philippi, which was one of the most important cities in Macedonia. The Roman colony had a large community of wealthy business owners and other affluent groups including retired

Fig. 1. *Saint Paul, Saint Sylvain (or Silas) and Saint Timothy on a boat* - from miniature, 13th century / © Selva/Leemage / Bridgeman Images.

Roman soldiers. On the Sabbath, the apostles found a place of prayer by the riverside and began to preach to a group of women. Among those women was Lydia, a well-respected seller of purple goods. Purple dye was the most difficult and costly to create, so her business made her extremely wealthy. Lydia was a worshipper of God, and as she listened to Paul, God opened her heart. She approached them after they finished speaking, and they baptized her and her entire household. She invited them to stay in her home, and soon her home became a hub for the small Christian community.

Unfortunately, not all who heard Paul and Silas speak felt as moved as Lydia. As they were walking to a place of prayer, they passed a slave girl possessed by a fortune-telling spirit, and she called out to them, saying, *"These men are servants of the Most High God, who proclaim to you the way of salvation!"* (Acts 16:17). She followed the men for several days until Paul commanded the spirit to leave her, and it did. However, when her owners saw that Paul and Silas had ruined their source of income, they forced them in front of the magistrates and accused them of disturbing their city. The crowd became so enraged that the magistrates tore Paul and Silas' clothing and instructed the crowd to beat them with rods. When they were satisfied with the beating, Paul and Silas were thrown in prison.

That night in prison, behind bars with their feet fastened in stocks, Paul and Silas sang hymns and prayed to God. As the other prisoners listened to them worship, there was an earthquake that released the locked doors and unfastened all the shackles. When the jailer arrived the next morning and saw the open prison doors, he drew his sword in desperation and moved to end his life because he thought the prisoners had escaped. He knew that if his prisoners had escaped, his punishment would be much worse than death. Just as he was about to deal himself a finishing blow, Paul cried out, *"'Do not harm yourself, for we are all here'"* (Acts 16:28). The jailer was astonished by Paul and Silas' presence, and he threw himself at their feet and asked how he could be saved. They told him the Word of the Lord. The jailer took them to his home where he washed their wounds, and they baptized him and his household.

In the morning, the magistrates ordered the police to release Paul and Silas, and the jailer told the men that they could go in peace. But Paul was unsatisfied and said, *"'They have beaten us publicly, uncondemned, men who are Roman citizens, and have thrown us into prison;*

Map 2. *Paul's Second Missionary Journey*/ bible-mapper.com.

Fig. 2. *Monument Apostle Paul -* Church St. Nicholas, Kavala Greece.

Fig. 3. P*aul and Silas in prison,* Hatherell, William (1855-1928) / Private Collection / © Look and Learn / Bridgeman Images.

and do they now throw us out secretly? No! Let them come themselves and take us out" (Acts 16:37). When the magistrates heard that Paul and Silas were Roman citizens, they apologized to them and released them from prison. They still asked them to leave the city because of the uproar they had caused. After Paul and Silas visited Lydia, they continued their journey.

The three conversions in Macedonia ensured that the Word reached three different socio-economic groups: the wealthy business class, the servant and slave classes, and the bureaucratic class. These groups would have had little interaction with each other, and so by planting the seed in one person of each class, Paul and Silas effectively began a city-wide wave of conversions in nearly every part of the social structure.

Christian Persecution in Thessalonica

After they were driven out of Philippi, they passed through two cities and focused on Thessalonica. In Thessalonica, Paul and Silas faced an even stronger backlash from the community. Paul's missionary strategy was to find cities that could serve as missionary outposts, to reach other towns and cities in each region. Thessalonica was an ideal city for such a purpose. It was the capital of the Macedonian region and had a population of approximately 100,000 souls. The city was accessible by major roads, the east-west Egnatian Way, a north-south trade route, and a natural port to the Aegean Sea.

As was his custom, Paul preached first to the Jews in the city's synagogue and then to the Gentiles of the city. He had a few converts from among the Jews. However, he made tremendous missionary inroads with the Gentile God-fearing community, including some of the leading women of the city (Acts 17:4). This did not sit well with the Jewish leadership. They saw Paul's message of unity under Christ and his practice of sharing the Gospel with Gentiles as a direct affront to the Jewish tradition of separation, and this affront invalidated his teachings. They incited a riot and attacked the members of the new church, specifically a man named Jason, while looking for Paul and his leadership team.

"But the Jews were jealous, and taking some wicked men of the rabble, they formed a mob, set the city in an uproar, and attacked

the house of Jason, seeking to bring them out to the crowd. And when they could not find them, they dragged Jason and some of the brothers before the city authorities, shouting, 'These men who have turned the world upside down have come here also, and Jason has received them, and they are all acting against the decrees of Caesar, saying that there is another king, Jesus.' And the people and the city authorities were disturbed when they heard these things. And when they had taken money as security from Jason and the rest, they let them go.'"
(Acts 17:5-9)

The charges brought by the Jewish mob against Jason and the other believers were serious—to identify someone as king instead of Caesar could have deadly consequences. After Jason and the young believers were released from their incarceration, they urged Paul to flee to safety in Berea. Paul's time in Thessalonica was cut short. It appears that he was in the city for less than a month. Considering that Paul would teach in Ephesus for almost three years, this was much less time than he would have liked. The Jews of Thessalonica continued zealously to pursue Paul and his companions.

In Berea, Paul and Silas had greater success with the Jewish population. They were eager to hear the Gospel, and many converted. Quite a few Greek Gentiles converted as well, including those of high social standing. However, after the Thessalonian Jews heard that Paul was preaching in Berea, they sent a mob there to agitate the community. The new members of the church sent Paul to Athens via boat, and Silas and Timothy went back to Thessalonica until Paul gave the word for them to join him.

Paul Continues to Preach

While in Athens, Paul saw the many idols of the gods and goddesses that the Athenian pagans worshipped. He preached in the synagogues, but he also preached in the marketplace to whomever happened to hear him. Because the Athenians were fond of philosophical discourse, they were very interested in Paul's teachings, and they asked him to speak in the Areopagus, saying, "'May we know what this new teaching is that you are presenting? For you bring some strange things to our ears. We wish to know therefore what these things mean'" (Acts 17:19-20). The Areopagus was a large outcropping used for oratory and political purposes, and many gathered to listen to Paul's sermon. Standing on the rock surrounded by pagans, Paul addressed the crowd:

"'Men of Athens, I perceive that in every way you are very religious. For as I passed along and observed the objects of your worship, I found also an altar with this inscription: 'To the unknown god.' What therefore you worship as unknown, this I proclaim to you. The God who made the world and everything in it, being Lord of heaven and earth, does not live in temples made by man,

Fig. 4. *St Paul in the Areopagus,* by Giovanni Ricco' (1817-1873). / De Agostini Picture Library / A. Dagli Orti / Bridgeman Images.

nor is he served by human hands, as though he needed anything, since he himself gives to all mankind life and breath and everything. And he made from one man every nation of mankind to live on all the face of the earth, having determined allotted periods and the boundaries of their dwelling place, that they should seek God, and perhaps feel their way toward him and find him. Yet he is actually not far from each one of us, for 'In him we live and move and have our being,' as even some of your poets have said, 'For we are indeed his offspring.'

Being then God's offspring, we ought not to think that the divine being is like gold or silver or stone, an image formed by the art and imagination of man. The times of ignorance God overlooked, but now he commands all people everywhere to repent, because he has fixed a day on which he will judge the world in righteousness by a man whom he has appointed; and of this he has given assurance to all by raising him from the dead.'"
(Acts 17:22-30)

After hearing the Gospel, some of the crowd mocked Paul, but others asked him to come back and speak more. Some Athenians joined him and believed in Jesus.

Paul traveled from Athens to Corinth, where he met an Italian Jew named Aquila and his wife Priscilla. They had been exiled from Rome with the rest of the Jews by Emperor Claudius' edict, and because they were tentmakers, Paul worked with them. Every Sabbath Paul preached in the synagogue and tried to persuade Jews and Greeks to believe the Gospel. By the time Silas and Timothy arrived, however, the Jews had begun to revile him, and so Paul took the Gospel to the Gentiles. It was then that Paul had a vision where the Lord said, "'Do not be afraid, but go on speaking and do not be silent, for I am with you, and no one will attack you to harm you, for I have many in this city who are my people'" (Acts 18:9-10). Paul continued to preach for a year and a half in Corinth, converting many people, including the leader of the synagogue and his family.

Then, the Jews made a united attack against Paul, and they brought him before a Roman tribunal. These Jews wanted Paul to face the punishment of Rome for spreading an illegal religion, a crime against the empire. They accused him of persuading people to worship God in an unlawful manner, but Proconsul Gallio refused to rule on the

Fig. 5. *Trial of the Apostle Paul before Gallio (oil on canvas), Bodarevski, Nikolai K. (1850-1921) / Regional Art Museum, Uzhgorod / Bridgeman Images.*

matter because it did not pertain to vicious crime and involved Jewish customs. He did not see the division between the Jewish and the Christian faiths—to Gallio, Paul was a Jew just like his accusers, and therefore he had not broken Roman law, and it was not up to him to settle Jewish religious disputes. He told them to settle the matter themselves and forced them from the tribunal.

After staying a little longer in Corinth, Paul set sail for Syria with Aquila and Priscilla. He preached in Ephesus, but when they asked him to stay longer, he declined and promised to return should God call him. He then traveled to Caesarea and Antioch, encouraging the churches there before going through Galatia and Phrygia and strengthening the communities along the way. In Ephesus, a native Jew of Alexandria named Apollos began to speak about Jesus. Though he knew his scripture and spoke eloquently, he did not know the Gospel—he only knew about the baptism of John. Upon hearing Apollo speak, Aquila and Priscilla told him the full story of Jesus, and Apollos became a powerful advocate for Christ (Acts 18:24-28).

1 THESSALONIANS: Pleasing to God, Not to Men

After experiencing the fervor of Jewish opposition in Thessalonica, Paul penned two letters to the small but growing Christian community. At the heart of Paul's message to the Thessalonians is a call to maintain their focus on pleasing God rather than men. The church in Thessalonica was passionate in their zeal for the Lord; however, they were easily swayed by external intimidation and internal confusion. The challenges stemmed from the way they were founded as a congregation: Paul was only able to teach there for a few days before he was chased out of town, leaving the new converts with a lot of questions.

However, despite its fiery trials and beginnings, the church in Thessalonica flourished in faith, but the pressures on the young congregation continued. For this reason, Paul sent Timothy back to minister to them while he continued alone to Athens and then to Corinth. Timothy's report back to Paul prompted the first letter to the Thessalonians.

Fig. 6. Gustave Dore Bible: *St Paul preaching to the Thessalonians* (engraving), Dore, Gustave (1832-83) / Private Collection / © Look and Learn / Bridgeman Images.

Paul primarily encouraged them to fear God more than men and seek to please God rather than men. The pressure of persecution was on, but God has his own pressure to apply in a day of ultimate judgment of the wicked. The two letters address the concerns that Paul had for the young congregation and helped clarify theological questions related to the afterlife and the second coming of the Lord.

By the time of his second letter, minor issues and problems had developed into more major concerns. The three main concerns centered on the ongoing persecution, continued questions, and persistent misunderstandings about the second coming and the practical idleness of some members within the community of the church.

LITERARY OUTLINES

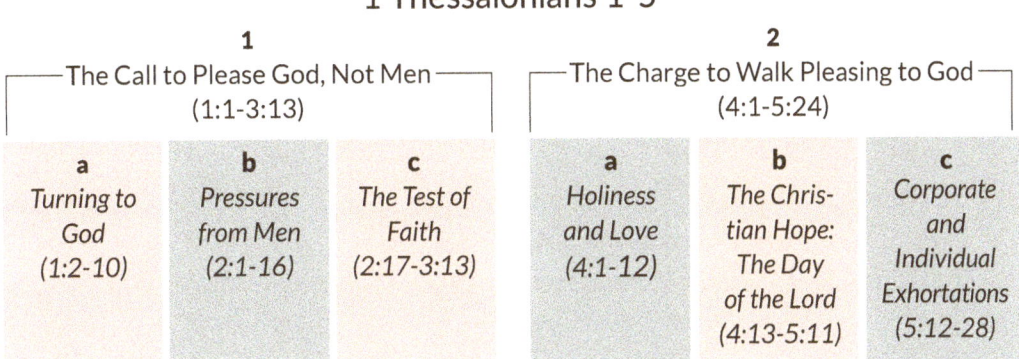

The Call to Please God, Not Men

This letter is addressed from Paul, Silvanus (Silas), and Timothy, the missionary team who first brought the Gospel to the Thessalonians. In the first three chapters of the letter, Paul reveals his concerns and assurances that the young church in Thessalonica remains focused on pleasing God rather than men.

Because of Paul's untimely retreat to Berea (see Acts 17) due to the hostile reception of the Jews in Thessalonica, he did not know whether the seeds of faith they planted continued to bear fruit. His fear was that Satan's attacks would continue against the church and that they would fall.

"For this reason, when I could bear it no longer, I sent to learn about your faith, for fear that somehow the tempter had tempted you and our labor would be in vain."
(1 Thessalonians 3:5)

Turning to God (1 Thessalonians 1:1-10)

Paul begins his letter by giving thanks to God for the steadfastness of the church's faithfulness in the Gospel, their character of love, and their hope in the Lord Jesus Christ. It is a testimony that they are indeed chosen by God (1 Thessalonians 1:2-4).

The church had embraced the word of the Gospel *"in much affliction, with the joy of the Holy Spirit"* (1 Thessalonians 1:6), and it had multiplied that faith by their strong witness to the Christian life and their preaching across Macedonia and Achaia. They had become the missionary hub that Paul was hoping and praying for by the sheer power of God and the truth of his Word.

Pressures from Men

Paul's overarching concern is that the Thessalonians would cave into the pressure and persecution from their fellow citizens. He first lifts his own example of perseverance in declaring the Gospel in the midst of much conflict and his shameful treatment in Philippi and Thessalonica. Paul gives the key to his strength of character in the truth of the Gospel:

"For our appeal does not spring from error or impurity or any attempt to deceive, but just as we have been approved by God to be entrusted with the gospel, so we speak, not to please man, but to please God who tests our hearts."
(1 Thessalonians 2:3-4)

Paul's own motivations in preaching the Gospel to them flow out of a deep singular desire to please God alone. The new believers in Thessalonica embraced the message of the Gospel through the apostle Paul *"not as the word of men, but as what it really is, the word of God"* (1 Thessalonians 2:13). So, they have become imitators of Paul and all faithful Christians in Judea who seek to please God even in the face of human pressure from their own countrymen. Their persecutors are compared with the unbelieving Jews who displease God and oppose all mankind (by their opposition to an apostolic mission to the Gentiles). They are the ones who killed both the Lord Jesus Christ and the prophets and drove the apostles out of Judea. (1 Thessalonians 2:15-16)

The Test of Faith

Paul now reveals his concern that the Thessalonians would give in to peer pressure and persecution. He was torn away from them, and yet his heart was invested in seeing them grow in their faith. But Satan hindered his return to them. Paul likely is referring to the unbelieving Jews from Thessalonica who continued to pursue him and stir up violence against them in Berea, thus forcing him to depart by sea to Athens and then Corinth (see Acts 17:13 cf. Rev. 2:9; 3:9).

Instead of returning to them in person, he sacrificially traveled on alone leaving Silas in Berea and sending Timothy back to Thessalonica to establish these two new churches (1 Thessalonians 3:1). Paul's deep concern for the church is that they would be assaulted by Satan as well and the labor for the Gospel would be in vain (1 Thessalonians 3:5). The powers that lurked behind the human persecutions and temptations are Satan and the spiritual forces of evil (cf. Ephesians 6:10-12).

The report from Timothy when he rejoined Paul in Corinth greatly encouraged Paul.

"But now that Timothy has come to us from you, and has brought us the good news of your faith and love and reported that you always remember us kindly and long to see us, as we long to see you—for this reason, brothers, in all our distress and affliction we have been comforted about you through your faith. For now we live, if you are standing fast in the Lord."
(1 Thessalonians 3:6-8)

THE CHARGE TO WALK PLEASING TO GOD

Having been reassured that the Thessalonian church was focused properly on pleasing the Lord and not buckling under the pressures of human and Satanic temptation and violence, Paul now focuses on strengthening that posture with theological and practical encouragement on how *"you ought to walk and to please God, just as you are doing, that you do so more and more"* (1 Thessalonians 4:1).

Holiness and Love

Paul summarized the Christian walk as a life of increasing and abundant *"love for one another and for all"* and *"blameless hearts of holiness before God."* Holiness for the Thessalonians primarily is in keeping their hearts from sexual immorality. As in our own culture, much of the Gentile culture was focused on licentiousness and lust. For Paul, sexual impurity not only is a transgression against God but also against Christian brothers. Sexual promiscuity is personal and spiritual adultery (1 Thessalonians 4:11-12).

Paul had no concerns about their mutual love for one another. He does make a minor mention of some who were not *"minding their own affairs"* and *"working with their own hands."* He reminds them to *"walk properly before outsiders and be dependent on no one"* (1 Thessalonians 4:12). This will develop into a full-fledged issue for Paul that he will address in detail in 2 Thessalonians 3:1-18.

THE CHRISTIAN HOPE: The Day of the Lord

The main theological concept motivating the Thessalonians is the Christian hope of ultimate victory in Christ at his Second Coming. This *"Word from the Lord"* is a powerful motivation and encouraging truth. As the Old Covenant prophets wrote, there is a coming *"Day of the Lord"* (1 Thessalonians 5:2; cf. Zechariah 14:5).

This day will bring ultimate restoration for those who are living to please the Lord. Also, the day will be a day of destruction and wrath for those who have rebelled against the Lord and have rejected his salvation in Jesus Christ (1 Thessalonians 5:3, 9).

Timothy likely had reported their interest about this teaching to Paul because of their interest in those who had died before the coming of the Day of the Lord. Paul explains that whether one has died or is still alive when the day comes, it will be a day of restoration and resurrection for the righteous (1 Thessalonians 4:16). He describes a great meeting of the Lord Jesus in the air as he descends in a triumphal military victory march to the Earth to establish eternal reign of God.

"For this we declare to you by a word from the Lord, that we who are alive, who are left until the coming of the Lord, will not precede those who have fallen asleep. For the Lord himself will descend from heaven with a cry of command, with the voice of an archangel, and with the sound of the trumpet of God. And the dead in Christ will rise first. Then we who are alive, who are left, will be caught up together with them in the clouds to meet the Lord in the air, and so we will always be with the Lord."
(1 Thessalonians 4:15-17)

The Christian hope of a glorious future should motivate and encourage the believer to present faithfulness and diligent labor in preparation for the day (1 Thessalonians 5:11). Unfortunately, if a person hyper-focuses on the future they can become idle in the present. In the last section of the letter, Paul encourages the right balance considering the Lord's coming. (1 Thessalonians 5:12-23)

2 THESSALONIANS: Worthy of the Calling

In his second letter to the church in Thessalonica, Paul returns to the themes of persecution, Christian hope, and idleness. Misunderstandings have taken root in the young congregation concerning the Second Coming and how to live in its light. The difficulties of establishing their faith in sound teaching and practice is compounded by the continuing persecutions. Their challenge was to live lives worthy of their calling in Jesus Christ while continuing to face great challenge.

2 Thessalonians 1-3

1	2	3
Concerns about Persecution (1:1-10).	Concerns about the Day of the Lord (2:1-12)	Corporate and Individual Exhortations (5:12-28)

Concerns about Persecution

Paul is grateful to God and commends them for their "steadfastness and faith" (2 Thessalonians 1:4) and in *"all your persecutions and in the afflictions that you are enduring"* (2 Thessalonians 1:4). Their knowledge and their hope in the Day of the Lord continues to strengthen them in the assurance of their promised relief from affliction and their coming vindication as God will judge *"those who do not know God and on those who do not obey the gospel of our Lord Jesus"* (2 Thessalonians 1:8). They will suffer *"eternal punishment"* away from the presence of the Lord. The saints will be *"glorified."* The key for all people is to be found *"worthy of his calling"* in that day (2 Thessalonians 1:11-12). This is Paul's prayer for them:

"To this end we always pray for you, that our God may make you worthy of his calling and may fulfill every resolve for good and every work of faith by his power, so that the name of our Lord Jesus may be glorified in you, and you in him, according to the grace of our God and the Lord Jesus Christ."
(2 Thessalonians 1:11-12)

Concerns About the Day of the Lord

Clearly, the Day of the Lord was a precious doctrine to the Thessalonian Christians—it was a driving hope! However, someone had introduced a teaching that the day already had happened and that they had somehow missed it (2 Thessalonians 2:1). Paul is not sure how they had received this teaching, but he resolves to set them straight in their understanding.

The key sign that he gives them is the advent of the *"man of lawlessness"* and the *"mystery of lawlessness"*. This is a person who will proclaim himself to be God and will seek to draw all unbelievers to himself. This will have the purpose in the divine economy of revealing human corruption for the fullness of evil that it is—that it may ultimately and finally be condemned (2 Thessalonians 2:9-12). Also, Paul reassures them that this has not happened yet.

The key is to remain firm in their faith now.

"But we ought always to give thanks to God for you, brothers beloved by the Lord, because God chose you as the firstfruits to be saved, through sanctification by the Spirit and belief in the truth. To this he called you through our gospel, so that you may obtain the glory of our Lord Jesus Christ. So then, brothers, stand firm and hold to the traditions that you were taught by us, either by our spoken word or by our letter."
(2 Thessalonians 2:13-15)

Concerns About Idleness

Their concern about the Day of the Lord had produced an idleness among some of the members. They were so heavenly minded that they produced no earthly good. That is not the Christian life that leads to salvation. It was not what Paul taught them or modeled for them. Paul gives a strong warning against idleness and then practical advice on how to deal with it. The concept is simple: *"no work, no food"* (2 Thessalonians 3:10).

These two letters are a real encouragement to any church or individual struggling with trials in this life. They also can be a powerful warning against idle Christianity, which is so prevalent among comfortable Christians in times of ease and plenty.

The Day of the Lord is not an idle promise, and therefore it must be met with active faith and good works despite fear of persecution. As Paul carried the Gospel across the nations, getting closer to the seat of Roman power, he inspired hope for a better future and eternal peace; especially among people who felt crushed by demonic and political forces even as those political forces chased him from city after city. Paul's testimony is a reminder of the way the Gospel dispels evil and disrupts the spiritual world as it restores hope and grace to God's people.

CHAPTER 4 NOTES:

CHAPTER 5
The Cross and Resurrection

OBJECTIVE: The maturing Christian will understand the theology of the cross and the resurrection and its practical application for life.

INTRODUCTION

Acts 18-20 describes Paul's efforts to spread the Gospel in Corinth, Ephesus, and small towns along the way. Preaching to mostly pagan communities, Paul presented freedom from idolatry and dark practices for those who believed in Jesus, and he had great success in planting churches and winning converts. These cities were ripe for liberation from the devil. Despite facing opposition in Corinth, Paul established a successful church there, and his extant communications with the Corinthian church comprise the biblical books 1 and 2 Corinthians.

The Christian Corinthians were plagued by the city's pagan practices and false teachers, and Paul's letters charge the Corinthians to abstain from sexual immorality, idol-tainted food, and hatefulness. He placed moral boundaries on their *"freedom in Christ"* and encouraged them to focus on practicing godly love. Like Paul's other epistles, 1 and 2 Corinthians were intended to settle theological conflicts in the early church.

> **Review of Paul's Earlier Missionary Journeys**
>
> *Paul's 1st Missionary Journey to Galatia*
>
> • Letter to the Galatians
>
> *Paul's 2nd Missionary Journey to Macedonia*
>
> • Letters 1st and 2nd Thessalonians

The Roman State of Affairs

Between 52-56 A.D., the Roman Empire experienced yet another change of leadership. After the death of Claudius in 54 A.D. 16-year-old Nero took the title of emperor. Unlike his predecessor, who struggled with what scholars identify as either Tourette syndrome or cerebral palsy, Nero was young and robust. The last years of Claudius' reign demonstrated little action, and similarly, the first five years of Nero's reign were stagnant. However, this was because his mother, Agrippina, ruled through him and murdered the majority of his political opponents. It was rumored that Agrippina also poisoned Claudius to hasten his death. Though most of the empire would not have known about the court gossip, it is important to note the immorality and hubris of the Roman elite. Not only did they worship former emperors as gods, but also they did not hesitate to kill each other and torture outsiders and criminals. Christianity was truly radical in calling for moral and spiritual purity, and the burgeoning Christian movement would face increasing persecution as it gained followers.

The Roman Emperors in the New Testament

Tiberius   14-37 A.D.   As ruler during Jesus' ministry, Tiberius is referenced in John 19:12,15 when the Jews shouted to Pilate at Jesus's trial *"If you release this man, you are not Caesar's friend... we have no king but Caesar."*

Caligula   37-41 A.D.   The Scriptures do not mention Caligula despite his chaotic reign.

Claudius I   41-54 A.D.   The Book of Acts mentions Claudius twice. Acts 11:28 mentions him in reference to the prophet Agabus and his prophecy of a famine that would come *"over all the world (this took place in the days of Claudius)."* He is noted a second time in Acts 18:1-2, when Paul meets Priscilla and Aquila on their way to Corinth after the emperor *"had commanded all the Jews to leave Rome."*

Nero   54-68 A.D.   Paul appeals to Nero in Acts 25:11. Nero became increasingly anti-Christian as his rule continued, and he blamed the Christians for the fire that erupted in 64 A.D.

At the same time, Jerusalem was in upheaval. The city had experienced severe famines over several years, and by 52 A.D., the different groups in the city were weakened physically and spiritually but still fixed in contention. Christian persecution had increased steadily, and the Christian church in Jerusalem was in dire need of aid. Paul took up a collection from among every congregation that he began or visited, to provide the Jerusalem Christians with much needed resources.

Paul in Corinth

Paul traveled from Athens to Corinth, where he met an Italian Jew named Aquila and his wife Priscilla. They had been exiled from Rome with the rest of the Jews by Emperor Claudius' edict in 49 A.D. Because they were tent makers, like Paul, he worked with them. Every Sabbath, Paul preached in the synagogue and tried to convince Jews and Greeks of the Gospel. By the time Silas and Timothy arrived, however, the Jews had begun to revile him, and so Paul took the Gospel to the Gentiles. It was then that Paul had a vision where the Lord said, *"Do not be afraid, but go on speaking and do not be silent, for I am with you, and no one will attack you to harm you, for I have many in this city who are my people"* (Acts 18:9-10). Corinth was a relatively wealthy city with a large pagan population. Despite the many local pagan temples and rampant sexual immorality, Paul achieved some success there. Paul continued to preach for a year and a half in Corinth, converting many people, including the leader of the synagogue and his family. He set up a church in Corinth, maintained communication with the congregation, and gave advice as problems arose.

Map 1. *Paul's Third Missionary Journey*

Then, the Corinthian Jews made a united attack against Paul, and they brought him before a Roman tribunal. These Jews wanted Paul to face the punishment of Rome for spreading an illegal religion, a crime against the empire. They accused him of persuading people to worship God in an unlawful manner because he proclaimed a savior greater than the Emperor. However, Proconsul Gallio refused to rule on the matter because it did not pertain to a vicious crime and involved Jewish customs. He did not see the division between the Jewish and the Christian faiths—to Gallio, Paul was a Jew just like his accusers, and therefore he had not broken Roman law because the God he proclaimed was also the Jewish God. It was not up to him to settle Jewish religious disputes, and he could not distinguish Jesus from Yahweh. He told them to settle the matter themselves and forced them from the tribunal.

After staying a little longer in Corinth, Paul set sail for Syria with Aquila and Priscilla. He preached briefly in Ephesus, but when they asked him to stay longer, he declined and promised to return should

Fig.1. After preaching in Corinth, the Jews tried to have Paul tried and condemned before the Roman proconsul Gallio; the official refused to hear a dispute based on 'words and names and your own law' (Acts 18:15). *Trial of the Apostle Paul* (oil on canvas), Bodarevski, Nikolai K. (1850-1921) / Regional Art Museum, Uzhgorod / Bridgeman Images.

God call him. He then traveled to Caesarea and Antioch, encouraging the churches there before going through Galatia and Phrygia and strengthening the communities along the way. In Ephesus, a native Jew of Alexandria named Apollos began to speak about Jesus. Though he knew his scripture and spoke eloquently, he did not fully know the Gospel. Upon hearing Apollos speak, Aquila and Priscilla told him the full story of Jesus, and Apollos became a powerful advocate for Christ (Acts 18:24-28). Apollos laid the foundation for Paul's mission in Ephesus.

Paul in Ephesus

Paul traveled from Corinth to Ephesus, where he encountered some men he recognized as disciples (Acts 19:1). He questioned them about their knowledge of the Holy Spirit, asking, *"'Did you receive the Holy Spirit when you believed?'"* (Acts 19:2). But the men responded in the negative: they had never heard of the Holy Spirit. They had been baptized *"into John's baptism"* (Acts 19:3), and so Paul shared the Gospel with them and baptized them in Jesus' name. The Holy Spirit entered the 12 men when Paul laid his hands on them, and they began to speak in tongues and make prophecies.

Paul taught in the synagogue of Ephesus for three months, spreading the Gospel and persuading the Jewish people to accept Jesus. But when members of the synagogue became belligerent in their disbelief, Paul and his team went to teach in the hall of Tyrannus, a place where Gentiles gathered to listen. The Holy Spirit had filled Paul so fully that even the touch of his handkerchief could heal a sick believer and cast out evil spirits, and soon word of Paul's miracles spread throughout the town.

When the sons of a Jewish high priest heard of Paul's success in invoking Jesus Christ to cast out demons, they invoked Jesus over a possessed man, saying *"'I adjure you by the Jesus whom Paul proclaims'"* (Acts 19:13). But to their surprise, the demon answered back, *"'Jesus I know, and Paul I recognize, but who are you?'"* (Acts 19:15). The possessed man leapt on them, furiously beating them until they ran out of the house naked and bleeding. When the residents of Ephesus heard about this, they felt afraid of the Lord, and those who had practiced magic and dark arts recognized the error of their ways. They piled their magic books together and burned them in the town square, despite their collective value of 50,000 pieces of silver. By burning the books, they freed themselves from their past and opened themselves to Jesus Christ. Paul was able to stay in Ephesus for quite a while because of their submission to the Lord, teaching and preaching to the believers there.

After this success in Ephesus, Paul resolved to return to Jerusalem. Jerusalem had faced famines and hardships in the past few years, and Paul wanted to bring financial aid to the city. He sent Timothy and Erastus into Macedonia. But despite the relative peace in Ephesus, a couple of craftsmen managed to incite a riot because of Paul's teachings. A silversmith named Demetrius, whose livelihood was crafting silver shrines to Artemis, the city's pagan patron goddess, noticed that following Paul's arrival, he had lost business. It was commonplace for cities in Ancient Greece and the Mediterranean to have a patron deity with dedicated temples to their particular entity. This way, pagans had to travel to other cities to worship in whatever particular temple each city housed, generating revenue for the city's economy. Part of the pagan Gentile backlash to the Gospel was the threat the Word posed to their economic traditions.

Fig. 2. *St Paul at Ephesus.* Residents who were engaged in exorcism burn the books / engraving in "The Bible illustree" by Gustave Dore (1832-1883) - Engraving from "The Dore Bible" © S. Bianchetti/Leemage / Bridgeman Images.

When he heard Paul preach that *"gods made with hands are not gods"* (Acts 19:26), Demetrius organized the other craftsmen in protest. They were afraid that the worship of Artemis would fade, and they would lose an important source of income. They angrily proclaiming the divinity of Artemis and caused confusion across the city. The protesting craftsmen dragged two of Paul's companions to the theater to question them. Paul wanted to join his friends and minister to the pagan craftsmen, but the other disciples would not let him. The crowd raged for several hours until a town clerk assured them of the permanence of Artemis' place as patron goddess of Ephesus. He directed the angry men to file a civil lawsuit instead of gathering in public, as they were in more danger of being charged with inciting a riot than Paul and the Christians were for proclaiming their faith. He dismissed the assembly, and they dispersed (Acts 19:35-41).

Fig. 3. *The fall of Eutychus from the window* (chromolitho), English School, (19th century) / Private Collection / © Look and Learn / Bridgeman Images.

Paul Prepares for Departure

Once the riot had settled, Paul decided to leave for Macedonia. He passed through the region, encouraging the Christian communities along the way, until he entered Greece. Paul spent three months ministering in Greece, but after he heard of yet another plot by the Jews to dispose of him, he returned to Macedonia with his team. They sailed to Troas, where they stayed for a week. The first day they were in Troas, Paul gave a lengthy sermon to the believers in the city. People gathered to listen in a large crowd, and a young man named Eutychus listened from his third-floor window. Paul spoke for so long, though, that young Eutychus fell asleep and fell out of his window. Those who rushed to his side proclaimed him dead, but Paul picked him up and said, *"Do not be alarmed, for his life is in him"* (Acts 20:10). The next morning, the young man woke up, and the believers of Troas were amazed and comforted by Paul's miracle.

Paul and his team rushed from Troas towards Jerusalem, but they stopped in Miletus where Paul called for the elders of Ephesus. Not knowing what would happen to him in Jerusalem, Paul delivered a farewell speech to the Ephesian elders:

"You yourselves know how I lived among you the whole time from the first day that I set foot in Asia, serving the Lord with all humility and with tears and with trials that happened to me through the plots of the Jews; how I did not shrink from declaring to you anything that was profitable, and teaching you in public and from house to house, testifying both to Jews and to Greeks of repentance toward God and of faith in our Lord Jesus Christ. And now, behold, I am going to Jerusalem, constrained by the Spirit, not knowing what will happen to me there, except that the Holy Spirit testifies to me in every city that imprisonment and afflictions await me. But I do not account my life of any value nor as precious to myself, if only I may finish my course and the ministry that I received from the Lord Jesus, to testify to the gospel of the grace of God. And now, behold, I know that none of you among whom I have gone about proclaiming the kingdom will see my face again. Therefore, I testify to you this day that I am innocent of the blood of all, for I did not shrink from declaring to

you the whole counsel of God. Pay careful attention to yourselves and to all the flock, in which the Holy Spirit has made you overseers, to care for the church of God, which he obtained with his own blood. I know that after my departure fierce wolves will come in among you, not sparing the flock; and from among your own selves will arise men speaking twisted things, to draw away the disciples after them. Therefore, be alert, remembering that for three years I did not cease night or day to admonish every one with tears. And now I commend you to God and to the word of his grace, which is able to build you up and to give you the inheritance among all those who are sanctified. I coveted no one's silver or gold or apparel. You yourselves know that these hands ministered to my necessities and to those who were with me. In all things I have shown you that by working hard in this way we must help the weak and remember the words of the Lord Jesus, how he himself said, 'It is more blessed to give than to receive.'"
(Acts 20:18-35)

Then they prayed together, and the elders wept and kissed Paul. They walked him to his ship, and they felt deep sorrow that they would never see him again. With that, Paul left for Jerusalem, knowing that he would meet violence but full of grace and joy in the Lord.

1 CORINTHIANS
INTRODUCTION: Concerning Spiritual People

Paul planted a church in Corinth on his second missionary journey (see Acts 18). Corinth was the capital city in the province of Achaia. It was a wealthy city due to its prominence as a port city and its location on a primary trade route. Corinth was famous for its highbrow culture and arts as well as for its rampant sexual immorality and temple prostitution.

Perhaps the most beloved and well-known passage in all of scripture is found in this letter, 1 Corinthians 13. It is Paul's ode to love.

"If I speak in the tongues of men and of angels, but have not love, I am a noisy gong or a clanging cymbal."
(1 Corinthians 13:1)

While 1 Corinthians 13 is arguably one of the best definitions of love, the occasion for its authorship was not primarily to address young couples who are about to be married! Rather, it serves as the convicting conclusion of a long confrontational letter to a group of Christians who had a very deep misunderstanding of what it truly means to be *"Spiritual People."*

1 Corinthians: Authentic Spiritual Maturity

Violations against the Resurrected Temple of the Lord (1-6)	Violations against the Resurrected Body of the Lord (7-16)
• *Divisions* • *Sexual Immorality* • *Lawsuits Against Believers*	• *Marriage and Sex* • *Food Sacrificed to Idols* • *Expressions of the Body in Worship* • *The Sacrament of the Body* • *The Church As the Body: Spiritual Gifts* • *Resurrection of the Body*

The members of church in Corinth were converts from the pagan Gentile culture of the city. In some ways, they were falling back into cultural practices and notions from their pagan history, visiting pagan temples and engaging in the sexual immorality of temple prostitution. The theological justification for their behavior was grounded in a super-spiritualized view of themselves as having already attained *"angelic"* status which was evidenced (in their minds) by *"eloquent wisdom"* and *"speaking in the tongues of angels."* From the apostle's perspective this was just misguided and immature arrogance (1 Corinthians 4:18-19, 5:2) and prideful boasting (1 Corinthians 1:29, 3:21, 5:6, 13:4). This put the Corinthian church at an impasse with Paul and his Gospel teachings. The crux of the issue centered around two main topics: Spirit and Body. A dualism had surfaced within this church that led to abuses and misunderstanding related to how to live as spirit-filled people in an earthly body.

The church in Corinth was a relatively young congregation planted by the apostle Paul sometime around 49-51 A.D. (see Acts 18). The situation that had caused the letter called 1 Corinthians had been brewing over a three-year period following his departure from them. Paul had written to the church over concerns he had pertaining to their syncretism with the pagan temple worship and the sexual immorality of the culture (1 Corinthians 5:9). In addition, he had received at least one report of the situation in the Corinthian church from *"Chloe's people"* (1 Corinthians 1:11). It is also clear from 1 Corinthians that he had received a letter from them brought by members from the church (1 Corinthians 16:15-17).

The letter and reports that Paul received indicate a growing divergence between the church in Corinth and Paul. His letter (1 Corinthians) is written to address the concerns he has for them and the concerns they have about him. The letter divides along these two main concerns. He first addresses the reports he has heard about them in Chapters 1-6. In Chapters 7-15, he addresses several concerns that they have about Paul and his teachings.

1 CORINTHIANS		Chapters 1-16
Letter Opening		1:1-9
Responding to Reports: Violations against the Temple of the Lord (1-6)	*Violations against the Unity of the Temple of God—Divisions Caused by False Wisdom*	1:10-4:20
	Violations against the Sanctity of the Temple—Sexual Immorality and Lawsuits	5:1-6:20
Responding to Concerns About Paul and his Teachings: Bodies and the Body of Christ (7-15)	*The Sexual Body: Marriage and Sex*	7:1-40
	Food for the Body	8:1-11:1
	Expressions of the Body in Worship	11:2-16
	The Sacrament Body of Christ: The Lord's Supper	11:17-34
	The Church as Body: Spiritual Gifts	12:1-14:40
	Resurrection of the Body	15:1-58
Letter Conclusion		16:1-24

RESPONDING TO REPORTS: Violations Against the Temple of the Lord

Paul uses two metaphors to address the false teachings and practices that had infiltrated the Corinthian church: the temple and the body. The Corinthians had developed a misunderstanding of the relationship between body and spirit. This misunderstanding was bearing fruit in a marked arrogance causing divisions among themselves and with Paul. In addition, it was also manifesting in the form of fleshly immoral behavior. In the first section of his letter, Paul uses the theme of the Temple of the Lord to address reports that he had received about the beliefs and practices of the church (1 Corinthians 3:11).

Violations Against the Unity of the Temple of God—Divisions Caused by False Wisdom

In this section, Paul is concerned with the integrity of the church and its message. Their divisions are *"destroying God's temple"* (1 Corinthians 3:17). At the root of the divisions and quarreling that have manifested is a marked arrogance that they have become *"spiritual beings"* akin to the angels because of a *"wisdom"* they have received apart from Paul. The main division is with Paul and his Gospel message. Paul writes to them:

"And I, when I came to you, brothers, did not come proclaiming to you the testimony of God with lofty speech or wisdom. For I decided to know nothing among you except Jesus Christ and him crucified."
(1 Corinthians 2:1-2)

Paul's challenge to the Corinthians is that true spiritual persons are humbled by the message of the cross. That is not eloquent wisdom from a worldly perspective—on the contrary, it is foolishness. Their arrogance about their state of being as *"spiritual"* had revealed that they were still quite worldly.

"But I, brothers, could not address you as spiritual people, but as people of the flesh, as infants in Christ. I fed you with milk, not solid food, for you were not ready for it. And even now you are not yet ready, for you are still of the flesh. For while there is jealousy and strife among you, are you not of the flesh and behaving only in a human way?"
(1 Corinthians 3:1-3)

Paul seeks to help them understand that true spiritual people see themselves as submissive to the Holy Spirit of God. Their quarrels with one another and Paul only serve to destroy the temple of the Holy Spirit:

"Do you not know that you are God's temple and that God's Spirit dwells in you? If anyone destroys God's temple, God will destroy him. For God's temple is holy, and you are that temple."
(1 Corinthians 3:16-17)

God's Spirit manifests not in puffed-up arrogance, but in weakness. In the weakness of our humanity, his power is displayed in glory. They saw Paul's weakness as a mark of worldliness; Paul asserts the opposite (1 Corinthians 4:1-20).

Violations Against the Sanctity of the Temple—Sexual Immorality and Lawsuits

The arrogance of the Corinthians in their overestimation of their spirituality also had manifested in a peculiar misappropriation of the use of their bodies. The three instances that had been reported to Paul (perhaps by Chloe's people) were blatant inappropriate sexual relationships, lawsuits among believers in pagan courts, and temple prostitutes.

As God's holy and redeemed people, the Corinthians should manifest God in their earthly existence and life. Unfortunately, their arrogance had blinded them to their own ungodliness:

"Your boasting is not good. Do you not know that a little leaven leavens the whole lump? Cleanse out the old leaven that you may be a new lump, as you really are unleavened. For Christ, our Passover lamb, has been sacrificed. Let us therefore celebrate the festival, not with the old leaven, the leaven of malice and evil, but with the unleavened bread of sincerity and truth."
(1 Corinthians 5:6-8)

As with Old Testament believers, sin must be purified by sacrifice and a fresh start made in "sincerity and truth." The sacrifice has been made by Christ as a Passover Lamb, what remained was for the Corinthians to manifest his holiness in a sanctified or holy life. Instead, their behavior was scandalizing the sacrifice of Jesus proclaimed in the Gospel. Also, their lawsuits in the secular courts against fellow believers showed the message of reconciliation as practically meaningless.

The continuation of temple visits and partaking of temple prostitution was a violation of the temple of the Holy Spirit:

"Or do you not know that he who is joined to a prostitute becomes one body with her? For, as it is written, 'The two will become one flesh.' But he who is joined to the Lord becomes one spirit with him. Flee from sexual immorality. Every other sin a person commits is outside the body, but the sexually immoral person sins against his own body. Or do you not know that your body is a temple of the Holy Spirit within you, whom you have from God? You are not your own, for you were bought with a price. So glorify God in your body."
(1 Corinthians 6:16-20)

Again, Paul builds on the theme of our bodies as the Temple of the Holy Spirit. Bodies are valuable to God. The Spirit and the Body are interconnected. What we do with our bodies is related to our spiritual personhood, and vice versa. Our spiritual relationship with God necessitates a holiness of life with respect to the body. From here, Paul will use the occasion of the letter written by Corinthians to him as the opportunity to teach the theology of our human bodies and the Body of Christ.

Responding to Concerns About Paul and His Teachings—Bodies and the Body of Christ

In 1 Corinthians, Chapters 7-11, Paul addresses errors about individual bodies. The Corinthians had arrived at some erroneous beliefs about their individual bodies, how those bodies relate to sexual relationships in marriage (1 Corinthians 7), eating, drinking, and in relationship to food sacrificed and dedicated to idols (1 Corinthians 8-11).

In Chapters 12-15, Paul turns to the corporate body of Christ. He first addresses expressions of the body in worship. Then, he discusses the implications of the bread and wine of communion as the Body and Blood of Christ. Next, he turns to spiritual gifts and unity of the Body of Christ as a spiritually gifted church. Finally, in Chapter 15, he focuses on the resurrection of the body.

The Sexual Body: Marriage and Sex

The Gospel of Luke provides us with the content of the Apostle Paul's teaching of the story of Jesus. The Corinthians' confusion about marriage and the embodied life in this age likely stemmed from the recorded words of Jesus to the Sadducees in Luke 20:34-36:

"And Jesus said to them, 'The sons of this age marry and are given in marriage, but those who are considered worthy to attain to that age and to the resurrection from the dead neither marry nor are given in marriage, for they cannot die anymore, because they are equal to angels and are sons of God, being sons of the resurrection.'"
(Luke 20:34-36)

While we do not have the entire set of letters written by Paul to the Corinthians, we can glean from his response to them that there were some Corinthians who had conceived of themselves as being of the character of the resurrected age. In other words, they thought of their bodies as equal to the angels and were no longer giving of themselves in the context of marriage. Paul pulls them back to this age in their bodies, yet at the same time affirming their orientation to the age to come (Chapter 15).

Eschatology of the New Testament

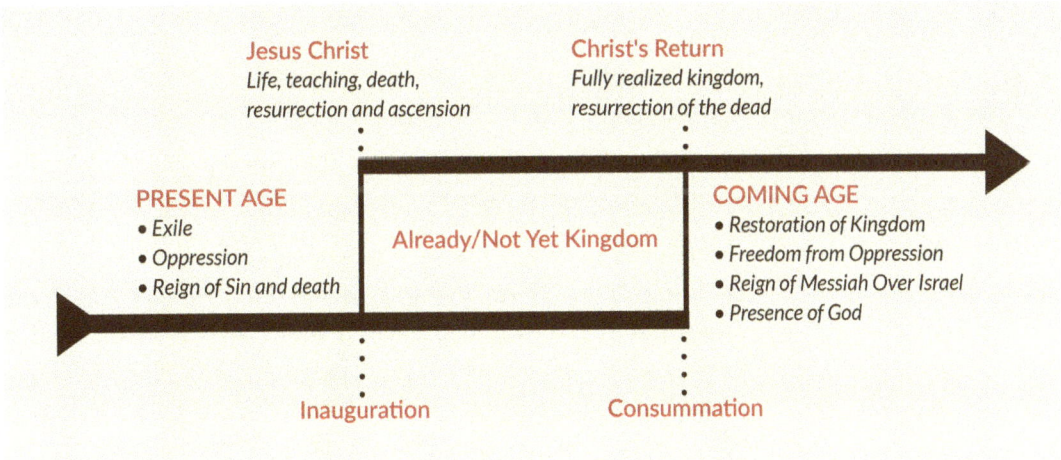

Some in the church had begun the practice of denying the sexual rights of their partners in marriage. This likely contributed to the sexual immorality among some of the members addressed in Chapters 5 and 6. Paul argues that marriage is the appropriate God-ordained context for sexual expression for those who otherwise would be tempted to sexual immorality by falling prey to the temptations of Satan because of lack of self-control. Indeed, it is wrong to deny a marriage partner (1 Corinthians 7:3-5). Paul affirms that we are still living in *"this age"* (Luke 7:34).

At the same time, Paul affirms the future orientation toward the resurrection age yet to come for those who can live according to the calling of celibacy to be *"free from anxieties"* that come with living in this age. Paul himself had adopted this practice as his own personal discipline as a way of expressing *"undivided devotion to the Lord;"* however, he recognized that not all are able to live this way because of *"strong passions"* (1 Corinthians 7:35, 7:36). It is not a sin to marry—it is appropriate as God's provision for this age.

Food for the Body

Paul now expands on a principle he provided in Chapter 5 regarding the association of the body with idolatry. He wrote:

"I wrote to you in my letter not to associate with sexually immoral people—not at all meaning the sexually immoral of this world, or the greedy and swindlers, or idolaters, since then you would need to go out of the world. But now I am writing to you not to associate with anyone who bears the name of brother if he is guilty of sexual immorality or greed, or is an idolater, reviler, drunkard, or swindler—not even to eat with such a one. For what have I to do with judging outsiders? Is it not those inside the church whom you are to judge? God judges those outside. 'Purge the evil person from among you.'"
(1 Corinthians 5:9-13)

The challenge is how to live the embodied life as the *"temple of the Lord"* in this age. What does it mean to live in this world but not of this world? They are not separate from unbelieving idolaters, for that would mean, *"you would need to go out of the world"* (1 Corinthians 5:10). But they are to avoid idolatry within their midst as the body of Christ. Practically speaking, how are they to work this out?

This section also deals with the Christian's relationship to food that has been sacrificed to idols. Apparently, there were some who were advocating that because of their super-spiritual knowledge, they had the right to partake of food sacrificed to idols in the temple and marketplaces without consequence or concern for conscience.

Paul addresses the issue by dividing the question in two parts. Paul forbids eating sacrificed food at temples in the presence of idols for (1) ethical reasons (1 Corinthians 8:1-13) and (2) theological reasons (1 Corinthians 10:1-22). Ethically speaking, those who think their freedom gives them rights of conscience to do whatever they please need to be very careful not to cause the weak to stumble. Theologically, the pagans are sacrificing to demons in their idolatry. God is jealous for his people.

"You cannot drink the cup of the Lord and the cup of demons. You cannot partake of the table of the Lord and the table of demons. Shall we provoke the Lord to jealousy? Are we stronger than he?"
(1 Corinthians 10:21-22)

Paul defends his own freedom but uses his personal example of not seeking to place stumbling blocks before anyone as an example to be followed (1 Corinthians 9:1-27). Paul makes allowance for eating food sacrificed to idols which is sold in the marketplace and eaten in private homes. Idols are nothing, and food is food. But if someone explicitly invests the food with idolatry, it is not to be eaten. (1 Corinthians 10:23-11:1)

Expressions of the Body in Worship

This section is particularly difficult to understand because we do not know precisely what expressions were taking place in worship by the women. They saw themselves as already having attained the fullness of the resurrection. As Paul and Jesus taught, they rightly were recognizing their equality and freedom in Christ. In Paul's letter to the Galatians, he wrote:

"There is neither Jew nor Greek, there is neither slave nor free, there is no male and female, for you are all one in Christ Jesus."
(Galatians 3:28)

However, it would appear from the issues raised in the letter that certain women were, as a sign of their freedom, exercising the gifts of prayer and prophecy in corporate worship without their traditional head coverings. He is careful to reassert their equality under God and the interdependence of men and women (1 Corinthians 11:12). The issue is similar to the that of eating food sacrificed to idols. The exercise of women's freedom in boldness was creating contention between the sexes. Paul warns against such contentiousness.

THE SACRAMENT OF THE BODY OF CHRIST: The Lord's Supper

The Corinthians' arrogance over their super-spiritual state also was affecting the way they partook of the Lord's Supper:

"Whoever, therefore, eats the bread or drinks the cup of the Lord in an unworthy manner will be guilty concerning the body and blood of the Lord."
(1 Corinthians 11:27)

What does it mean to eat and drink in *"an unworthy manner?"* Paul raised two concerns. First, there were divisions and factions among them. Second, some were putting their own selfish appetites ahead of the body—even to the point of some of the poorer members of the church not being able to participate in the common meal.

We see a continuation of these patterns. There is a marked arrogance and self-centeredness among some members of the church, that, in Paul's perspective, failed to recognize the body of Christ. A body is not the individual members but the whole. He now turns to the theme of spiritual gifts and speaking in tongues.

THE CHURCH AS BODY: Spiritual Gifts

The Corinthians had exalted the spiritual gift of speaking in ecstatic speech as the defining mark of the truly spiritual. In exalting this one gift among their membership, they had neglected, discouraged, and even despised the many other gifts that God gives to the Body of Christ. Staying with the paradigm of body, Paul describes the church as the human body with many different and important parts, all interdependent and equally vital to the other.

Paul is now ready to address the fundamental problem in the Corinthian church. The church, in its arrogance concerning knowledge and wisdom; its assertion of rights and freedoms to the neglect of the weaker brethren; marital commitments; and, cultural norms, had proven itself to be spiritually immature. Paul turns to his most clear exposition on what it means to be spiritually mature. He calls for the church to follow in the *"most excellent way of love"* (1 Corinthians 13).

"If I speak in the tongues of men and of angels, but have not love, I am a noisy gong or a clanging cymbal. And if I have prophetic powers, and understand all mysteries and all knowledge, and if I have all faith, so as to remove mountains, but have not love, I am

nothing. If I give away all I have, and if I deliver up my body to be burned, but have not love, I gain nothing.

Love is patient and kind; love does not envy or boast; it is not arrogant or rude. It does not insist on its own way; it is not irritable or resentful; it does not rejoice at wrongdoing, but rejoices with the truth. Love bears all things, believes all things, hopes all things, endures all things."
(1 Corinthians 13:1-7)

Just because a person or group is spiritually gifted does not mean that they are spiritually mature. In considering themselves as super-spiritual, the Corinthians had shown themselves to be *"envious, boastful, arrogant and rude"* (2 Corinthians 13:4). In insisting on their own way, they had violated Christ's way of love.

Moreover, in their focus on lesser gifts of prophecy and speaking in tongues as if they were signs of the age to come, they really were finding security in things of *"this age"* that will *"pass away"* (1 Corinthians 13:8) Human knowledge and wisdom in this age is partial. They were really just behaving like children following *"childish ways"* that they should rightly place behind them:

"When I was a child, I spoke like a child, I thought like a child, I reasoned like a child. When I became a man, I gave up childish ways."
(1 Corinthians 13:11)

The primary expression of the resurrected age will be the expression of love. If Corinthian Christians truly desired to orient their lives to their future hope, it would be a marked orientation to the way of love.

2 CORINTHIANS
Introduction

Paul wrote 2 Corinthians from Macedonia some time around 55-56 A.D. The purpose for Paul's second letter to the Corinthians was as a follow up to a stern letter written with "many tears" to the Corinthian Church mentioned in 2 Corinthians 2:3-4.

"And I wrote as I did, so that when I came I might not suffer pain from those who should have made me rejoice, for I felt sure of all of you, that my joy would be the joy of you all. For I wrote you out of much affliction and anguish of heart and with many tears, not

to cause you pain but to let you know the abundant love that I have for you."
(2 Corinthians 2:3-4)

2 Corinthians: Chapters 1-13

Paul Defends His Legitimacy as an Apostle (1:1–7:16)	Paul's Appeal for Generosity Toward the Christians in Judea (8:1–9:15)	Paul's Confrontation of the Super Apostles (10:1–13:10)	Closing Greetings (13:11–14)

For this reason, it is believed that there was a fourth letter written to the Corinthians. The first letter is mentioned in 1 Corinthians 5:9; the second is referenced in 1 Corinthians; the third is the *"many tears"* letter mentioned in 2 Corinthians 3-4; and, the fourth is 2 Corinthians.

The letter addresses three issues. First, Paul's legitimacy as an apostle was being called into question because of his suffering and struggles in his ministry, Chapters 1-7. Paul argues that it is his sufferings, struggles, and weakness that make his apostleship legitimate as a sign of sharing in the sufferings of Christ and the power of his Spirit.

Second, in Chapters 8-9, Paul calls the Corinthian church to participate in the offering that he is collecting for the persecuted believers in Judea. Paul encourages the believers in Corinth to be generous out of their abundance.

Finally, in Chapters 10-13, Paul returns to the subject of the *"super-apostles"* of the Corinthian church who were stirring up dissention and undermining the apostolic authority of Paul. He confronts them in their arrogant boasting. He challenges their legitimacy by a comparison to his own credentials as an apostle.

Paul's Defends His Legitimacy as an Apostle

The main focus of 2 Corinthians is in Paul's defense of his own legitimacy as an apostle. His concern is not as much with himself as it is with the believers in the Corinthian church and their faith and commitment to the Gospel of Jesus Christ.

Greetings and Introduction

Paul identifies himself as *"an apostle of Christ Jesus by the will of God"* (2 Corinthians 1:1). He is writing not only to the Christians in Corinth but also to the province of Achaia. His opening prayer is a blessing of God for his comfort in afflictions and sufferings. This opening blessing reveals the crux of the issue addressed by the letter. A group of so called *"super-apostles"* (2 Corinthians 11:5; 12:11) had infiltrated the Corinthian church and were calling into question the apostolic authority of Paul by pointing to his sufferings and afflictions.

Paul sees the afflictions that he has suffered as the foundation of his legitimacy. He is sharing *"abundantly in Christ's sufferings"* (2 Corinthians 1:5). For Paul, suffering is a reason to bless God for in suffering we are forced to *"rely not on ourselves, but on God who raises the dead"* (2 Corinthians 1:9).

PAUL'S BOAST IN CHRIST: His Sincerity toward Them

The issue of boasting will come up again later in the letter. The *"super-apostles"* likely pointed to their own status, successes and eloquence as evidence to their supremacy over Paul and the other apostles. Paul points not to his success but to his personal relationship with and sincerity towards the Corinthian Christians.

His concern is that his delay in visiting them could be misconstrued as a broken promise (2 Corinthians 1:15-24). He explains that the delay in his visit was to spare them the pain of a difficult and inevitable confrontation (2 Corinthians 2:1). His absence provided the necessary space for them to exercise the church discipline called for in his last letter and for forgiveness and restoration of the sinner (2 Corinthians 2:2-11).

Paul's sincerity in his tearful accountability and gracious accommodation toward the Corinthians should be compared to the *"peddlers of God's word"* (2 Corinthians 2:17) who are doing ministry for their own gain rather than to serve others and Christ.

PAUL'S LETTER OF RECOMMENDATION: The Spirit in Them

Paul continues in his defense of his apostolic ministry by providing *"letters of recommendation"* (2 Corinthians 3:1). The *"letters"* are the ministry of the Holy Spirit of God at work within them. Earlier he spoke of his desire to have a second experience of grace with them.

The first experience of grace was in the proclamation of the Gospel and the outpouring of the Holy Spirit into the hearts of the believers. Paul compares the ministry of Moses and the letters on stone to his own ministry written with *"the Spirit of the living God…on tablets of human hearts"* (2 Corinthians 3:3), the second experience.

Paul's exposition of Exodus 32-34 highlights the supremacy of God's glory revealed in the new covenant in Jesus Christ as compared with the old covenant through Moses. The primary difference between the two is in the locus of divine glory.

Moses displayed a reflected and fading glory. As awesome as the light shining from his face was, it was nothing in comparison to the glory of Christ—a transfigured glory shining from within his own divine personhood. Those who behold the face of Jesus Christ are themselves transfigured from within by the divine Spirit of God, because the Spirit is the Lord.

Paul's conclusion is that his letter of recommendation is an *"open statement of the truth"* as opposed to the *"disgraceful, underhanded ways"* of those who *"practice cunning or to tamper with God's word"* (2 Corinthians 4:2). The Gospel speaks for itself in the changed lives of those who are being saved and changed by it. Therefore, Paul has no need to commend himself; the fruit of the ministry of the Gospel is commendation enough.

"For what we proclaim is not ourselves, but Jesus Christ as Lord, with ourselves as your servants for Jesus' sake. For God, who said, 'Let light shine out of darkness,' has shone in our hearts to give the light of the knowledge of the glory of God in the face of Jesus Christ."
(2 Corinthians 4:5-6)

The awesome power of God's glory in us leads to an awesome ministry of reconciliation through us. Paul now returns to the pressing issue used by the "super-apostles" to question the value and legitimacy of his ministry—namely, his own physical suffering.

PAUL'S MINISTRY OF RECONCILIATION:
Treasure in Jars of Clay

Paul argues that his own external suffering highlights the surpassing glory that shines within his heart and ministry.

"But we have this treasure in jars of clay, to show that the surpassing power belongs to God and not to us. We are afflicted in every way, but not crushed; perplexed, but not driven to despair; persecuted, but not forsaken; struck down, but not destroyed; always carrying in the body the death of Jesus, so that the life of Jesus may also be manifested in our bodies."
(2 Corinthians 4:7-10)

The ministry of reconciliation will lead to physical death and eternal life. Just as Jesus was crucified in the flesh, so too must the minister of the Gospel humbly accept the call to suffering for the Gospel's sake. Knowledge of the death and resurrection enables the minister of the Gospel to maintain a radical outlook on life and death. From a worldly point of view, it may even seem crazy (2 Corinthians 5:13). But from a Christian point of view, it is the reconciling power of God.

God has chosen to use those who are in Christ be instruments of his new creation. Paul calls this the *"ministry of reconciliation"* that has been entrusted to all Christians as a holy calling.

"All this is from God, who through Christ reconciled us to himself and gave us the ministry of reconciliation; that is, in Christ God was reconciling the world to himself, not counting their trespasses against them, and entrusting to us the message of reconciliation."
(2 Corinthians 5:18-19)

The heart of Paul's ministry is in this ministry of reconciliation. He is a divine ambassador calling all people to a reconciled relationship with God—including the Corinthians!

"Therefore, we are ambassadors for Christ, God making his appeal through us. We implore you on behalf of Christ, be reconciled to God. For our sake he made him to be sin who knew no sin, so that in him we might become the righteousness of God."
(2 Corinthians 5:20-21)

This message of grace and forgiveness has been at the heart of Paul's service to them. The *"super-apostles"* are leading them away from this message of grace. Paul is calling them back to it. Paul is willing to undergo any indignity, pain or tribulation to see this grace fulfilled in the lives of the people of the Corinthian church.

> *"And we all, with unveiled face, beholding the glory of the Lord, are being transformed into the same image from one degree of glory to another. For this comes from the Lord who is the Spirit."*
> *(2 Corinthians 3:18)*

PAUL'S CHALLENGE TO REPENTANCE:
The Joy of Godly Grief

The humility and suffering of Paul, coupled with the glory and power of the Gospel should drive the Corinthians toward the joy of repentance, and indeed it has! Paul could care less about his own personhood; his desire is for their salvation through repentance to Jesus Christ and holiness (2 Corinthians 6:1-7:1).

Paul had been bold with them in confronting the sin within their congregation in his letter of tears. Perhaps this was part of the reason why they were questioning the relationship with Paul and turning toward the *"super-apostles."* Paul had not minced words in confronting some wrong within their congregation. He realizes that the letter caused the church some measure of pain and grief. He even had mixed feelings about sending it! (2 Corinthians 7:8) But his letter produced a godly grief within the congregation that led to the joys of repentance and restoration.

"As it is, I rejoice, not because you were grieved, but because you were grieved into repenting. For you felt a godly grief, so that you suffered no loss through us. For godly grief produces a repentance that leads to salvation without regret, whereas worldly grief produces death."
(2 Corinthians 7:9-10)

Paul's Appeal for Generosity Toward the Christians in Judea

In Chapters 8 and 9, Paul shifts subjects and turns to the task of collecting an offering for the persecuted Christians in Judea. Paul is in Macedonia. He has been completely surprised by the generosity of the Macedonian Christians. The contrast with the Corinthians could not be starker. Macedonia is extremely poor but abounding in generosity; the Corinthians are exceedingly rich, but will they excel in generosity?

The Macedonian church is impoverished, and yet they gave not only financially, but begged to give of themselves in participation. Paul praises the Macedonians as a godly example to be emulated by the Corinthians. He challenged them to excel in matching their generous witness. (2 Corinthians 8:7) Paul says that if they will freely give to the Jerusalem Christians, God will match their generosity in blessings back to them (2 Corinthians 9:11-15).

Paul's Confrontation of the "Super-Apostles"

In the final three chapters of 2 Corinthians, Paul returns his attention to the so called "super-apostles." He recognizes that he is engaged in spiritual warfare with these false teachers. He is now ready to do battle with them directly.

It has come to Paul's attention that the *"super-apostles"* say this of him: *"His letters are weighty and strong, but his bodily presence is weak, and his speech of no account"* (2 Corinthians 10:10). But they do not know the Apostle Paul. They have mistaken his humility for weakness of character. Paul chooses to boast in his weakness and sufferings to magnify Christ and to demonstrate his love for whom he serves. Paul commends himself to them as the one who first brought them the Gospel (2 Corinthians 10:14). He has never asked anything for himself in return (2 Corinthians 11:7). On the contrary, the Gospel came to Corinth at the expense and generosity of other congregations—even impoverished Macedonia! (2 Corinthians 11:9) He calls out the *"super-apostles:"*

"For such men are false apostles, deceitful workmen, disguising themselves as apostles of Christ. And no wonder, for even Satan disguises himself as an angel of light. So it is no surprise if his servants, also, disguise themselves as servants of righteousness. Their end will correspond to their deeds."
(2 Corinthians 11:13-15)

No, Paul's credentials come in the form of his sufferings for the Gospel and Jesus Christ (2 Corinthians 11:23-33). He could boast in his superior revelation from God, but he is embarrassed to do so as himself (2 Corinthians 12:1-7). The Lord has given him a "thorn in the flesh" to keep him from being proud (2 Corinthians 12:7). Paul's desire is that the church would heed his words from him and respond to his apostolic authority. His greatest fear is that they would be led astray by these false teachers.

"For I fear that perhaps when I come I may find you not as I wish, and that you may find me not as you wish—that perhaps there may be quarreling, jealousy, anger, hostility, slander, gossip, conceit, and disorder. I fear that when I come again my God may humble me before you, and I may have to mourn over many of those who sinned earlier and have not repented of the impurity, sexual immorality, and sensuality that they have practiced."
(2 Corinthians 12:20-21)

> "The point is this: whoever sows sparingly will also reap sparingly, and whoever sows bountifully will also reap bountifully. Each one must give as he has decided in his heart, not reluctantly under compulsion, for God loves a cheerful giver."
> *(2 Corinthians 9:6-7)*

But Paul hopes and prays that his fears will not be realized as the Corinthian Christians respond to the call to godly sorrow and repentance as well as accountability with the false teachers. His desire is that the church will *"aim for restoration, comfort one another"* (2 Corinthians 13:11). Paul's extant letters to the Corinthians provide insight into the practical and theological issues converted Gentiles faced while offering wisdom that still rings true today.

CHAPTER 5 NOTES:

CHAPTER 6
The Gospel of God

OBJECTIVE: The Maturing Christian will understand the sovereign plan of salvation revealed in the Gospel.

INTRODUCTION

Paul's letter to the Romans encapsulates the lessons he taught the Gentile believers as he made his third missionary journey (53 A.D.). Though many of the epistolary books of the New Covenant sought to resolve specific conflicts within the early church, Paul's letter to the Romans focuses on creating and maintaining a peaceful, faith-based community of believers. The broad theological foundation he provides explains the need for salvation, the redemptive gift of Jesus Christ, and the practicalities of creating a relationship with the Lord. He discusses the implications of redemptive history as it pertains to Jewish and Gentile communities and describes the manifestation of faith in personal and communal practices. Paul promised to visit Rome after he completed his trip to Jerusalem, but his imprisonment and trial in Jerusalem meant that Paul would reach Rome by different circumstances than he imagined at the end of his letter (Romans 15:22-29).

Overview of Paul's Third Missionary Journey

Before embarking on his third missionary journey, Paul spent time in Syrian Antioch building the community and preaching extensively. Syrian Antioch became a hub for Christianity, and it served as a home base for Paul as he traveled. He left Syrian Antioch and first visited Galatia and Phrygia. From Phrygia, he returned to Ephesus. He spent a little over two years teaching in Ephesus, first to the Jews and then to the Gentiles, who were significantly more receptive to his message. Paul revisited Macedonia and Greece after a riot broke out in Ephesus. From a region in western Greece known as Achaia, he traveled to Troas and Assos and continued to Miletus. In Miletus, a coastal town near Ephesus, Paul delivered a farewell speech to the

Map 1. *Paul's Third Missionary Journey*/www.biblemapper.com/Used with permission.

Ephesian elders. There he boarded a boat and sailed around Rhodes and past Cyprus. He and his party rested for a week in Tyre before making the trip to Caesarea. Despite the foreboding prophecies made by several believers about Paul's fate in Jerusalem, Paul pressed on to the city. Paul completed his third missionary journey in Jerusalem.

INTRODUCTION TO ROMANS

The Letter to the Romans has been one of the most influential books in the New Testament. Many of the greatest leaders in the Christian church were converted or deeply influenced by the letter. Christian thought leaders such as St. Augustine, Martin Luther, and John Wesley trace their initial conversion and spiritual awakening to verses from the Letter to the Romans. The letter is Paul's most systematic and dynamic presentation of the Gospel of Jesus Christ.

Paul's aim in writing the letter is to set forth a clear and well-developed presentation of the Gospel and its implications for the church and the world. He clearly identifies this purpose in his opening statements:

"Paul, a servant of Christ Jesus, called to be an apostle, set apart for the gospel of God, which he promised beforehand through his prophets in the holy Scriptures, concerning his Son, who was descended from David according to the flesh and was declared to be the Son of God in power according to the Spirit of holiness by his resurrection from the dead, Jesus Christ our Lord, through whom we have received grace and apostleship to bring about the obedience of faith for the sake of his name among all the nations, including you who are called to belong to Jesus Christ." (Romans 1:1-6)

Paul specifically addressed the church in Rome. Because his exposition is more positive than negative, it does not appear that Paul is addressing a particular problem as he does in some of his other letters. Rather, he is providing a broad theological foundation for the church, one that will be readily accessible with little need for contextual adjustments to address other audiences. His main theme is the theological and personal application of the incarnation, death, resurrection, and ascension of Jesus Christ. Paul clearly understands this to be the fulfillment of everything the Jewish scriptures hoped for in the Messiah and the Messianic age. He also sees the message of the

Gospel as having wide implications not just for the Jewish people but *"among all the nations,"* (Romans 1:5) including the church in Rome.

Original Audience: The Church in Rome

The Roman church had, by this point, become something of a missionary outpost. Located in the capital city of the Roman Empire, the church had a global reach for presenting the Gospel. Paul expressed gratitude to the church for their strong witness saying, *"I thank my God through Jesus Christ for all of you, because your faith is proclaimed in all the world"* (Romans 1:8).

It appears from the letter that Paul had not visited the church in Rome, though he deeply wanted to do so (Romans 13). The letter laid the groundwork for a future preaching-teaching visit. It may have served as a surrogate for a more personal instruction. Paul's delay is revealed in Romans 15:22-33 where he describes his journey to Jerusalem to deliver a gift to the impoverished saints there.

Paul's delay in visiting Rome became the occasion for writing this letter. It has had a tremendous impact over time. Had he gone to Rome earlier, the letter to the Romans would not have been written. That is why one commentator calls Paul's Jerusalem letter "The Gift that Changed the World." Sometimes God prevents us from doing what we want so he can accomplish an even greater purpose.

Structure of Romans

ROMANS Topic	Passage
Introduction to the Revelation of the Gospel	1:1 - 1:17
The Revelation of the Justice of God	1:18 - 3:20
The Revelation of the Grace of God	3:21 - 8:39
The Revelation of the Plan of God	9:1 - 11:36
The Revelation of the Will of God	12:1 - 15:13
Concluding Greetings and Benedictions	15:14 - 16:27

INTRODUCTION TO THE REVELATION OF THE GOSPEL

In Paul's introduction, we see his thesis for the book:

"For I am not ashamed of the gospel, for it is the power of God for salvation to everyone who believes, to the Jew first and also to the Greek. For in it the righteousness of God is revealed from faith for faith, as it is written, 'The righteous shall live by faith.'"
(Romans 1:16-17)

Over the course of his letter, Paul systematically works through the major themes of this statement. First, he establishes the universal human need for salvation from the judgment of a holy God. Every person on this planet desperately needs the message of salvation held out in the Gospel. This is why Paul is not ashamed to bring this message. This is covered in the first three chapters.

Second, Paul expands on how God has revealed his salvation in the person and work of Jesus Christ. Paul calls this salvation *"righteousness"* or *"justification,"* and he describes it as a gift offered to all humanity. He explains that the way a person receives this righteousness is by responding in what he calls *"the obedience of faith"* in Jesus. In Chapters 3-8, Paul explains how this righteousness works and is appropriated in our lives through belief.

In Chapters 9-11, Paul explains the unfolding plan of a sovereign God who offers the Gospel to and through the Jewish people and then to the rest of the world. He wrestles with the implications of God's sovereignty and the human responsibility to carry out the plan of salvation, *"to the Jew first and also to the Greek."*

Finally, Paul expands on how those who have believed in the Gospel will *"live by faith."* Not only do the *"righteous"* receive eternal life because of faith, but the righteous will manifest their faith tangibly in the character and actions of their lives. Chapters 12-15 discuss the implications of the Gospel through the discernment of God's will and the applications of his will in our individual lives and among the believing community.

The Revelation of God's Justice

In Romans 1:18 – 3:20, Paul makes a systematic case that all people are alike in that they are under the judgment of God because of sin and rebellion. Paul begins his discussion of our need for salvation, describing the wrath of God revealed against the rebellion of the pagan Gentile societies (Romans 1:18-32). He then demonstrates the fallacy of self-justification by addressing the self-righteous moralist (Romans 2:1-16). He calls out those who exempt themselves from the judgment of God due to their Jewish status as heirs of God's law (Romans 2:17-38). He concludes with a compilation of stinging quotes from the Hebrew scriptures revealing the universality of human sin and rebellion in all people. So that *"the whole world may be held accountable before God"* (Romans 3:19).

The Wrath of God

Paul begins his argument with a rather jarring statement:

"For the wrath of God is revealed from heaven against all ungodliness and unrighteousness of men, who by their unrighteousness suppress the truth."
(Romans 1:18)

Fig. 1. St Paul holds the sword with which he was martyred by decapitation, and appears to address us, in token of his great powers as a preacher. *St Paul* (oil on canvas), Batoni, Pompeo Girolamo (1708-87) / Basildon Park, Berkshire, UK / National Trust Photographic Library/John Hammond / Bridgeman Images.

The Gospel is necessary because all humankind is in danger of God's righteous judgment. Before Paul tells the Good News, he awakens his audience with the bad news. Humanity is intrinsically rebellious to God and his self-revealed nature. It has willfully held down and rejected the truth about God and failed to give him the worship and glory that he is due. The consequences of this rebellion have been immense. God has given them over to the depravities of their minds, hearts, and desires. Many of the things that we so often label as "sins" are really the consequences of willful rebellion against the worship of God.

The Critical Moralist

Paul anticipates that some will seek to exempt themselves from the blanket condemnation, so he states that all moralistic judgment is ultimately self-condemning because all people have sinned. The moralist's commitment to law and conscience only results in condemnation, because no one can keep the laws of God perfectly. God's justice for those who break his law is perfect in its impartiality and exactitude. He even will judge the "secrets of men" (Romans 2:16).

The Self-Righteous Jew

Paul offers eight self-confident statements of Jewish self-righteousness:

"But if you call yourself a Jew and rely on the law and boast in God and know his will and approve what is excellent, because you are instructed from the law; and if you are sure that you yourself are a guide to the blind, a light to those who are in darkness, an instructor of the foolish, a teacher of children, having in the law the embodiment of knowledge and truth ...."
(Romans 2:17-20)

Then he turns the tables on this self-confidence by highlighting the Jewish hypocrisy when it comes to keeping the law: *"While you preach against stealing, do you steal?"* (Romans 2:21). The Jewish faith reveals God's oracles and high standards. But in revealing those righteous standards, they also demonstrate human sinfulness by way of contrast. The light of God flows from the words of the Jewish people, yet their own lives are characterized by just as much darkness as the rest of humanity (Romans 3:5-8).

ALL have sinned!

Paul's dramatic conclusion is that every person, including himself, has sinned and is deserving of God's wrath and condemnation (Romans 3:9). With a barrage of quotations from the Old Testament, Psalms, and prophetic writings, he summarizes this section:

"None is righteous, no, not one;
  no one understands;
  no one seeks for God.
All have turned aside; together they have become worthless;
  no one does good,
  not even one."
"Their throat is an open grave;
  they use their tongues to deceive."
"The venom of asps is under their lips."
  "Their mouth is full of curses and bitterness."
"Their feet are swift to shed blood;
  in their paths are ruin and misery,
and the way of peace they have not known."
  "There is no fear of God before their eyes."
(Romans 3:10-18)

If the book of Romans were to end there, it would be a gloomy book indeed! However, Paul has laid the groundwork for the great Gospel of God through Jesus Christ. The laws of God and the consciences of men stop every mouth from self-justification and hold the entire world *"accountable to God"* (Romans 3:19) The law condemns us—it cannot save us. Our universal sin and the revelation of God's wrath and judgment against human sin means that we all have a universal need for salvation.

The rest of Romans reveals the solution to the need for salvation, the New Covenant. Paul describes the grace offered to all people through faith in the person and works of Jesus Christ.

The Revelation of the Grace of God

If Chapters 1-3 were about the revelation of God's wrath and judgment due to human sin, Chapters 3:21-8:39 are about God's revelation of grace and righteousness through Jesus Christ.

God's Righteousness Revealed and Examined

Romans 1:18 begins: *"For the wrath of God is revealed from Heaven …"*

Romans 3:21 begins: *"But now, the righteousness of God has been manifested …"*

The words *"But now"* indicate a major turning point in Paul's presentation. He concluded the last section with a withering indictment of all of humanity. *"none is righteous, no, not one"* (Romans 3:10). But God has overcome this dilemma through sending his son:

"But now the righteousness of God has been manifested apart from the law, although the Law and the Prophets bear witness to it—the righteousness of God through faith in Jesus Christ for all who believe. For there is no distinction: for all have sinned and fall short of the glory of God, and are justified by his grace as a gift, through the redemption that is in Christ Jesus, whom God put forward as a propitiation by his blood, to be received by faith." (Romans 3:21-25a)

Paul explains the righteousness of God will not come from sinful humanity following the law but by a gift of gracious forgiveness and redemption through the cross of Jesus Christ. As he explains, a gift is not earned as some type of compensation but rather is accepted and received through faith in Jesus.

He anticipates there will be intellectual objections to this idea and

Revelation of the Grace of God

1. God's Righteousness Revealed and Examined (Romans 3:21-4:25)
2. God's People United with Christ (Romans 5:1-6:23)
3. God's Law and Christian Discipleship (Romans 7:1-25)
4. God's Spirit in God's Children (Romans 8:1-39)

confronts possible objections directly. The first objection is that such a scheme eliminates a person's ability self-confidently to boast in their own *"self-righteousness."* Paul agrees—there is no longer any room to boast in self. Because righteousness is a gift given and not a reward earned, the person who receives this gift has no grounds to boast in it (Romans 3:27-31).

In the second objection, Paul anticipates that this way of considering righteousness would make a pious Jew uncomfortable. He rhetorically asks, *"What then shall we say was gained by Abraham, our forefather, according to the flesh?"* (Romans 4:1). This is a reference to the covenant sign of circumcision. Paul then uses Abraham as the primary illustration: even Abraham did not receive righteousness because of his obedience to the commandment to be circumcised, but rather he received it for his belief in *"him who justifies the ungodly"* (Romans 4:5). He believed in God, "and it was counted to him as righteousness" (Romans 4:3). Indeed, he says if Abraham got what was due to him with regard to the law, he would receive judgment.

"'Blessed are those whose lawless deeds are forgiven,
and whose sins are covered;
blessed is the man against whom the Lord will not count his sin.'"
(Romans 4:7-8)

Continuing, Paul argues that Abraham became the model and father of all who share his faith in the God *"who gives life to the dead and calls into existence the things that do not exist"* (Romans 4:17). Those who would share in Abraham's faith are called to *"believe in him who raised from the dead Jesus our Lord, who was delivered up for our trespasses and raised for our justification."* (Romans 4:24-25). Theologians refer to this as the *"imputation of righteousness;"* that the righteousness of God is *"credited to us"* even though we do not deserve it—it is a gift to all who believe in Jesus.

God's People United with Christ

Now Paul turns from explaining how the Gospel works and is appropriated by faith to a description of the benefits of being given this righteousness. In Romans 5:1-11, Paul tells of six marvelous results of being made righteous or justified by faith in Christ. Each benefit begins with a *"we,"* emphasizing the unity of the body of Christ. Paul then compares two humanities: one in Adam and one in Christ. We are all born into Adam and in him die. Those who believe in Jesus are given new life—eternal life (Romans 5:12-21).

Chapter 6 describes the actual change that will take place in our lives through the transformation into unity with Jesus Christ. Paul uses the metaphor of Jesus' physical cross and resurrection to describe the spiritual death and resurrection that takes place in the life of a believer. The sinful nature is put to death, and we are given a new resurrected nature in Jesus Christ. This concept is difficult to describe, so Paul uses another metaphor—slavery and freedom. By our human nature and wills, we are enslaved to sin. However, Jesus is in the process of liberating us from our sinful nature through a process of renewal and inner transformation called sanctification.

God's Law and Christian Discipleship

The process of sanctification is not accomplished through external means such as commandments and laws, but rather by internal renewal through the gift of the Holy Spirit. In Chapter 7, Paul discusses the effects of the external commandments of God on a person controlled by the sinful nature. Even though God's commandments are right and good, they accomplish death in our lives. What the believer has that the law cannot accomplish is the inward liberating power of the Holy Spirit.

God's Spirit in God's Children

In the final chapter of this section, Paul explores how the Holy Spirit liberates the sinful will from the power of the sin nature (Romans 8:1-11). He describes the work of the Spirit as a process of interaction and transformation in accordance with the divine purposes and will of God. The Holy Spirit works as a type of interpreter between God the Father and the children of God. Those who have the Spirit of God can be assured of absolute security and goodness in their relationship and love from God. No matter what forces and threats assault the people of God, there is nothing that can separate them from him. This would have been particularly reassuring to the Roman Christians who faced persecution because of their faith.

"No, in all these things we are more than conquerors through him who loved us. For I am sure that neither death nor life, nor angels nor rulers, nor things present nor things to come, nor powers, nor height nor depth, nor anything else in all creation, will be able to separate us from the love of God in Christ Jesus our Lord."
(Romans 8:37-39)

> **Revelation of the Plan of God**
> 1. *Israel's Fall: God's Purpose of Election*
>   (Romans 9:1-33)
> 2. *Israel's Fault: God's Dismay Over Her Disobedience*
>   (Romans 10:1-21)
> 3. *Israel's Future: God's Long-Term Design*
>   (Romans 11:1-32)
> 4. *Doxology*
>   (Romans 11:33-36)

THE REVELATION OF THE PLAN OF GOD

Chapters 3-8 are about God's revelation of grace and righteousness for believers in Jesus Christ. Chapters 9-12 reflect on the larger plan of God's salvation for all people in the world.

In this section, Paul teaches about the revelation of divine sovereignty and human responsibility with a focus on the Jewish rejection of the Messiah. He discusses how ultimately the hardness of the human heart among Jew and Gentile alike will be overcome through the faithful preaching of the Gospel and the internal calling of the Holy Spirit to the praise of God's glory.

Israel's Fall: God's Purpose of Election

Ultimately, salvation is entirely dependent on the sovereignty of God. Paul reflects with *"great sorrow"* over the rejection of the Messiah by many of the Jewish people. For Paul, this is a very personal and difficult truth. He has *"great sorrow and unceasing anguish"* for the members of his own family who have rejected Jesus despite their unique role in redemptive history (Romans 9:2). Using the story of Israel's history, he demonstrates that salvation has been the prerogative of God's election and choosing. (Romans 9:6-18)

Paul anticipates that his audience will be left with a question of the justice of the divine election of some and not all without any basis other than mysterious divine purpose.

"What shall we say then? Is there injustice on God's part? By no means!"
(Romans 9:14)

Paul argues that mercy does not have to be fair. God will have mercy on whom he has mercy (Romans 9:15). Fairness means justice, and no one wants that. Though he exercises mercy, God is completely just in exercising judgment on those he determines need it, such as Pharaoh (Romans 9:17).

We are the Lord's creation, and he will determine who is saved and who is not. God is in control. Does this somehow negate human responsibility? (Romans 9:19) Not at all! We are on the horns of a logical mystery. God is in control of determining his elect unto salvation *"not from the Jews only but also from the Gentiles,"* and human beings are held responsible for our rebellious choices and actions (Romans 9:24).

Israel's Fault: God's Dismay Over Her Disobedience

Again, does God's sovereignty in election somehow negate human responsibility? Not at all! It is precisely because of the willful stubbornness of the Jewish people that they have rejected the Messiah. They sought *"to establish their own, they did not submit to God's righteousness"* (Romans 10:3). And again, he says of the Jewish rejection: *"All day long I have held out my hands to a disobedient and contrary people"* (Romans 10:21).

Paul holds out hope for the Gentiles and the Jewish people in the Gospel. Quoting the promise from the prophet Joel, *"… everyone who calls upon the name of the Lord shall be saved"* (Joel 2:32). Paul argues for a chain of causality leading to salvation that includes both the human responsibility of preaching, hearing, believing, calling on the Lord, and the divine sovereignty in sending out messengers of the Gospel and quickening hearts in election (Romans 9:13).

So, what of the Jewish people? Is there any hope for them that they would hear and believe? Yes of course! According to Paul, God currently is electing a remnant (Romans 11:5).

Israel's Future: God's Long-Term Design

Paul explains that God's ultimate plan is the grafting in of the Gentiles by God's grace even while Israel is going through a time of hardening. However, he warns Gentile believers not to be too haughty in their salvation and Jewish unbelief. God can easily judge the haughty.

"Note then the kindness and the severity of God: severity toward those who have fallen, but God's kindness to you, provided you continue in his kindness. Otherwise you too will be cut off."
(Romans 11:22)

God has a larger plan that includes all the people of this world, and it is mysteriously unfolding in his time. It is this unfolding plan that requires a certain trust and fear of the sovereign Lord. Salvation is according to his plan. For this reason, Paul calls the Christian to marvel in the glorious wonder of God:

"Oh, the depth of the riches and wisdom and knowledge of God! How unsearchable are his judgments and how inscrutable his ways!

'For who has known the mind of the Lord, or who has been his counselor?'

Or 'who has given a gift to him that he might be repaid?'
For from him and through him and to him are all things. To him be glory forever. Amen."
(Romans 11:33-36)

Manifesto on Evangelism

Based on Romans 10-11, John Stott, in his commentary on Romans, delineates an eight-point evangelism manifesto, which is summarized as follows:

1. The **need for evangelism**: evangelism is necessary because until people hear and receive the gospel they are lost. (Romans 1-3; 10:13-14)

2. The **scope of evangelism**: the whole human race must be given the chance to hear the gospel. (Romans 1:5; 3:22; 9:4; 10:2, 12, 18; 11:23; 16:26)

3. The **incentive to evangelism**: evangelism arises from the love and longing of the heart. (Romans 9:1ff; 10:1)

4. The **nature of evangelism**: evangelism is sharing with others the good news of Christ crucified and risen. (Romans 9:30-10:13; particularly 10:6ff.)

5. The **logic of evangelism**: evangelism demands the sending out of evangelists, so that people may call on Christ for salvation. (10:13ff.)

6. The **result of evangelism**: evangelism brings such blessings to those who believe, that it arouses the envy of others. (10:19; 11:11, 4)

7. The **hope for evangelism**: evangelism has hope of success only if it rests on the election of God. (10:1, 14, 17, 21)

8. The **goal of evangelism**: evangelism introduces converts into the people of God, and so brings glory to God. (9:17; 22ff.; 11:30ff.)

The Revelation of the Will of God

Drawing on his other letters, Paul offers guidance on the practical application of the Gospel to resolve any potential conflict in the church. As Paul contemplates the implications of the Gospel, one way to frame this last section is using the theme of relationships. At the heart of the Gospel is the message of how God has reconciled and redeemed our relationship with him. In view of this renewed and redeemed relationship, our human relationships are transformed as well.

The Revelation of the Will of God: Transformed Relationships	Romans 12:1-16-16:27
Our Relationship to God: Consecrated Bodies and Renewed Minds	Romans 12:1-2
Our Relationship to Ourselves: Soberly Understanding Spiritual Gifts	Romans 12:3-8
Our Relationships to One another: Love in the Family of God	Romans 12:9-16
Our Relationship to Our Enemies: Not Retaliation but Service	Romans 12:17-21
Our Relationship to the State: Conscientious Citizenship	Romans 13:1-10
Our Relationship to the Day: Living in the "Already" but "Not yet"	Romans 13:11-14
Our Relationship to the Weak: Welcoming, and Not Despising or Judging	Romans 14:1-15:13
Conclusion: The Providence of God and the Ministry of Paul	Romans 15:14-16:27

Consecrated Bodies and Renewed Minds

In the first two verses of Chapter 12, Paul calls the Romans to rise above the practices of the world, *"to present your bodies as a living sacrifice, holy and acceptable to God, which is your spiritual worship"* (Romans 12:1). On a basic level, this means abstaining from immoral and degrading behaviors. Living a Christian life in Rome would have been difficult—not only was it the capital city of an oppressive pagan empire, but also it was the epicenter of extreme immorality. However, Paul also is reminding them of the transformative properties of the Holy Spirit. The Spirit cleanses the hearts and minds of those who offer themselves to God, and this renewal is the first step in maintaining a relationship with him. The mind transformed by the Holy Spirit interacts with the world in a different way.

Soberly Understanding Spiritual Gifts

Paul warns the Roman Christians of valuing certain spiritual gifts over others. They should consider their own gifts because each one has an important purpose. He compares the church to the body: not all members have the same function, and the diversity of functions among members is what comprises the body of Christ. As members of the body of Christ, we should use our gifts to the best of our ability to further the faith: *" … if prophecy, in proportion to our faith; if service, in our serving; the one who teaches, in his teaching; the one who exhorts, in his exhortation; the one who contributes, in generosity;*

the one who leads, with zeal; the one who does acts of mercy, with cheerfulness" (Romans 12:6-8). By exercising our spiritual gifts, we please the Lord.

Love in the Family of God

The message of the Gospel is ultimately one of love—God's love for his people and Jesus' expression of love through suffering. Paul now addresses interpersonal relationships within the body of Christ. He charges the Roman Christians to:

"Let love be genuine. Abhor what is evil; hold fast to what is good. Love one another with brotherly affection. Outdo one another in showing honor. Do not be slothful in zeal, be fervent in spirit, serve the Lord. Rejoice in hope, be patient in tribulation, be constant in prayer. Contribute to the needs of the saints and seek to show hospitality. Bless those who persecute you; bless and do not curse them. Rejoice with those who rejoice, weep with those who weep. Live in harmony with one another. Do not be haughty, but associate with the lowly. Never be wise in your own sight."
(Romans 12:9-16)

Believers must mirror Jesus' radical love in their earthly communities. Paul paints a picture of relational care where each member of the church does his or her best to contribute to the group as a whole and also to extend empathy, love, and understanding to individuals. These rules of love and harmony also apply to those who persecute and curse them.

Because the transformed mind rises above the practices of the world, human justice has no place in the Christian community. Instead of retaliating when wronged, Christians should turn the other cheek. Paul elaborates on how to respond to evil words and deeds: *"Beloved, never avenge yourselves, but leave it to the wrath of God, for it is written, 'Vengeance is mine, I will repay, says the Lord.' To the contrary, 'If your enemy is hungry, feed him; if he is thirsty, give him something to drink; for by doing so you will heap burning coals on his head'"* (Romans 12:19-20). The Lord is the only one who can pass judgement, and yet he provided an avenue for forgiveness through Jesus Christ. Paul reminds his audience that they are called to practice forgiveness and grace just as Jesus did.

Conscientious Citizenship

Paul pivots from interpersonal relationships to the relationship between governments and citizens. As citizens of the Roman Empire pledged allegiance to the one true God, it is possible the Roman Christians felt conflicted about their loyalty. The Roman emperor was worshipped as a deity, but they recognized a power higher than the emperor, which called their allegiance to the government into question. As members of the Kingdom of God, how were they to interact with their earthly government? According to Paul, *"For there is no authority except from God, and those that exist have been instituted by God"* (Romans 13:1). He argues that rulers and authorities are only a threat to those who break the law, and those who follow the law have no reason to fear the government. Those who enforce the law are *"an avenger who carries out God's wrath on the wrongdoer. Therefore one must be in subjection, not only to avoid God's wrath but also for the sake of conscience"* (Romans 13:4-5). He goes on to remind them of their obligation to pay taxes and to give honor and respect to whom it is owed.

Paul describes love as the fulfillment of the law because the commandments *"... are summed up in this word: 'You shall love your neighbor as yourself.' Love does no wrong to a neighbor, therefore love is the fulfilling of the law"* (Romans 13:9-10). Being a good citizen and a good neighbor means meeting societal obligations with respect and demonstrating love to the entire community. It is only when one acts outside of love that the law demands justice.

Living in the "Already", but "Not Yet"

In Paul's letters to the other communities, he discusses the pitfalls associated with misunderstanding the timing of Christ's return. The Galatians had an under-realized sense of eschatology. They believed the Day of the Lord was so far in the future that they returned to the Old Covenant laws as if Christ's kingdom had not been inaugurated. They needed to step into the *"Already/Not Yet"* kingdom. Paul had to push them forward to realize more of the implications of the coming age.

Conversely, the Thessalonians mistakenly believed the Day of the Lord and Christ's return was so close at hand that they stopped working. They had a hyper-realized eschatology manifest with an over-preoccupation with the Day of the Lord as if it was about to happen any day now. Paul had to spur them into action by extending their eschatological horizon.

The Corinthians had an even over-realized eschatology because they were behaving as though the consummation had already taken place and they were attempting to over realize the coming age. Paul had to remind them that Jesus hadn't yet returned and pull them back into the *"Already/Not Yet"* kingdom.

Eschatology of the New Testament

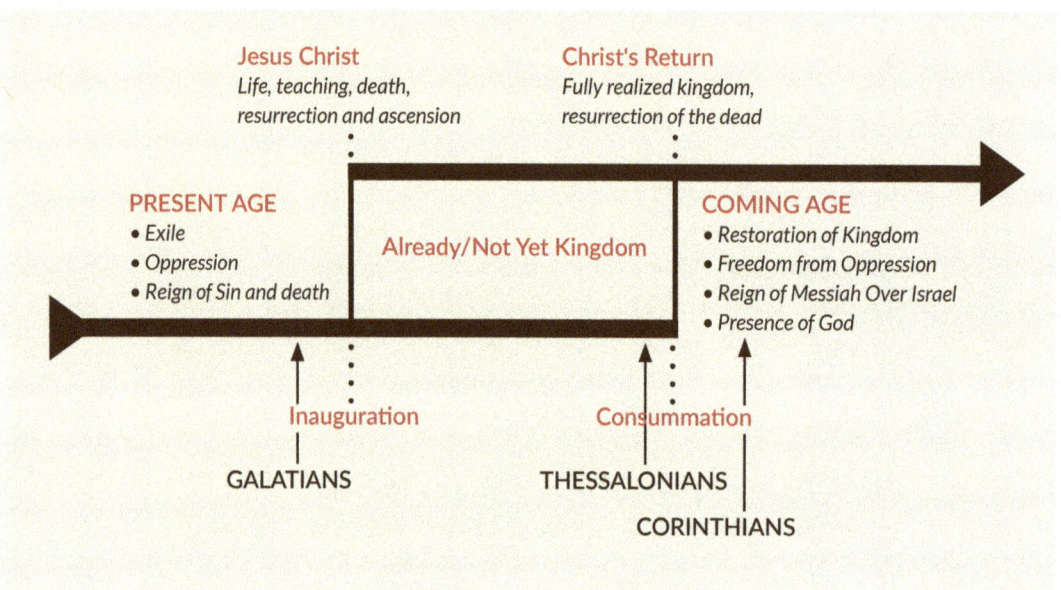

Because the Day of the Lord is an easily misunderstood but hope-inspiring promise, Paul takes some time at this point in the letter to encourage the Roman Christians with the proximity of their salvation. Paul writes, *"Besides this you know the time, that the hour has come for you to wake from sleep. For salvation is nearer to us now that when we first believed. The night is far gone; the day is at hand. So then let us cast off the works of darkness and put on the armor of light"* (Romans 13:11-12).

The salvation of the Lord was closer than it ever had been for the Romans. Like a bride waiting for her wedding, Christians wait for the Day of the Lord. Paul tells the Romans that now that they have accepted Christ, they should ensure their behavior matches the promise of the salvation to come: *"Let us walk properly as in the daytime, not in orgies and drunkenness, not in sexual immorality and sensuality, not in quarreling and jealousy. But put on the Lord Jesus Christ, and make no provision for the flesh, to gratify its desires"* (Romans 13:13-14). The day has not yet arrived, but they should prepare by embracing all that is good.

Welcoming Instead of Despising or Judging

Paul then addresses a timelessly derisive issue: passing judgment on the diets and worship practices of others. The Roman church, like the majority of the early churches, had a mixture of Jewish and Gentile members. These two cultures had different eating practices, yet they would have shared a common table as congregants, which doubtlessly lead to internal conflict.

However, it does not matter who eats meat and who eats only vegetables because all who participate in worshiping the Lord are worthy in his sight. Paul writes, *"Who are you to pass judgment on the servant of another? It is before his own master that he stands or falls. And he will be upheld, for the Lord is able to make him stand"* (Romans 14:4). It does not matter if one person prefers to worship on a particular day and his neighbor worships on another because *"The one who observes the day, observes it in honor of the Lord. The one who eats, eats in honor of the Lord, since he gives thanks to God, while the one who abstains, abstains in honor of the Lord and gives thanks to God"* (Romans 14:6).

Essentially, the means and method of honoring God do not matter so long as they glorify him. Everyone in the community of Christ should give each other the grace to engage with God in their personal way. Everyone experiences and expresses spiritual maturity in a different way, and Paul instructs the Romans to respect those differences. However, differences in diet and worship should not cause someone to stumble in their practice. Paul uses himself as an example:

"I know and am persuaded in the Lord Jesus that nothing is unclean in itself, but it is unclean for anyone who thinks it unclean. For if your brother is grieved by what you eat, you are no longer walking in love. By what you eat, do not destroy the one for whom Christ died. So do not let what you regard as good be spoken of as evil. For the kingdom of God is not a matter of eating and drinking but of righteousness and peace and joy in the Holy Spirit. Whoever thus serves Christ is acceptable to God and approved by men. So then let us pursue what makes for peace and for mutual upbuilding."
(Romans 14:14-19)

The path to spiritual maturity is personal and calling someone's relationship with the Lord into question because of their food choices might cause them to stumble in self-doubt. Paul says, *"The faith that you have, keep between yourself and God"* (Romans 14:22). Those with strong faith should shore up their weaker brothers and sisters, not bring them down with judgment. Paul charges the Romans to live in harmony with each other, to encourage each other to glorify God, to *"... welcome one another as Christ has welcomed you, for the glory of God"* (Romans 15:7).

The Ministry of Paul

Paul concludes his letter by summarizing his ministry and the ways God helped him achieve such depth and breadth of evangelism. Particularly, he is proud that he brought the Gospel to so many Gentiles. He reaffirms his conviction to preach the Gospel in new places. He also explains his delay in visiting Rome—he is on his way to Jerusalem to take them the donations from Macedonia and Achaia. After he has completed that journey, he plans to visit Rome on his way to Spain. Paul asks for their prayers as he travels:

"I appeal to you, brothers, by our Lord Jesus Christ and by the love of the Spirit, to strive together with me in your prayers to God on my behalf, that I may be delivered from the unbelievers in Judea, and that my service for Jerusalem may be acceptable to the saints, so that by God's will I may come to you with joy and be refreshed in your company. May the God of peace be with you all. Amen."
(Romans 15:30-33)

The end of Paul's letter features a long greeting to a number of specific people, including women, and a greeting from the members of his travel party. He offers some summary advice and closes his letter with the doxology.

Paul's Journey to Jerusalem

As Paul continued his trip to Jerusalem, he encountered several ill-boding prophecies predicting his fate, but he stayed the course. Paul and his group traveled by boat from Miletus after Paul said goodbye to the elders of Ephesus.

When they landed in the Syrian city of Tyre, they found the disciples there and stayed for a week. The disciples in Tyre spoke through the Holy Spirit and warned Paul not to continue his journey to Jerusalem, but Paul remained undeterred. They left Tyre for Caesarea, where they stayed with Philip the evangelist. While they were at Philip's house, a prophet called Agabus arrived from Judea. Taking Paul's belt, he bound his own-

Fig. 2. *Paul says farewell,* 2002 (w/c on paper), Harlin, Greg (b.1957) / Private Collection / Wood Ronsaville Harlin, Inc. USA / Bridgeman Images.

hands and feet with it and said, *"Thus says the Holy Spirit, 'This is how the Jews at Jerusalem will bind the man who owns this belt and deliver him into the hands of the Gentiles'"* (Acts 21:11). When they heard Agabus' prophecy, the people broke down in tears and begged Paul to stay in Caesarea. But Paul would not be persuaded. He replied, *"What are you doing, weeping and breaking my heart? For I am ready not only to be imprisoned but even to die in Jerusalem for the name of the Lord Jesus"* (Acts 21:13). A few days later, Paul arrived in Jerusalem.

The church in Jerusalem excitedly welcomed Paul, and they listened intently as he told them of the things God had done for the Gentiles through his ministry. Though they understood why Paul preached to the Gentiles and why he preached that Jewish Christians should abandon the laws of Moses, the Jewish population resented Paul for these teachings. The church members knew that Paul's reputation as someone who communed with Gentiles would precede him, and so they encouraged him to purify himself with some other believing Jews as a symbol of his accordance with the Jewish customs.

On the seventh day of Paul's purification, some Jews from Asia recognized him in the temple. They accused him of not only teaching against the law but also of defiling the temple. Because they had seen him the previous day with a Gentile, they assumed he had brought his Gentile companion into the temple, and they stirred the crowd into a frenzy. The riotous attitude spread to the entire city, and they seized Paul and dragged him out of the temple. The crowd wanted to kill him, but the Roman authorities had heard about the violent crowd and quickly sent the tribune and soldiers to quell the conflict. Upon seeing the soldiers, the crowd stopped beating Paul. The tribune arrested Paul and asked the crowd what he had done, but the crowd was so uproarious that he couldn't understand what they said.

The soldiers carried Paul to the barracks, where he got the attention of the tribune. Paul identified himself and asked to speak to the angry crowd, and the tribune agreed. Paul stood on the steps and addressed the mob. He spoke to them in Hebrew and told them his testimony: how he had persecuted Christians until the Lord struck him blind and how he came to believe in Jesus. The crowd listened intently, but when he had finished speaking, they still condemned him. The tribune took Paul back into the barracks and ordered that the soldiers whip him into confession. But when Paul was positioned for the flogging, he asked the centurion nearby, *"Is it lawful for you to flog a man who is a Roman citizen and uncondemned?"* (Acts 22:25). The centurion ran to the tribune to ask his advice. They both returned to Paul, where the tribune asked Paul about his citizenship. The tribune had purchased his citizenship for a large sum of money, but Paul was a citizen by birth. Legally, the tribune and centurion had made a grave transgression against Paul, and they felt afraid.

Even still, they did not free him, but instead they took him to the Sanhedrin to find out why the Jews had accused him.

Once in front of the council, Paul declared his innocence in God, but the high priest ordered that someone strike him on the mouth for saying such a thing. Paul challenged the high priest, *"'God is going to strike you, you whitewashed wall! Are you sitting to judge me according to the law, and yet contrary to the law you order me to be struck?'"* (Acts 23:3). He did not know that the priest he addressed was the high priest. After admitting his mistake, Paul identified himself as a Pharisee when he realized that half of the council were Pharisees and the other half were Sadducees. He added, *"'It is with respect to the hope and resurrection of the dead that I am on trial'"* (Acts 23:6), because he knew the Pharisees and Sadducees fundamentally disagreed on the existence of resurrection, angels, and spirits. The council broke out in debate, and it became so heated that the tribune removed Paul from the council, fearing he would be injured.

The Beginning of Paul's Journey to Rome

That night, the Lord appeared to Paul and encouraged him, saying *"'Take courage, for as you have testified to the facts about me in Jerusalem, so you must testify also in Rome'"* (Acts 23:11). The next day, 40 angry Jews made a pact to abstain from eating and drinking until they had killed Paul. Informing the chief priests and elders of their plan, they asked that the council summon Paul so that they could lay in wait and kill him on his way. Though the council agreed, Paul's nephew caught wind of the plan, and he went to the barracks to tell Paul of the plot to kill him. Paul got a centurion to escort his nephew to the tribune, where he told the tribune of the ambush to kill Paul. The tribune ordered 200 soldiers, 70 horsemen, and 200 spear men to escort Paul to Felix the governor. In the dead of night, the soldiers took Paul to Caesarea and presented him to the governor, who agreed to give him a hearing.

Fig. 3. *The Roman soldiers take Paul by night from Jerusalem,* Dixon, Arthur A. (1872-1959) / Private Collection / Bridgeman Images.

CHAPTER 6 NOTES:

CHAPTER 7
The Spirit and the Church

OBJECTIVE: The maturing Christian will understand the role of the Holy Spirit in loosing the chains of oppression and setting the human spirit free to develop into a new ordering of human relationships.

INTRODUCTION

Even as the world bound Paul in chains and falsely accused him, he recognized the freedom of his heart, and the letters he wrote during his imprisonment reflect his confidence in God's salvation. Paul wrote seven extant letters while he awaited trial after trial on the road to Rome. Four of these letters, Ephesians, Colossians, Philippians, and Philemon, concentrate on maintaining a new life in Christ while navigating the new societies and relationships emerging at the time. Each letter addresses a different conflict in the church: steadfastness, false teachers, persecution, and human slavery.

He offered the Ephesians preventive medicine to avoid the mistakes of other churches while examining the cosmology of Christianity. Cosmology is the study of how the universe is ordered. The New Covenant writings answer the big theological and philosophical questions quite differently than the cultures of the day.

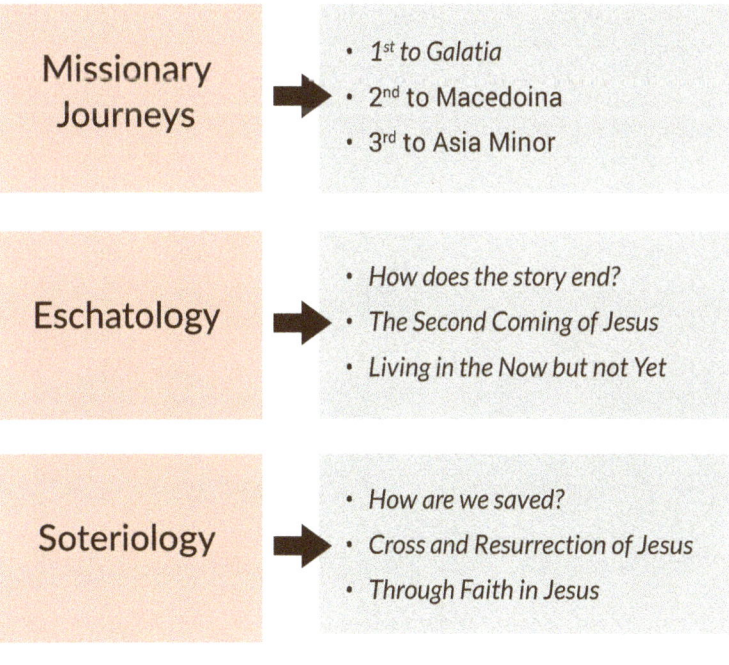

He gave radical surgery to the Colossians, instructing them to cut out the false teachings spreading throughout their church. Paul encouraged the Philippians by giving them a heavenly perspective with which to view their earthly struggles. He wrote to Philemon on the subject of freedom from human slavery. Though Paul remained in custody, his confidence and assurance in God's plan for conquering evil never wavered, and he shared his strength with others through his letters.

Religion in the Roman Empire

The official religion of the Roman Empire followed the ancient Greek pantheon of gods. It represented the antithesis of Christianity, and the philosophical differences between the two religions explain the confusion of Gentile converts and the Roman backlash against Christianity. The polytheistic religion practiced in Roman society was a mixture of foreign deities, international cults, and as the empire progressed, the imperial cult. It absorbed new territories and the deities of that region. This was a means of promoting social stability. With the exception of Judaism, the Roman Empire pressed its culture into nearly every group they conquered, while allowing some religious freedom. The imperial cult served as an advertisement for new territories, and by worshipping their deified royalty, citizens demonstrated their loyalty to the empire. Rejecting the state religion was a treasonous action.

Fig. 1. The Caesar Cult envisioned the emperor as a divine-human, son of god. Here is Caesar Augustus as Jove, Jupiter, holding scepter and orb (first half of century A.D.) State Hermitage Museum, Saint Petersburg, Russia.

Those who worshipped the Roman pantheon of gods and goddesses relied on a transactional philosophy rather than one of faith: if they said the right prayer and offered the correct sacrifice or offering, then they would receive a favorable outcome. They had little understanding of divine grace. They believed that upon death, they would enter the underworld, which was more like the Roman Catholic purgatory than heaven. The Christian concepts of salvation by faith would have been entirely foreign; as for most pagan Romans, faith did not play a role in their practices. There was no life after death, reunion with God, or divine forgiveness. Indeed, the Christian concept of a single God with ultimate power who granted salvation to those who believed would have been almost unimaginable for the pagans. Even the Jewish belief systems of the time emphasized observance of law rather than salvation by grace.

As Christianity spread throughout the empire, the pagan religions lost their foothold among their former followers as more of them turned to the salvation possible in Jesus Christ. The Roman Empire began to see Christianity as a major threat not only because it placed a single authority over their own, but also because it reflected an entirely different outlook, one incompatible with legalistic Rome.

Fig. 2. This model of the Temple of Artemis, at Miniatürk Park, Istanbul, Turkey, attempts to recreate the probable appearance of the first temple.

Paul's Imprisonment in Caesarea

After his transport to Caesarea, Paul waited in Felix the governor's custody for five days before the Jewish high priest Ananias arrived with some elders. Ananias son of Nebedeus officiated as high priest in Jerusalem from about 47 A.D. to 52 A.D. His party included a spokesperson called Tertullus. Ananias and his group explained their grievance against Paul to Felix, so Felix summoned Paul to defend himself. Before Paul could say anything, Tertullus accused him of attempting to profane the temple, describing him as *"… a plague, one who stirs up riots among all the Jews throughout the world … a ringleader of the sect of the Nazarenes"* (Acts 24:5). When the governor allowed Paul to speak, he denied Tertullus' accusations. Paul explained:

"But this I confess to you, that according to the Way, which they call a sect, I worship the God of our fathers, believing everything laid down by the Law and written in the Prophets, having a hope in God, which these men themselves accept, that there will be a resurrection of both the just and the unjust. So I always take pains to have a clear conscience toward both God and man. Now after several years I came to bring alms to my nation and to present offerings. While I was doing this, they found me purified in the temple, without any crowd or tumult."
(Acts 24:14-18)

Fig. 3. *Saint Paul in Prison,* 1627 (oil on panel), Rembrandt Harmensz. van Rijn (1606-69) / Staatsgalerie, Stuttgart, Germany / © Selva/Leemage / Bridgeman Images.

The Jews had no evidence of their accusations, and it was unclear which laws had been broken. Felix knew quite a bit about the Way, but he decided to postpone his judgment until the tribune who had witnessed the disturbance arrived. He ordered Paul to return to custody and granted him privileges so his friends could visit him.

Paul's imprisonment in Caesarea was more like house arrest. After a few days, Felix and his wife Drusilla sent for Paul and listened to him speak about the Gospel. But when Paul's discussion of righteousness, self-control, and judgment alarmed and frightened Felix, he sent Paul away, promising to hear more at a later date. Paul remained in his custody, writing and praying. Felix hoped that Paul might bribe him for his release, so he regularly talked with Paul during the last two years of his governorship, but Paul offered him nothing but the Gospel, so Felix did not reopen his case. After two years, Porcius

Festus took over the governorship, and Felix left Paul in prison as a favor to the Jews.

Paul Appeals to Caesar

A few days after Porcius Festus took office, he traveled to Jerusalem where the chief priests and elders presented their case against Paul. They urged Festus to send Paul to Jerusalem, hiding their plan to ambush and kill him. Instead, he invited the chief priests and elders to travel with him to Caesarea and present their case in front of the tribunal. After a week, Festus returned to Caesarea with the Jews. The Jews who accused him of a number of serious charges could not prove any of them. Paul denied that he had committed any offense against the Jews, the temple, or Caesar. Festus admired the fervor of the Jews, and so seeking to do them a favor, he asked Paul if he wanted to be tried in Jerusalem. Paul replied,

> "I am standing before Caesar's tribunal, where I ought to be tried. To the Jews I have done no wrong, as you yourself know very well. If then I am a wrongdoer and have committed anything for which I deserve to die, I do not seek to escape death. But if there is nothing to their charges against me, no one can give me up to them. I appeal to Caesar."
> (Acts 25:10-11)

Paul's Letters from Prison (A.D. 61-62)

Ephesians
Colossians
Philipians
Philemon

Map 1. *Paul's 4th Missionary Journey.*

Festus left and discussed the matter with his council. When he returned, he told Paul, *"To Caesar you have appealed; to Caesar you shall go"* (Acts 25:12).

A few days later, Agrippa and his wife Berenice visited Festus in Caesarea. As they broke bread together, Festus, perplexed by Paul's case, explained the trial and Paul's appeal to the king. After he told Agrippa about it, he asked to hear Paul's argument for himself. The next day, as Paul stood before King Agrippa, Festus announced Paul's case and stated that although he had decided to send him to Caesar, he could not identify the charges against him. The king gave Paul license to speak for himself, and he delivered his testimony to the crowd. He spoke of his former life as a Pharisee and persecutor of Christians, his miraculous conversion on the road to Damascus, his mission to spread the Gospel, and his faith in Jesus Christ. As Paul spoke, Festus interrupted him and accused him of being mad. But Paul replied,

"I am not out of my mind, most excellent Festus, but I am speaking true and rational words. For the king knows about these things, and to him I speak boldly. For I am persuaded that none of these things has escaped his notice, for this has not been done in a corner. King Agrippa, do you believe the prophets? I know that you believe."
(Acts 26:25-27)

King Agrippa asked Paul if he were trying to convert him to be a Christian, and Paul answered: *"Whether short or long, I would to God that not only you but also all who hear me this day might become such as I am—except for these chains"* (Acts 26:29). Satisfied with Paul's answers and testimony, the king, the governor, and the rest of his party withdrew. Behind closed doors, they agreed that Paul did not deserve death or punishment, and if he had not appealed to Caesar, Paul could have been set free. But because Paul sought an audience with Caesar, he was required to remain imprisoned.

EPHESIANS: Preventive Medicine

Paul likely wrote his letter to the church in Ephesus at the same time he wrote to the church in Colossae, while he was imprisoned. The two letters were written to address concerns with false teachers and corruption of Christian practices. Ephesus is about 100 miles to the west of Colossae. One might describe the letter to Colossae as *"radical surgery,"* and the letter to Ephesus as *"preventive medicine."*

Compared with Colossians, Ephesians is more general and positive in its tone, and does not appear to address a specific false teaching or practice. Rather, its purpose is to lay a strong foundation for the preaching of the Gospel. With Jesus Christ as the cornerstone, the church would be strong, united, and mature; able to face every stormy *"wind"* or *"wave"* of false teaching or ungodly practice.

The letter to the Ephesians may have been a circular letter intended to be copied, circulated, and read by many different congregations around the region. This may account for why the letter contains fewer personal greetings and acknowledgements than Paul's other letters. Some of the earliest copies of the letter do not have the audience identifier *"in Ephesus"* in the first verse.

"Paul, an apostle of Christ Jesus by the will of God,
To the saints who are in Ephesus, and are faithful in Christ Jesus."
(Ephesians 1:1)

This letter, along with the letter to Philemon and the letter to the church in Colossae, were hand delivered by Tychicus and Onesimus, two of Paul's personal assistants. (see Ephesians 6:21; Acts 20:4; Colossians 4:7; 2 Timothy 4:12; Titus 3:12; Philemon). Paul intended the letters that he wrote to be copied and shared among all the churches in the region (see Colossians 4:16).

The Church in Ephesus

The church in Ephesus was started by the apostle Paul. His visits are recorded in Acts. He left Apollo, Aquila, and Priscilla to build a mission congregation there (Acts 18:24-26). Early the following year, Paul stayed in Ephesus for two years and made it a base of missionary outreach from which *"… all the residents of Asia heard the word of the Lord, both Jews and Greeks"* (Acts 19:10). His missionary efforts from Ephesus to the region were so effective that the idol makers rioted.

"And you see and hear that not only in Ephesus but in almost all of Asia this Paul has persuaded and turned away a great many people, saying that gods made with hands are not gods. And there is danger not only that this trade of ours may come into disrepute but also that the temple of the great goddess Artemis may be counted as nothing, and that she may even be deposed from her magnificence, she whom all Asia and the world worship."
(Acts 19:26-27)

The work that Paul had accomplished in Ephesus was substantial despite all the opposition and persecution he encountered. The letters to the region serve to strengthen that good work for the long-term administration of the Gospel in Asia Minor.

On his last journey to Jerusalem, the apostle landed at Miletus, and after summoning the elders of the church from Ephesus, he delivered to them a farewell charge as he expected never to see them again. The final charge to the elders of the Church in Ephesus resonates with the letter to the church. He voices concern for their strong leadership in *"… the word of his grace, which is able to build you up"* in the face of the threat of false teachers that Paul characterizes as *"fierce wolves"* who will speak *"twisted things"* to draw away disciples (Acts 20:29-32).

Paul's purpose in writing the letter is clearly pre-emptive. He is seeking to ward off the theological problems that were plaguing other congregations in the region. If those twisted teachings and practices were to take root in Ephesus, it could be disastrous for the entire Christian community in Asia. For this reason, the letter provides a strong dose of preventative medicine for churches in every generation.

Ephesians' Literary Structure

Passage	Content	Theme	Structure	Mood
1:1–14	Salutation and benediction for all God's blessings in Christ	Salvation	New life	*Indicative: What God has done for believers in Christ*
1:15–23	Prayer of thanksgiving for knowing God's glorious work in Christ			
2:1–10	Saved by grace through faith in Christ			
2:11–22	Gentiles and Jews are united in Christ	Reconciliation	New society	
3:1–13	Paul's calling to preach the gospel of Christ to the Gentiles			
3:14–21	Prayer of intercession for Christ's love, power, and glory in the church			
4:1–16	Exhortation to use a diversity of gifts to promote unity in the body of Christ	Sanctification	New Standards	*Imperative: What God tells believers to do in Christ*
4:17–32	Exhortation to put off the old self and put on the new self in Christ			
5:1–21	Exhortation to walk in the love and the light of Christ			
5:22–33	Husbands and wives	Domestic Duties	New Relationships	
6:1–9	Parents and children, masters and servants			
6:10–20	The full armor of God	Spiritual Warfare		
6:21–24	Closing greetings and benediction			

---

[1] http://www.esvliterarystudybible.org/search?q=Ephesians+1

The book of Ephesians divides neatly into two main sections. In Chapters 1-3, Paul is primarily speaking in the indicative verb tense about the new life and society being formed in Jesus Christ. In the second half of the book, Chapters 4-6, Paul moves toward the application of this new life and community, first, to day-to-day life in the church as a maturing body and, second, to individuals and households living within a world that is under spiritual assault by the forces of evil.

INDICATIVE: What God Has Done for Believers in Christ

The heart of Paul's life and ministry is what he calls the *"Gospel of Salvation."* In Chapter 1, Paul praises God for the blessings and benefits of the Gospel of Salvation in the lives of the church in Ephesus. In Chapter 2, he explains precisely how the Gospel of Salvation works through grace and faith in Jesus Christ. He outlines the larger implications of the Gospel as an outworking of the plan of God for global reconciliation among all people. In Chapter 3, Paul reflects on the cosmic and spiritual realities at work in the interplay between the administration of the Gospel on Earth among the nations and the impact of God's work on the rulers, powers, and authorities in the heavenly realms.

SALVATION: New Life

After his epistolary greetings, Paul describes in rich language the new life given to *"the saints"* in Jesus Christ. Before he can talk about it, he overflows in blessing and thanksgiving to God for the gift of the Gospel of Salvation. God is working out a glorious plan of salvation for humankind in Jesus Christ. Paul speaks of the *"riches of his grace..."*"...

"which he lavished upon us, in all wisdom and insight making known to us the mystery of his will, according to his purpose, which he set forth in Christ as a plan for the fullness of time, to unite all things in him, things in heaven and things on earth."
(Ephesians 1:8-10)

God has a plan for cosmic unity that is being brought into operation—right now! Paul is overwhelmed with praise and gratitude that he and the members of the Church in Ephesus are privileged to be a part of it. At the heart of the plan is the death and resurrection of Jesus Christ and the outpouring of the Holy Spirit. These two powerful forces are saving the world, one person at a time.

The forces of evil in *"this world," "the prince of the power of the air,"* and *"the passions of our flesh"* are on a course that will result in death, bondage, and the wrath of God (Ephesians 2:1-3). But the Lord, who is *"rich in mercy"* and of *"great love,"* has made a way of salvation through faith in the grace offered by the cross and resurrection of Jesus (Ephesians 2:4) and through resurrection power at work through the indwelling gift of the Holy Spirit (Ephesians 1:13, 17-23; 2:8-10).

The application of the Gospel comes through the agency of the gift of the Spirit manifesting itself in believing faith in Jesus Christ and in the outworking of a "holy life" in Christ:

"For by grace you have been saved through faith. And this is not your own doing; it is the gift of God, not a result of works, so that no one may boast. For we are his workmanship, created in Christ Jesus for good works, which God prepared beforehand, that we should walk in them."
(Ephesians 2:8-10)

RECONCILIATION: New Society

The fruit of the Gospel of Salvation is global and cosmic unity. The grace and spiritual power offered through Jesus Christ and the Holy Spirit is universal in scope. They are being offered and received by all nations, Gentile and Jew alike. Before the coming of Jesus Christ, nations and people were estranged from one another. But now the reconciliation of the nations to God through the Jewish Messiah provides the occasion for radical reconciliation among human peoples, tribes, and nations.

"But now in Christ Jesus you who once were far off have been brought near by the blood of Christ. For he himself is our peace, who has made us both one and has broken down in his flesh the dividing wall of hostility by abolishing the law of commandments expressed in ordinances, that he might create in himself one new man in place of the two, so making peace, and might reconcile us both to God in one body through the cross, thereby killing the hostility."
(Ephesians 2:13-16)

Again, the heart of what makes this possible is the cross of Jesus Christ and the uniting gift of the Holy Spirit (Ephesians 2:16,18).

Paul draws on the covenantal promises given through the Old Testament prophets of a united humanity built together as a living temple with Jesus Christ as *"the cornerstone"* (Ephesians 2:20).

The problem for international unification on earth throughout history has been a result of rebellion by powers, rulers, and authorities in the heavenly spiritual realms. The reunification of people with God through the cross and Holy Spirit has the reversing effect of unseating rebellious spiritual authorities and powers in the heavenly realms. It is for this reason that Paul is devoted to praying for the spiritual strengthening of the people of the church in the spiritual power and love of God:

"For this reason I bow my knees before the Father, from whom every family in heaven and on earth is named, that according to the riches of his glory he may grant you to be strengthened with power through his Spirit in your inner being, so that Christ may dwell in your hearts through faith—that you, being rooted and grounded in love, may have strength to comprehend with all the saints what is the breadth and length and height and depth, and to know the love of Christ that surpasses knowledge, that you may be filled with all the fullness of God."
(Ephesians 3:14-19)

IMPERATIVE: What God Tells Believers to Do in Christ

The Gospel of Salvation has practical implications for every believer and new community in Christ. The theory translates into practical reality. In Chapters 4 and 5, Paul addresses the application of the Gospel to corporate church administration, unity, maturity in truth and love, and personal spiritual holiness of life (Ephesians 4:1-5:21). He then exhorts the church to manifest the reconciliation in Christ through all interpersonal and household relationships. Finally, he redefines the nature of the conflict to be primarily a spiritual conflict with Satan and the spiritual forces of evil in heavenly realms (Ephesians 6:10-24).

SANCTIFICATION: New Standards

As Paul has stated previously, the church is the primary locus of the new society being built in Christ. So, he first turns his attention to maintaining the unity of the church in the truth of the Gospel. Frequently, evil uses two forces, schism and heresy, to thwart the plan of God. It is imperative that the leaders of the church work together as a unified body to grow strong in Christ (Ephesians 4:1-6).

While there is a diversity of gifts and peoples within the membership of the church, that diversity was given to help strengthen a unified and built-up body of Christ that is mature and immovable in the truth:

"... so that we may no longer be children, tossed to and fro by the waves and carried about by every wind of doctrine, by human cunning, by craftiness in deceitful schemes. Rather, speaking the truth in love, we are to grow up in every way into him who is the head, into Christ, from whom the whole body, joined and held together by every joint with which it is equipped, when each part is working properly, makes the body grow so that it builds itself up in love."
(Ephesians 4:14-16)

The second component to the new life and new society in Christ is to manifest and walk in the spirit-filled life. There will be a marked contrast between those who are not saved and still under bondage and those who are saved and free in Christ. The new self and new creation will be reflected in the Christian's manner of speech, self control of emotions, character of grace and forgiveness, and sexual purity (Ephesians 4:17-5:7). Christians are called to walk as children of the light, reflecting God's glory and his spirit of love, holiness, and truth (Ephesians 4:8-21).

NEW RELATIONSHIPS: Domestic Duties and Spiritual Warfare

The new life and new society in Christ redefines the relationships Christians have at the household level (Ephesians 5:22-6:9). Also, it redefines their relationships with adversaries and enemies (Ephesians 6:10-24).

Paul ended the last section with an exhortation: *"… do not get drunk with wine, for that is debauchery, but be filled with the Spirit"* (Ephesians 5:18). We are filled in three ways:

1. By addressing one another with psalms, hymns and spiritual psalms (corporate worship);

2. By giving thanks in everything (Eucharist);

3. By submitting to one another out of reverence for the Lord (relationships).

In Ephesians 5:22-6:9, Paul expands on what it looks like to be filled with the Holy Spirit by submitting to one another out of reverence for the Lord. He begins with a focus on the marital relationship and describes a manner of mutual submission between husband and wife. He then turns to children and parents (Ephesians 6:1-4); and then to household servants and masters (Ephesians 6:5-9). Relationships in Christian households should reflect the sacrificial love of Jesus Christ.

Fig. 4. Our battle is not against flesh and blood. *Archangel Michael Defeating Satan,* c.1636 (oil on canvas), Reni, Guido (1575-1642) / Santa Maria della Concezione, Rome, Italy / Bridgeman Images.

"Husbands, love your wives, as Christ loved the church and gave himself up for her, that he might sanctify her, having cleansed her by the washing of water with the word, so that he might present the church to himself in splendor, without spot or wrinkle or any such thing, that she might be holy and without blemish."
(Ephesians 5:25-27)

The world's formation of household relationships is based on domination and power. Christ overcomes the world through mutual humility and love.

The way Christ conquers the world is through mysteriously overcoming the spiritual forces of evil. Paul redefines the battleline away from "flesh and blood" and toward Satan and the spiritual forces of evil:

"Put on the whole armor of God, that you may be able to stand against the schemes of the devil. For we do not wrestle against flesh and blood, but against the rulers, against the authorities, against the cosmic powers over this present darkness, against the spiritual forces of evil in the heavenly places."
(Ephesians 6:11-12)

The spiritual battle requires spiritual armor and weapons. Paul goes through each piece of armor in detail (Ephesians 6:13-17). Likewise, the weaponry is spiritual as well, the Word of God and the Spirit of God (Ephesians 6:17-20).

If the church will take the letter to the Ephesians to heart, it will be strong for fulfillment of God's plan to bring the kingdom of God on Earth as it is in heaven.

PAUL'S LETTER TO THE COLOSSIANS
Radical Surgery

What Paul addresses generally in Ephesus, he addresses specifically in Colossae. For this reason, if the letter to the Ephesians is *"Preventive Medicine,"* the letter to the Colossians is *"Radical Surgery."* The locus of concern for Paul was this congregation.

Paul's concerns pertained to a false teaching that was being foisted upon the Colossian Christians. There were some teachers who were seeking to delude and captivate the church through spiritual intimidation and manipulation.

We cannot know the precise nature of the false teaching; however, we can discern some sense of it from the specifics of the text. Paul's reference to the Sabbath and circumcision shows that the teachers were promoting some form of Judaism (Colossians 2:16, 2:11, 4:11). However, it appears that this teaching was not merely a Jewish practice based in strict legalism, of the sort that the church in Galatia and perhaps even Rome were being pressured to embrace.

This false teaching emphasized a form of *"super spirituality"* that *"qualified"* (Colossians 1:12) or *"disqualified"* (Colossians 2:18) people from the inner circle of elite believers on the basis of their angel worship, spiritual visions, and forms of physical asceticism or *"severity to the body"* that had little to do with union with Jesus Christ (Colossians 2:18-19).

COLOSSIANS

Topic	Passage
Paul's Heart Prayer for the Church: The Truth of the Gospel of Jesus Christ	1:1-14
The Supremacy of the Gospel of Jesus Christ: His Person and Work	1:15-23
Paul's Stewardship of the Gospel of Jesus Christ	1:24-2:5
The Sufficiency of the Gospel of Jesus Christ Alone	2:6-23
Seeking the Life of Jesus Christ	3:1-4:6
The Servants of Jesus Christ	4:7-18

Not only does Paul directly address the false beliefs and practices promoted by these teachers but also, he reasserts and encourages faith in the uniqueness and primacy of the person of Jesus Christ—he is the embodiment of the divine and thus wholly to be relied upon. He reminds them of their knowledge and understanding of the Gospel message that proclaims the full sufficiency of the redeeming work of Jesus Christ on the cross for salvation. And practically, he reaffirms the spiritual freedom and liberty they have as those who live by faith in the power of the Holy Spirit over the *"earthly"* and *"of the flesh."*

PAUL'S HEART PRAYER FOR THE CHURCH: The Truth of the Gospel of Jesus Christ

Paul introduces himself as an *"apostle"* of Christ Jesus *"by the will of God"* (Colossians 1:1). Paul uses other titles for himself such as a *"servant"* or *"prisoner for Christ Jesus."* The emphasis to the Colossians was on his authority as an authorized representative of Jesus Christ by God's ordination. As with all of Paul's opening prayers, we gain true insight into the concerns that occasioned the letter. His concern is for the continued maturity of the church in the Gospel message, the word of truth that they have received from Epaphras.

Epaphras had learned the Gospel from Paul himself while Paul was teaching in Ephesus. He then brought the *"word of truth"* back to the Colossae and established a new congregation. The degree of separation from the apostle, could have left a vulnerability to false teachers. As was happening in other congregations, pseudo-leaders were imposing themselves into the body and teaching a false understanding of the Christian life. Paul's purpose and prayer is that they would become stronger in the original message they had received both in their knowledge, understanding and beliefs, and in their manner of Christian life.

"And so, from the day we heard, we have not ceased to pray for you, asking that you may be filled with the knowledge of his will in all spiritual wisdom and understanding, so as to walk in a manner worthy of the Lord, fully pleasing to him, bearing fruit in every good work and increasing in the knowledge of God."
(Colossians 1:9-10)

For Paul, Christian beliefs and practice are intertwined. His prayer is that they would reach maturity in both. In addition, his prayer anticipates the false teaching that he will address in that he affirms that they are already *"qualified"* to receive a *"share of the inheritance as the saints of light."* The false teachers were using their own religious beliefs and practices as a standard to disqualify members of the church (see Colossians 2:16, 18, 1:12). For Paul, according to the Gospel the only qualification necessary is a faithful relationship with the Lord Jesus Christ.

The Supremacy of the Gospel of Jesus Christ: His Person and Work
Paul asserts Jesus as supreme in all things. The false teachers were asserting other things as primary, such as the worship of angels, festivals, Sabbath, and circumcision. By naming Jesus Christ as Lord, all other powers and authorities are diminished in their importance, becoming secondary at best. This is particularly relevant to the Colossians as the false teachers were asserting the primacy of mystical visions and angel worship (Colossians 2:18).

By proclaiming the supremacy of Jesus Christ (Colossians 1:15-23), Paul provides the foundation for his later applications regarding his own ministry, his stewardship of the Gospel, and the sufficiency of Christ alone for the salvation of the people of God. Paul is reasserting first principles in Jesus Christ and encouraging the Colossians not to shift away from their hope in Christ, lest they fall from their secure position in him:

"And you, who once were alienated and hostile in mind, doing evil deeds, he has now reconciled in his body of flesh by his death, in order to present you holy and blameless and above reproach before him, if indeed you continue in the faith, stable and steadfast, not shifting from the hope of the gospel that you heard, which has been proclaimed in all creation under heaven, and of which I, Paul, became a minister."
(Colossians 1:21-23)

Paul's Stewardship of the Gospel of Jesus Christ

Whenever the message of the Gospel is challenged, it is often on the basis of Paul's authority. At this time, he reasserts the foundation of his own ministry of the Gospel. It did not originate with him; he is merely a steward of a mystery revealed by God. The language he uses intentionally challenges the false teaching.

The claim of the false teachers (and it may have been just one person, see Colossians 2:18) for authority was on the basis of a secret revelation given to an elite few because of their special relationships with angels and because of detailed *"visions, puffed up without reason by his sensuous mind"* (Colossians 2:18). For Paul, the emphasis is on being a deacon or servant and not a puffed up, self-centered leader.

The Christian hope is not a secret given only to a select enlightened few who control a small sect. Paul points to the revelation of Jesus Christ—which is a mystery revealed to ALL the saints for EVERYONE in the world. Paul speaks of …

"... the mystery hidden for ages and generations but now revealed to his saints. To them God chose to make known how great among the Gentiles are the riches of the glory of this mystery, which is Christ in you, the hope of glory. Him we proclaim, warning everyone and teaching everyone with all wisdom, that we may present everyone mature in Christ. For this I toil, struggling with all his energy that he powerfully works within me."
(Colossians 1:26-29)

Paul points to Christ, the false teacher points to himself. Jesus holds all the *"hidden treasures of wisdom and knowledge"*—he alone is sufficient for salvation and life (Colossians 2:3).

The Sufficiency of the Gospel of Jesus Christ Alone

Because of their immaturity in Jesus Christ, the Colossian Christians were vulnerable to being manipulated by false leaders. Paul's concerns proved to be well-founded. In his second letter, to Timothy, he reveals *"… that all who are in Asia turned away from me"* (2 Timothy 1:15). Paul names Phygelus, Hermogenes (2 Timothy 1:15), and Alexander the Coppersmith (2 Timothy 4:14).

We do not know whether these are the same people about whom Paul was concerned in Colossae, but there were fractures in teaching and practice that were troubling. Paul had not been able to visit them *"face to face"* (Colossians 2:1). Paul's concern is that the church might be *"deluded"* by *"plausible arguments"* and taken *"captive by "philosophy and empty deceit, according to human tradition, according to the elemental spirits of the world and not according to Christ"* (Colossians 2:4,8).

At the heart of Paul's concern was the sufficiency of Jesus Christ and the Gospel for salvation. The false teachers were arguing for additional practices that included circumcision, keeping particular festivals, new moon celebrations, and Sabbaths. They were teaching rigorous physical asceticism: *"Do not handle. Do not taste. Do not touch"* (Colossians 2:21). They were teaching about hidden *"treasures of wisdom and knowledge"* (Colossians 2:3) of which only the initiated and enlightened were privy.

The Colossians were losing their freedom in Christ and allowing themselves to be manipulated and controlled by *"super-spiritual"* cult leaders who in their rigid lifestyle and secret visions and mystical talk of angels controlled those who were immature in their understanding of the Gospel. Paul reasserted that Jesus alone is sufficient. As for the other:

"These have indeed an appearance of wisdom in promoting self-made religion and asceticism and severity to the body, but they are of no value in stopping the indulgence of the flesh."
(Colossians 2:23)

Seeking the Life of Jesus Christ

In rejecting the self-made religion of the false teachers, Paul now paints a clear picture of what true life in Jesus Christ is like. The Colossians were right to seek and desire more. However, they should seek to go deeper by setting their mind on Christ and not on the things that are on earth. Christ is their life (Colossians 3:4). So, then, what does life in Christ look like?

First, there is an aspect of our character that needs to be *"put to death."* There are practices that need to be *"put away"* and *"taken off."* He calls all of this the *"old self."*

"Put to death therefore what is earthly in you: sexual immorality, impurity, passion, evil desire, and covetousness, which is idolatry. On account of these the wrath of God is coming. In these you too once walked, when you were living in them. But now you must put them all away: anger, wrath, malice, slander, and obscene talk from your mouth. Do not lie to one another, seeing that you have put off the old self with its practices ...."
(Colossians 3:5-9)

Paul encourages putting on the *"new self."* This is the *"life in Christ"* as it is *"being renewed in the image of the Creator"* (Colossians 3:10). The new self is free from the social, racial, and ethnic categories which create arbitrary pecking orders among human beings. In Christ, all are represented. In contrast with the *"old self"* the new self has its own character:

"Put on then, as God's chosen ones, holy and beloved, compassionate hearts, kindness, humility, meekness, and patience, bearing with one another and, if one has a complaint against another, forgiving each other; as the Lord has forgiven you, so you also must forgive. And above all these put on love, which binds everything together in perfect harmony."
(Colossians 3:12-14)

For Paul, the key is internal transformation through the peace and word of Christ. With the Colossians, the emphasis remains on the supremacy and sufficiency of Jesus Christ—the Christian life should be lived in every aspect unto him as the supreme Lord of all (Colossians 3:17).

This means that all human interactions should bring him honor: wives and husbands, children and parents, masters and servants. Christians are called to honor all, even those who are unjust in their treatment of others (Colossians 3:23-25). But Christian masters should all treat their servants justly and fairly, because all are bondservants to the Lord (Colossians 4:1).

The Servants of Jesus Christ

Paul concludes his letter with a long list of greetings and commendations from various people whom he holds up as examples and fellow servants in the Gospel of Jesus Christ. It is one thing to hear the principles explained and taught, but Christianity is better caught than taught. The notable examples Paul gives provide ample accountability for the Colossian congregation. While Paul is not able to visit them because of his imprisonment, they are not without his support.

The danger of false teaching (heresy) is that it leads to schism. Their unity is in Jesus Christ. They should not allow these false teachers to draw them away from Jesus, his body the Church, and the glorious life lived walking together with him. The Colossians need maturity in Christ, so at the end of Paul's letter is a list of mature believers with whom they can walk.

"Walk in wisdom toward outsiders, making the best use of the time. Let your speech always be gracious, seasoned with salt, so that you may know how you ought to answer each person."
(Colossians 4:5-6)

PAUL'S LETTER TO THE PHILIPPIANS
Partnership in the Gospel

The letter to the Philippians would be called in our day a missionary support letter. Paul is prayerful in his gratitude for the Philippians' steadfast *"partnership in the gospel from the first day until now"* (Philippians 1:5). His letter develops a theme of partnership in the Gospel.

Standing Tall Together in a Twisted and Crooked World

The general tone of Paul's letter to the Philippians is encouragement. When a person encourages, they breathe courage into a discouraged person or party. The church was facing difficulties due to external persecution, internal conflict, false teachers, and fallen members. They also shared deep concerns about Paul because of his imprisonment and impending death penalty. In this letter, Paul seeks to give the Philippians a heavenly perspective on earthly trials.

"But our citizenship is in heaven, and from it we await a Savior, the Lord Jesus Christ, who will transform our lowly body to be like his glorious body, by the power that enables him even to subject all things to himself."
(Philippians 3:20-21)

Using himself as an example in vulnerability, Paul allows them some insight into his own theological thought processes as he faces his own imprisonment and death sentence with courage in the Lord. He then provides some very practical encouragement to the members of the church that they too may stand up straight and tall for the Gospel of Jesus in the midst of a *"crooked and twisted generation"* (Philippians 2:15).

The Church in Philippi

While trying to minister in Asia, God had a different mission plan for Paul. In a vision, the Lord called him to go into Macedonia.

"And a vision appeared to Paul in the night: a man of Macedonia was standing there, urging him and saying, 'Come over to Macedonia and help us.' And when Paul had seen the vision, immediately we sought to go on into Macedonia, concluding that God had called us to preach the gospel to them."
(Acts 16:9-10)

In the very first city in Macedonia that Paul enters, he finds a convert. The city of Philippi is described as *"… a leading city in the district of Macedonia and a Roman colony"* (Acts 16:12). It was a city that prided itself in Roman culture and heritage as the site of a Roman military victory. The first converts to the church included Lydia, a merchant who sold purple dye, a demon possessed, *"fortune-telling"* slave girl, and the jailkeeper of the city Philippi (Acts 16:14, 16).

Paul's initial activity and the nature of the converts in Philippi caused quite a scene, and a political scandal ensued with the officials of the city (see Acts 16:11-40). They simply did not have a category for Christians or for Paul, who was both a Roman citizen and a loyal citizen of the Kingdom of God. The disruption and confusion caused by Paul certainly was not welcome in the city, and they asked him to leave:

"But Paul said to them, 'They have beaten us publicly, uncondemned, men who are Roman citizens, and have thrown us into prison; and do they now throw us out secretly? No! Let them come themselves and take us out.' The police reported these words to the magistrates, and they were afraid when they heard that they were Roman citizens. So they came and apologized to them. And they took them out and asked them to leave the city."
(Acts 16:37-39)

What began in conflict likely would have continued to be plagued with official trouble. The Christians who lived in Philippi would have been lumped in the same category as Paul. From the letter, we can see that they continued to have *"opponents"* who may have *"frightened"* them from "striving side by side for the faith of the gospel" (Philippians 1:27).

Those opponents may have been both unbelievers who lived as members of the *"crooked and twisted generation"* and false teachers who were promoting a form of heresy that Paul so firmly refuted in his letter to the Galatians. He warns them: *"Look out for the dogs, look out for the evildoers, look out for those who mutilate the flesh"* (Philippians 3:2).

The Philippian Christians were financial supporters of Paul's mission. His letter of encouragement to them was written with thanksgiving for their latest gift and it provides an update on the fruit of the ministry they are supporting.

Paul is writing to them from a prison in Rome. He mentions the Roman *"imperial guard"* (Philippians 1:17) and he sends greetings from the Christians in *"Caesar's household"* (Philippians 4:22). Paul was imprisoned in Rome starting around 62 A.D., ending with his martyrdom sometime between 64-67 A.D. So, the letter to the Philippians was written around 62 A.D. during his first imprisonment and period of house arrest in Rome. Therefore, it is often called one of his *"prison epistles"* along with the letters to Ephesians, Colossians, and Philemon.

Fig. 5. *St Paul in Prison*, English School, (20th century) / Private Collection / © Look and Learn / Bridgeman Images.

Literary Structure

PHILIPPIANS 1-4

    A *Prologue: 'Partnership in the Gospel' Theme Introduced with Prayerful Gratitude (1:1-11)*

        B *Comfort / Example: Paul's Safety and Right Thinking in the Midst of a Difficult 'Guarded' Situation (1:12-26)*

            C *Challenge: Stand Fast and Be United, Fulfilling Paul's Joy! (1:27-2.4)*

                D *Example / Action: Christ's Example of Humility and Suffering Before Glory, Then Related Behavioral Instructions (2:5-16)*

                    E *Midpoint: Caring Models of Gospel Partnership, Two of Which Are Sent to Help Immediately (2:17-3.1a)*

                D' *Example / Action: Paul's Example of Humbling and Suffering Before 'Upward Call' / Transformation, Then Instructions (3:1b-21)*

            C ' *Challenge: Stand Fast and Accentuate Existing Joy by the Reconciliation of Two Past Gospel Partners! (4:1-5)*

        B' *Comfort / Example: The Philippians' 'Guarded' Peace of Mind and Right Thinking in the Midst of an Anxious Situation (4:6-9)*

    A' *Epilogue: Partnership from the Past Renewed, with Expressed Gratitude (4:10-23)*

The letter to the Philippians follows a thematic structure known as chiasm. The theme of the letter, partnership in the Gospel, develops toward a central point (see E. 2:17-3:1a) and then reverses to the theme of partnership. Paul is using the occasion of financial partnership in the Gospel to encourage a deeper partnership in unity of thought and life application.

A, E, & A' PARTNERSHIP IN THE GOSPEL:
Gratitude and Renewal

The key theme, partnership in the Gospel, is first introduced in Chapter 1 and then renewed in Chapter 4. Paul is filled with gratitude for the Philippians, and his prayer is that they would be united in this Gospel both in the grace shown to them; in their mutual struggles and suffering for the Gospel; and, in the unified defense and proclamation of the Gospel to a lost world.

In the midpoint of the letter, Paul highlights two tangible examples of this partnership in action through the sending of help in the humble servants of the Gospel: Timothy and Epaphroditus (Philippians 2:17-3:1a).

B & B' COMFORT / EXAMPLE:
Under the Guard of Rome and of God

Both Paul and the Philippians were experiencing persecution due to their commitment to the Gospel. Paul was imprisoned for the Gospel by the imperial guard, From an earthly perspective, his imprisonment could cause tremendous worry and despair. Paul uses the example of his own sufferings to help the Philippians see a different way of looking at the persecution.

First, Paul sees the incredible fruit that is being brought forth by his imprisonment (Philippians 1:12-18). The entire guard is hearing Christ proclaimed, the faithful are being encouraged to boldness because of Paul's witness, but Paul's rivals are seeing an opportunity to gain a place in the pulpit for their own selfish gain. Yet, in all of these things Paul rejoices because *"Christ is proclaimed!"* (Philippians 1:18).

Second, Paul has a different way of looking at this life because of the resurrection life to come (Philippians 1:19-26). In a Shakespearean *"to be or not to be"* reflection, Paul reveals that whether he lives or dies, he is blessed in Jesus Christ. He knows that if he dies, it will result in being with Christ. His continued life means more fruitful labor with them. Either way, Paul proceeds with joy. Live or die, he simply can't lose!

In Chapter 4:6-9, Paul encourages the Philippians to lay aside anxiety in their own struggles by turning their worries over to God in prayer with thanksgiving and by setting their minds on that which is glorious and good. While he is under guard of Rome, their hearts and minds are guarded by the peace of God.

"And the peace of God, which surpasses all understanding, will guard your hearts and your minds in Christ Jesus."
(Philippians 4:7)

As citizens of Rome, they are guarded in persecution because of the Gospel. As citizens of heaven, they are guarded for eternal life.

C & C' CHALLENGE:
Stand Fast and Be United, Fulfilling Paul's Joy

Paul challenges them to stand fast in unity and joy. The oppositions and struggles they face could become an occasion for dissension and division. Indeed, there were two female leaders in conflict with one another, Euodia and Syntyche (Philippians 4:3). Paul challenges them to eschew conflict with one another and unite against the common enemy.

"Only let your manner of life be worthy of the gospel of Christ, so that whether I come and see you or am absent, I may hear of you that you are standing firm in one spirit, with one mind striving side by side for the faith of the gospel, and not frightened in anything by your opponents. This is a clear sign to them of their destruction, but of your salvation, and that from God."
(Philippians 1:27-28)

The unity in their relationships should be reflected in a remarkable character of joy! Paul encourages them to *"complete my joy"* by being united in mind and the character of humility exemplified in Christ (Philippians 2:2).

D & D' EXAMPLE / ACTION:
Humility and Suffering before Glory / The Example of Christ and Paul

To underscore his challenge to humility and unity of mind and joy, Paul points to the example of Jesus in 2.5-16 and then his own desire to share in Christ's example in his own life in 3:1b-21. Jesus is the supreme example of the type of humility that will lead to ultimate glory. Though he had every right to assert his own leadership and status in his divine nature, he humbled himself and took on the frail flesh of humanity even to the point of dying an ignoble death on a cross. The humility of Jesus led to his exaltation to the highest place in heaven and on Earth.

"Have this mind among yourselves, which is yours in Christ Jesus, who, though he was in the form of God, did not count equality with God a thing to be grasped, but emptied himself, by taking the form of a servant, being born in the likeness of men. And being found in human form, he humbled himself by becoming obedient to the point of death, even death on a cross. Therefore God has highly exalted him and bestowed on him the name that is above every name, so that at the name of Jesus every knee should bow, in heaven and on earth and under the earth, and every tongue confess that Jesus Christ is Lord, to the glory of God the Father."
(Philippians 2:5-11)

Paul uses the example of Christ's humility to call the Philippians to stand tall and bright as *"lights in the world"* in the midst of a sinful and fallen world (Philippians 2:15). The reason they can do this is because of the partnership with Christ and Paul, who has himself emptied himself for the sake of the Gospel.

Paul returns to the subject of humility leading to exaltation when he shares his own purpose to follow Christ Jesus in suffering so to somehow obtain the glory of the resurrection (Philippians 3:1b-21). To Paul, nothing else in this life really matters (Philippians 3:8). He will pursue the end of partnering with Christ at all personal cost and by any means possible (Philippians 3:10). Paul has made this pursuit the singular focus of his life. His challenge to the Philippians is to join him in partnership for the Gospel.

"Indeed, I count everything as loss because of the surpassing worth of knowing Christ Jesus my Lord. For his sake I have suffered the loss of all things and count them as rubbish, in order that I may gain Christ and be found in him, not having a righteousness of my own that comes from the law, but that which comes through faith in Christ, the righteousness from God that depends on faith—that I may know him and the power of his resurrection, and may share his sufferings, becoming like him in his death, that by any means possible I may attain the resurrection from the dead."
(Philippians 3:8-11)

PHILEMON

Despite being the shortest of Paul's letters, Philemon packs a powerful cultural application of the Gospel to one of the world's most egregious institutions, human slavery. Writing from prison, Paul is no stranger to bondage and suffering. He is comforted in Rome by a runaway slave from Ephesus named Onesimus. Onesimus was a slave to Philemon, a convert of Paul, and a leader in one of the house churches in Ephesus. Onesimus' name means *"useful"* or *"beneficial."*

Freedom is central to the Gospel. In his other letters, he expounds on freedom from the law, freedom from the sin nature, and freedom from the fear of death and Satan's reign. But how does that freedom in Christ apply to human slavery? Paul cautions against using our freedom in Christ as an occasion to sin or gratify the works of the flesh.

Onesimus, a slave and Christian convert, forced his way to freedom from his owner Philemon, a slave holder and Christian convert.

Onesimus fled to Paul. But Paul, exercising Solomonic wisdom in his application of Christian freedom, sent Onesimus back to his master with a letter in hand encouraging Philemon to release him and welcome him as an equal brother in Christ. Both men had much to lose in that moment for the sake of the Gospel. Paul also had found Onesimus useful to him in ministering to him in prison.

Legally, Philemon could ignore the urging of Paul and bring Onesimus back under the yoke of slavery—a risk Onesimus was willing to take in returning. But, for the sake of the Gospel, Philemon could welcome him back as a free brother and risk losing the economic advantage of a human slave. Paul could have asserted his rights and authority as an apostle and forced a resolution. All three men were called to sacrifice their rights to find a spirit-filled Gospel way where the flesh could have prevailed.

Fig. 6. *Onesimus of Byzantium coming back to his master Philemon with a letter of the apostle Paul* (epistle to Philemon) Engraving 19th century Private collection / © The Holbarn Archive/ Leemage /Bridgeman Images.

The fact that this letter survived in the New Testament bodes well for all behaving with integrity in the Gospel. Early church history records that the second Bishop of Ephesus was named Onesimus. In addition, he was called Onesimus of Byzantium and Ignatius of Antioch. He is thought to have died in 68 A.D.

The Gospel overturns the status quo, social norms, and worldly legalities. Indeed, the Gospel brings a new ordering to human relationships under Christ.

"(Formerly he was useless to you, but now he is indeed useful to you and to me.) I am sending him back to you, sending my very heart. I would have been glad to keep him with me, in order that he might serve me on your behalf during my imprisonment for the gospel, but I preferred to do nothing without your consent in order that your goodness might not be by compulsion but of your own accord. For this perhaps is why he was parted from you for a while, that you might have him back forever, no longer as a bondservant but more than a bondservant, as a beloved brother—especially to me, but how much more to you, both in the flesh and in the Lord."
(Philemon 1:11-16)

CHAPTER 7 NOTES:

CHAPTER 8
Letters From Departing Apostles

OBJECTIVE: The maturing Christian disciple will understand the importance of apostolic succession in passing the faith on to future generations.

INTRODUCTION

As time passed, the apostles realized an urgency to appoint new leaders. They still had wisdom to share, but because of physical limitations such as imprisonment and old age, they could not maintain the pace they had set earlier. As a result, they wrote letters to pass along their apostolic knowledge. Paul wrote his last few letters, 1 and 2 Timothy and Titus, from his home in Rome while under house arrest. He knew his earthy life was coming to an end, so he wrote to Timothy and Titus to offer advice on how to pastor a church and develop leadership.

Likewise, Peter penned two letters toward the end of his life. Peter's first letter of encouragement expands on the idea of a heavenly inheritance of the Promised Land. Peter's second letter discusses the importance of discerning false from true teachers; how to live according to Jesus; and the consequences of apostasy. The themes of 2 Peter are amplified by Jesus brother, Jude, in his short letter. Though the author of Hebrews is unknown, the letter describes how to continue worshiping the Lord by being vulnerable to him. These four themes of leadership, perseverance, discernment, and worship exemplify the values of church stewardship passed down through apostolic succession.

> **Letters from the Departing Apostles:**
>
> - *Developing Leadership:*
>   (1 & 2 Timothy, Titus)
>
> - *Rejoicing in Trials and Tribulations:*
>   (James & 1 Peter)
>
> - *Discerning False and True Teachers:*
>   (2 Peter & Jude)
>
> - *Persevering Worship:*
>   (Hebrews)

Paul Sails for Rome

Paul waited in Festus' custody for an audience with Caesar. Eventually Festus decided to send Paul and some other prisoners to Italy via boat. Festus handed them over to a centurion named Julius, and they all set sail by way of Asian ports. They landed first in Sidon, where Julius allowed Paul to see his friends. From there, the prisoners and guards sailed past Cyprus, along the coast of Cilicia and Pamphylia, and landed at Myra in Lycia. There they changed boats and boarded an Alexandrian ship bound for Italy.

They sailed toward Crete, but the voyage was becoming increasingly dangerous. Paul advised the centurion to take a different route as he foresaw that the rest of the voyage would cause the loss of the cargo, ship, and passengers' lives. However, the centurion only listened to the ship's owner and the pilot, and they continued on their dangerous course.

Soon, a strong wind caught the ship, and they were tossed about in a violent storm. In an attempt to save the ship by lightening the load, the crew began to throw cargo and gear overboard. For several days, the sea roiled, and everyone feared for their lives. They could not navigate because they could not see the sun or stars, and they were lost at sea with little food. Paul rebuked the crew for ignoring his advice, but he also offered hope: an angel of God had visited him and said, "Do not be afraid, Paul; you must stand before Caesar. And behold, God has granted you all those who sail with you" (Acts 27:24).

After two weeks of disorienting storms and no food, some of the sailors thought they were nearing land. That night, they put down a small dingy under the pretense of dropping anchors. However, they intended to escape despite Paul's warning. At dawn, Paul encouraged all 276 passengers and crew to break their fast and eat. As the sun rose, they spotted unfamiliar land. Because they no longer had an extra boat to travel to shore, they planned to run the ship aground. However, they struck a reef as they neared the beach, and so everyone floated on pieces of the ship or swam to shore.

Soon after landing, they found that the island was called Malta, and the natives built a fire to welcome all the shipwrecked passengers. After Paul was bitten by a viper and suffered no harm, the natives believed he was a god. Paul healed the ailing father of the island's chief, and then he healed the rest of the diseased people. The islanders were grateful and took care of Paul and the other passengers for three months. When they left in a ship that had wintered on the island, the islanders provisioned the ship with everything they might need.

After Malta, they called on several harbors before arriving in Rome. Some Roman brothers met Paul before he was taken back into custody. However, Paul was allowed to stay by himself in a house guarded by a soldier. After three days, Paul called the local Jewish leaders to his home and explained how the Jerusalem Jews had persecuted him and how he wished to speak with them about his faith. The Roman Jews had not heard any bad things about Paul, and because they were curious to hear more about the much-maligned Christian sect, they agreed to come back and listen to his testimony. When they returned, Paul testified all day about the kingdom of God and the legitimacy of Jesus as the Messiah. He convinced some, but others did not believe. For two years, Paul lived under house arrest, preaching to all who came to him.

Fig. 1. The work represents the beheading of the apostle Saint Paul, Apostle of the Gentiles, which according to tradition took place in Rome during the persecution against Christians decreed by the Emperor Nero. Simonet, Enrique, *The Beheading of Saint Paul/* oil on canvas/Málaga Cathedral/1887/WikiCommons.

Martyrdom and The Succession of Discipleship

While Paul preached in Rome, James, the brother of Jesus, suffered martyrdom in Jerusalem. The historian Eusebius recorded that after Paul left Jerusalem, the Jews who had sought to kill Paul decided to kill James instead. They summoned James the Just to answer questions about Jesus, but when he used their platform to preach and convince the listeners of Jesus' power, they threw him from the pinnacle of the temple. However, the fall did not kill him, so they gathered around him and stoned him. As they were throwing stones at James, one of the priests called for them to stop because James was praying for their forgiveness even as they killed him. Then one man hit James in the head with a fuller's club, delivering the fatal blow (Eusebius, Church History II, 23).

CHAPTER 8 Letters From Departing Apostles 187

The Fate of the Apostles

The Bible does not tell us the fate of all the Apostles. Historical records do not complete their stories either. However, the fate of many of them are known and others can be presumed. What is important is to remember is why they died. They all claimed to witness Christ's death and resurrection, that he was the long-sought messiah and savior of the world. In these claims they were unwavering and unrelenting.

APOSTLE	DATE OF DEATH	CIRCUMSTANCES OF DEATH
Stephen	34-36 A.D.	Stoned by the Sanhedrin.
James	44-45 A.D.	Herod Agrippa had him executed by sword. The executioner was so impressed by his faith that he was executed as well.
Philip	54 A.D.	Natural causes, or torture and crucifixion.
Matthew	60-70 A.D.	Nailed to the ground and beheaded by King Hytacus at Nad-davar, Ethiopia.
James the Lesser	63 A.D.	Thrown from the Temple and beaten with a fuller's club.
Peter	64 A.D.	Crucified upside down by a Roman executioner.
Paul	67 A.D.	Beheaded at the hands of Roman Emperor Nero in Rome.
Andrew	70 A.D.	Hanged on an olive tree in Patrae, Achaia.
Thomas	70 A.D.	Stabbed with a spear, tortured with red-hot plates and burned alive in India.
Nathanael (Bartholomew)	70 A.D.	Flayed and then crucified.
Matthias	70 A.D.	Unclear. Several traditions exist, including his death at Sebastopolis, stoning at Jerusalem by the Jews, and then beheading while hanging upon a cross.
Judas Thaddeus	72 A.D.	Beheaded with an axe in Syria.
Simon the Zealot	74 A.D.	Crucified by a governor in Syria.
John	94 A.D.	Natural causes but severely scarred after being thrown into boiling oil at the Latin Gate.

Extra-Biblical sources referenced.

Copyright, 2009 Reclaiming the Mind Ministries. May be reproduced unaltered from free.

https://www.christianity.com/church/church-history/timeline/1-300/whatever-happened-to-the-twelve-apostles-11629558.html

Like Stephen and the other martyred James (the brother of John and son of Zebedee), James the Just (the brother of Jesus Christ) died for his faith in Christ. Paul and Peter's fates were similar; they also became martyrs for Christ. After spending several years under house arrest, Nero ordered Paul's execution by beheading for proclaiming that Jesus was Lord over all, including Caesar. Soon after killing Paul, Nero ordered Peter's execution by crucifixion (Eusebius, Church History II, 25). Because Peter felt that he was not fit to die in the same way as Jesus, he was crucified upside-down. These men offered themselves to the Gospel, both in their actions as teachers and evangelists in life and their unwavering faithfulness in death. They bore wholehearted witness to the power of Jesus Christ by dying for their devotion. Their deaths as martyrs strengthened their testimony as apostles and secured their legacies as fathers of the church.

Paul's letters to Timothy and Titus express knowledge of his impending fate and his desire to create strong leaders to take his place. Paul understood the concept of apostolic succession—he and the other disciples were dying, and soon none of the 12 apostles would be around to spread the Gospel. They needed not only to pass on their knowledge but also to mold the next generation into responsible and faithful stewards of the growing churches. Apostolic succession is still a part of the church today. When a Bishop is consecrated, other clergy gather around him and pray that the Holy Spirit comes and equips him for this service. The laying on of hands is a symbolic transference of the apostolic teaching and witness.

Fig. 2. *Martyrdom of James the Just/* Venice Italy/Basilica di San Marco/ Photograph: Ekkehard Ritter. Image Collections and Fieldwork Archives, Dumbarton Oaks, Trustees for Harvard University, Washington, D.C.

1 TIMOTHY
Guarding the Gospel: Leadership 101

Paul's two letters to Timothy and his letter to Titus are called the Pastoral Epistles. In them, the apostle conveys his encouragement and instructions for pastoral leadership on philosophical, personal, and practical levels.

There are two main reasons for these letters: geography and time. First, Paul could only be in one place at a time. The delegation of leadership was important for Paul. He saw it as part of the future of a geographically broad Gospel movement. As Paul traveled from region to region, city to city, and town to town, many new congregations were planted. New leadership had to be developed in each region, city, and town. Coordination and support of those various congregations became critical for the Gospel.

The second issue is related to time. Paul was keenly aware that his days of fruitful ministry were numbered. The issue of succession is critically important to Paul as he empowered Timothy to lead and to identify more leaders for the churches. Each generation must keep in mind the needs of the next generation of believers.

In Asia Minor, we have letters that Paul wrote to the congregations in Colossae and Ephesus. From those letters, we learn that there were congregations in nearby cities and towns such as Laodicea. It is also apparent that Ephesus was an important hub church with strategic importance for the entire region of Asia Minor.

In his letters to the Thessalonians, we see how Paul used Timothy as a trusted proxy to support the ministry and leadership of the church in Thessalonica when he was unable to go there in person. In these letters, we see that Paul continues to entrust Timothy with the care of congregations. He has appointed him to serve as a regional leader in Ephesus, a bishop overseer.

In this way we see the first examples of apostolic succession and delegation at work in the personal and pastoral relationship between Timothy and Paul. For Paul, the issue is not merely the passing of a personal torch—for him it was critically important that the content and the character of the Gospel be guarded that it would be conveyed *faithfully* to the next generation of leaders.

Literary Structure

1 TIMOTHY : Guard the Gospel	Chapters 1-6
Topic	**Passage**
Guard the Doctrine: Unity, and Discipline	1:1-4:16
Doctrine Matters: False and True Teaching	1:3-20
Unity Matters: Peace in Worship	2:1-15
Discipline Matters: The Character of Leaders	3:1-4:16
Attend to the Pastoral Concerns	5:1-6:10
Final Charge: Guard the Church and Self	6:3-21

GUARD THE DOCTRINE: Unity, and Discipline

The primary focus of the first letter of Paul to Timothy is a call to guard the doctrine, unity and discipline of the church. Paul's concern is in three key leadership areas: false and true teaching, unity in worship, and godly character.

DOCTRINE MATTERS: False and True Teaching

Paul's concern for right belief and teaching is manifest in all of his letters. Here Paul is concerned about leadership in particular. One of the primary roles Paul is entrusting to Timothy is to *"charge certain persons not to teach any different doctrine"* (1 Timothy 1:3)

Doctrine means teaching. It is possible to teach things that are *"contrary to sound doctrine"* (1 Timothy 1:10). The key for Paul is that all teaching and doctrine be *"in accordance with the gospel of glory of the blessed God with which I have been entrusted"* (1 Timothy 1:11).

The succinct truth of the gospel message is: *"Christ Jesus came into the world to save sinners"* (1 Timothy 1:15). Paul will develop the content of the Gospel and all its nuances and applications in other letters. However, the key for Timothy is to guard the teaching of the Gospel as a soldier fights to win a battle, and to resist false teachers who have failed to be diligent stewards of the Gospel of God.

UNITY MATTERS: Peace in Worship

After addressing doctrine, Paul encourages unity in worship. Apparently, there were some scandals and divisions manifesting within the Ephesian church that not only were destroying the unity within the congregation with *"anger or quarreling"* but also had spilled out into public controversy (1 Timothy 2:8). Paul challenges Timothy to lead the flock into a unity of worship that is a blessing to those outside and inside the church *"dignified in every way"* (1 Timothy 2:2).

The ultimate vision of the church is a unified body that leads all humanity into unity with the one God through the one mediation in Jesus:

"This is good, and it is pleasing in the sight of God our Savior, who desires all people to be saved and to come to the knowledge of the truth. For there is one God, and there is one mediator between God and men, the man Christ Jesus, who gave himself as a ransom for all, which is the testimony given at the proper time. For this I

was appointed a preacher and an apostle (I am telling the truth, I am not lying), a teacher of the Gentiles in faith and truth."
(1 Timothy 2:3-7)

Apparently, there was controversy and conflict related to the freedoms and roles of women in worship. This, along with the quarrellings and vain discussions created by the false teachers, had done great harm to the unity of the church.

Paul encourages Timothy to adopt a policy for women in teaching roles as a way of resolving some of the controversies and bring peace to the worship life of the church.

DISCIPLINE MATTERS: The Character of Leaders

Paul then moves to encourage Timothy to be diligent in guarding leadership positions within the body of Christ. Timothy is charged to pay particularly close attention to issues of character and reputation.

"The saying is trustworthy: If anyone aspires to the office of overseer, he desires a noble task. Therefore an overseer must be above reproach, the husband of one wife, sober-minded, self-controlled, respectable, hospitable, able to teach, not a drunkard, not violent but gentle, not quarrelsome, not a lover of money. He must manage his own household well, with all dignity keeping his children submissive, for if someone does not know how to manage his own household, how will he care for God's church? He must not be a recent convert, or he may become puffed up with conceit and fall into the condemnation of the devil. Moreover, he must be well thought of by outsiders, so that he may not fall into disgrace, into a snare of the devil."
(1 Timothy 3:1-7)

Paul's concern is not only that a leader have a positive character within the body of Christ but also with outsiders. Character matters in leadership. For Paul, the Gospel itself is on display in the life of the people of the church, which he calls *"a pillar and buttress of the truth"* (1 Timothy 3:15). The members will take their lead from their overseers and deacons.

There are false teachers with poor character who do not follow the discipline of the truth. He calls them *"liars whose consciences are seared"* (1 Timothy 4:2). Timothy's charge is to guard his own discipline of character in godliness:

"Rather train yourself for godliness; for while bodily training is of some value, godliness is of value in every way, as it holds promise for the present life and also for the life to come."
(1 Timothy 4:7-8)

He is called to set the *"example"* of godly leadership to all the believers in the church in every aspect of his own life: in teaching, in unity, and discipline (1 Timothy 4:12). But the key thing for Paul is that Timothy persists in faithful teaching of the scriptures (1 Timothy 4:13). If Timothy will guard his own life in godliness and teaching, he will be fully equipped and trained to guard the leadership life of the church.

Attend to the Pastoral Concerns

Paul then turns his attention to general concerns of pastoral ministry: the respect and care of older men and widows (1 Timothy 5:1-16). He is teaching not only pastoral interpersonal skills to Timothy, but also providing practical instruction on the allocations of the common purse for widows and care of the needy within the body.

He also encourages Timothy to teach about respect for the leaders in the congregation in preserving both their livelihoods and their reputations (1 Timothy 5:17-21). However, because leadership is so important, Timothy should not be too hasty in promoting people into it (1 Timothy 5:22-24).

FINAL CHARGE: Guard the Church and Self

Paul's final charge to Timothy: *"guard the deposit entrusted to you"* (1 Timothy 6:20). As a minister of the Gospel, Timothy is being sent into a battle. He needs strong encouragement to see the importance of his ministry. Paul challenges Timothy:

"But as for you, O man of God, flee these things. Pursue righteousness, godliness, faith, love, steadfastness, gentleness. Fight the good fight of the faith. Take hold of the eternal life to which you were called and about which you made the good confession in the presence of many witnesses."
(1 Timothy 6:11-12)

2 TIMOTHY

Paul's second letter to Timothy continues to build on the theme of guarding the Gospel. Timothy likely has communicated to Paul his insecurities and timidity in the face of strong opposition from false teachers. Because of Paul's situation (being bound in chains and facing death), it is critical that Timothy become strong in the Lord. Paul provides Timothy with three metaphors—the soldier, the athlete, and the farmer—as a way of illustrating the type of leader Timothy needs to be.

Literary Structure

2 TIMOTHY : Guard the Good Deposit		Chapters 1-4
Topic		Passage
A. The Charge: Guard the Deposit		1:1-2:13
Paul's Charge to Timothy (1:4-6)	Paul's Example	4:6-8
1. Soldier: Avoid civilian entanglements	*I have Fought the Fight*	2:14-26
2. Athlete: Compete according to the rules	*I have Finished the Race*	3:1-3:17
3. Farmer: Work hard and enjoy the reward	*I have Kept the Faith/ Won the Prize*	4:1-8
B. Final Instructions		4:9-22

THE CHARGE: Guard the Deposit

Timothy is struggling with timidity. Paul writes to encourage Timothy to match his sincerity for the faith (1:3-5) with confidence in the task:

"For this reason I remind you to fan into flame the gift of God, which is in you through the laying on of my hands, for God gave us a spirit not of fear but of power and love and self-control."
(2 Timothy 1:6-7)

Paul holds up himself as a weak vessel who needed the Lord's strength and power to be effective. Confidence comes by God's resurrection power manifesting itself in the minister of the Gospel through his Holy Spirit. So Paul charges Timothy: *"By the Holy Spirit who dwells within us, guard the good deposit entrusted to you"* (2 Timothy 1:14). Paul is concerned about succession and he needs Timothy to be concerned about it, too! Paul has a vision to see the Gospel faithfully entrusted over multiple generations of servant leaders.

"You then, my child, be strengthened by the grace that is in Christ Jesus, and what you have heard from me in the presence of many witnesses entrust to faithful men who will be able to teach others also." (2 Timothy 2:1-2)

The task of guarding the deposit of the faith is critical. Paul gives Timothy three metaphors from everyday life to illustrate the tasks necessary to ensure the deposit can be transferred for five generations and more. The three metaphors are the soldier, the athlete, and the farmer.

"Share in suffering as a good soldier of Christ Jesus. No soldier gets entangled in civilian pursuits, since his aim is to please the one who enlisted him. An athlete is not crowned unless he competes according to the rules. It is the hard-working farmer who ought to have the first share of the crops. Think over what I say, for the Lord will give you understanding in everything." (2 Timothy 2:3-7)

SOLDIER: Avoid Civilian Entanglements, Please Your Commander

An obedient and disciplined soldier does not get entangled in civilian pursuits. There are those who want to quarrel over words and irreverent babble that spreads like gangrene. Timothy is to avoid getting involved with any of it. Here is where leaders go astray (see 2 Timothy 2:17-18). The key is in remaining focused on pleasing the commanding officer alone.

"But God's firm foundation stands, bearing this seal: 'The Lord knows those who are his,' and, 'Let everyone who names the name of the Lord depart from iniquity.'" (2 Timothy 2:19)

The good soldier flees these ungodly and immature pursuits and passions and focuses on the pursuit of *"righteousness, faith, love, and peace along with those who call on the Lord from a pure heart"* (2 Timothy 2:22).

ATHLETE: Compete According to the Rules

The second metaphor Paul employs is that of the athlete. The key in completion of the race is winning, yes, but winning according to the rules. There will be many people the church who want the benefits of the church and the faith but who do not desire to follow the rule of the church and faith.

Paul looks at the example of Jannes and Jambres, the names given to the Egyptian magicians mentioned in Exodus 7:8-13. These men who contended with Moses were posers and cheaters. They didn't compete according to the rules. They were *"disqualified regarding the faith"* (2 Timothy 3:8). Where does the athlete find the rulebook of the faith?

"All Scripture is breathed out by God and profitable for teaching, for reproof, for correction, and for training in righteousness, that the man of God may be complete, equipped for every good work."
(2 Timothy 3:16-17)

FARMER: Work hard and enjoy the reward

Paul then turns to his last metaphor, the farmer. Fundamental to the farmer's success is daily faithfulness to the hard work of tending the crops. Timothy is now encouraged to stick with the consistent hard work of ministry.

"I charge you in the presence of God and of Christ Jesus, who is to judge the living and the dead, and by his appearing and his kingdom: preach the word; be ready in season and out of season; reprove, rebuke, and exhort, with complete patience and teaching. For the time is coming when people will not endure sound teaching, but having itching ears they will accumulate for themselves teachers to suit their own passions, and will turn away from listening to the truth and wander off into myths. As for you, always be sober-minded, endure suffering, do the work of an

evangelist, fulfill your ministry."
(2 Timothy 4:1-5)

There are times when the minister does not feel like his hard work is bearing fruit. The people *"will not endure sound teaching"* (2 Timothy 4:3). However, Timothy must, like a farmer in season and out of season, stay faithful and *"do the work"* of a Gospel-preaching evangelist, thus fulfilling his ministry. The promise to the farmer is that there will be a prize. *"It is the hard-working farmer who ought to have the first share of the crops."* (1 Timothy 2:6). Paul holds himself up as an example of one who has lived what he has encouraged Timothy to live. He has been a soldier, an athlete, and a farmer. As a result, he knows that his hard work will be rewarded with a glorious prize.

"For I am already being poured out as a drink offering, and the time of my departure has come. I have fought the good fight, I have finished the race, I have kept the faith. Henceforth there is laid up for me the crown of righteousness, which the Lord, the righteous judge, will award to me on that day, and not only to me but also to all who have loved his appearing."
(2 Timothy 4:6-8)

The letter concludes by reflecting on the danger of a martyr's death that awaits Paul in the Roman Coliseum. Is Paul speaking metaphorically or literally?

"But the Lord stood by me and strengthened me, so that through me the message might be fully proclaimed and all the Gentiles might hear it. So I was rescued from the lion's mouth. The Lord will rescue me from every evil deed and bring me safely into his heavenly kingdom. To him be the glory forever and ever. Amen."
(2 Timothy 4:17-18)

The torch is being passed to the next leaders who will guard the good deposit. Paul has been faithful to the end, will we?

PAUL'S LETTER TO TITUS
Unfinished Business

Titus' main job in being sent to the island of Crete is to bring some order to the new churches that had been planted there by Paul and his missionary team. *"This is why I left you in Crete, so that you* might *put what remained into order, ..."* (Titus 1:5).

We do not read about any missionary activity of Paul in Crete in the Book of Acts, though Cretans were present in Jerusalem when the Holy Spirit was first given on the day of Pentecost (see Acts 2:11), and Paul's ship made port in Crete during his guarded escort to Rome (Acts 27:7ff). All we really know about Paul's establishment of the church at Crete is from this letter to Titus.

Paul's usual way of writing letters is to move from indicative teachings to imperative commands, from the theology of the Gospel to the practice of the Gospel. In the case of the Cretan church, that formula is reversed. Paul sees the primary concern as being more practical in nature.

Crete was infamous for the immorality among the general populace. Polybius, an ancient historian, wrote that it was "almost impossible to find ... personal conduct more treacherous or public policy more unjust than Crete" (Histories 6.47). Cicero wrote: *"Moral principles are so divergent that the Cretans ... consider highway robbery honorable"* (Republic 3.9.15). Paul quotes the 6th century B.C. Cretan Epimenides:

"One of the Cretans, a prophet of their own, said, 'Cretans are always liars, evil beasts, lazy gluttons.' This testimony is true. Therefore rebuke them sharply, that they may be sound in the faith ...."
(Titus 1:12-14)

Paul is concerned that the culture of Crete is so corrupt that the emphasis needs to be on accountability to the Christian way of life—how to live in godliness. In his opening greeting Paul underscores how he was sent:

"... for the sake of the faith of God's elect and their knowledge of the truth, which accords with godliness in the hope of eternal life, which God, who never lies, promised before the ages began and at the proper time manifested in his word through the preaching with which I have been entrusted by the command of God our Savior."
(Titus 1:1-3)

The truthfulness of God contrasts with the lying character on the people of Crete. Paul starts with the practical concerns pertaining to differentiating the Christian life *"which accords with godliness"* (Titus

1:1), from the corrupt surrounding culture. He then works his way back to the Gospel of salvation. Paul has three primary tasks of unfinished business for Titus. First, Titus is charged to appoint godly leaders in every town. Second, he is to teach the congregation the life that accords with Christian principles and practice. Finally, he is called to remind them of their salvation in Jesus Christ.

The outline of the letter to Titus logically follows Paul's three-part assignment: Appoint, Teach, Remind.

The Outline of Titus

TITUS	Chapters 1-3
Topic	Passage
Appoint for them godly leaders	Titus 1
Teach them to live the Christian Life	Titus 2
Remind them of their witness to the Gospel	Titus 3

Appoint for them Godly Leaders

The first order of business for Titus is to build a leadership team. Paul uses the terms elders and overseers interchangeably. There were several city-states (towns) on the island of Crete at the time. The first task is to have an elder in every one of these city-states. In this role, Titus is functioning as a regional bishop or overseer himself. Paul charges Titus:

"This is why I left you in Crete, so that you might put what remained into order, and appoint elders in every town as I directed you …."
(Titus 1:5)

As in 1 and 2 Timothy, there are certain qualifications required for leadership positions. In Crete, finding men who met Paul's criteria may have been a challenge. Nonetheless, Paul insists on a godly character marked by a good reputation, strong family life, self-control, and good works. The elder/overseer also needs to have the ability and commitment to teach sound doctrine. Likewise, he must have the character of a courageous leader who can stand up to others, correct false teaching and rebuke false practice.

In the same way he has a list of essential qualities, he also shares a list of beliefs, practices, and character traits that would disqualify a person from leadership (Titus 1:10-16). Titus is not to appoint people who manifest these disqualifications. Paul challenges him to silence them because of the detrimental effect their teaching is having on families.

Teach them the Christian Life

The second chapter of Titus focuses on Paul's charge to *"teach what accords with sound doctrine…"* (Titus 2:1). By that, Paul is concerned with practical matters.

He addresses Christian conduct and behavior not only among the men and the women as individuals but also in marriage relationships and parenting of children.

Titus is called to model such godly behavior in his own life so that he cannot be criticized:

> *"Show yourself in all respects to be a model of good works, and in your teaching show integrity, dignity, and sound speech that cannot be condemned, so that an opponent may be put to shame, having nothing evil to say about us."*
> *(Titus 2:7-8)*

For Paul, Christians must demonstrate both in their behavior and witness the reality of God's plan of salvation as presented in the Gospel from this present corrupt and evil age.

Correct Christian behavior flows directly from the outworking of God's plan of salvation. Jesus redeems people from *"lawlessness"* in order to *"purify for himself"* a new people who are internally motivated to do *"good works"* (Titus 2:11-14).

Remind them of their witness to the Gospel

The last section in the letter to Titus places an emphasis on the witness to the Gospel to the unredeemed population on Crete. The people of

Crete had an insubordinate character. However, it is in their obedience and submission to good order and in engagement in good works that the Christians could stand out as witnesses for the Gospel.

"Remind them to be submissive to rulers and authorities, to be obedient, to be ready for every good work, to speak evil of no one, to avoid quarreling, to be gentle, and to show perfect courtesy toward all people."
(Titus 3:1-2)

The transformed life of the Christian is a testimony to the salvation found in Jesus Christ. The converts on Crete were at one time no different in character from the people of their island. However, because of salvation, the grace of God, and the *"washing of regeneration and renewal of the Holy Spirit,"* these Christians had *"become heirs according to the hope of eternal life"* (Titus 3:5-7). They must now live into that hope and distinguish themselves from the culture in which they live. If anyone doesn't manifest this character, he shows himself to be *"warped and sinful"* and *"self-condemned"* (Titus 3:11). Titus has his charge: Appoint, Teach, Remind. Good people do good works.

THE FIRST LETTER OF PETER
A Living Hope

There are two letters attributed to St. Peter in the New Testament. The early church held that the Gospel of Mark may summarize the Gospel teaching of Peter (see 1 Peter 5:12). The letter was written sometime around 60-63 A.D. while Peter was Bishop of Rome (see 1 Peter 5:13, Babylon is an early church name for Rome). He used the services of a secretary named Silvanus (Silas) whom Peter describes as a *"faithful brother"* (1 Peter 5:12).

As one of the first 12 disciples and the most preeminent among them, Peter's teaching is vital to all of the churches, not only in his day but for all time. While the specific audience he addresses is in Asia Minor, this letter was circulated widely. The church has grouped the letters of Peter within a larger section of the New Testament known as the *"General Epistles"* or the *"Catholic Epistles."* In this case, catholic means the united and universal church across geography and time. The other Catholic Epistles are James, 2 Peter, 1, 2, 3 John, and Jude.

The main focus of 1 Peter is on living holy lives as exiles facing the day of visitation and judgment. For Peter, the *"time of judgment"* (1 Peter 4:17) has begun with the people of God tested in the *"genuineness of your faith"* (1 Peter 1:7) through a *"fiery trial"* (1 Peter 4:12). Peter's concern in his letter is not only the salvation and judgment of the exiled people of God, but also for the unbelieving souls of the Gentiles. Ultimately, all people will have to *"give account to him who is ready to judge the living and the dead"* (1 Peter 4:5). Therefore, the witness of the Christian life confirms their own personal salvation (1 Peter 1:7).

Literary Structure

1 PETER: A Living Hope — Chapters 1-5

Topic	Passage
A Heavenly Inheritance: Salvation at the End of Times	1:1-13
A Living Temple: The Redeemed People of God	1:14-2:10
A Sojourn in Exile: Glorifying God Among Unbelievers	2:11-3:13
A Fiery Trial: Suffering in the Flesh for God's Ultimate Glory	3:13-5:14

A LIVING HOPE: Salvation at the End of Times

Peter addresses his letter to the *"elect exiles of the Dispersion"* (1 Peter 1:1). Before the coming of Jesus Christ, this could have referred only to Jews who had been exiled from the Promised Land because of the Assyrian, Babylonian, Persian, Greek, and Roman occupations of the geographic region called Israel. The hope of the exiles was a return to the *"Inheritance of the Land,"* a *"Restored Temple,"* and a *"Messianic Davidic King."*

Peter proclaims the restoration of the inheritance of land, temple, and king. Only the restoration offered in the New Covenant is more important than that of the hopes of pre-Jesus Israelite exiles. Peter is describing *"a living hope through the resurrection of Jesus Christ from the dead, to an inheritance that is imperishable, undefiled, and unfading, kept in heaven"* (1 Peter 1:3-4).

Yes, there is a promised inheritance of land, but it is no longer to be seen in geographic Israel. The true inheritance is being kept in heaven. The nature of the exiled people of God changes after the coming of Jesus Christ. Their hope is not in a salvation from a geographic exile and a return to a geographic plot of land. The living hope is a salvation from this present age to the inheritance of a New Heaven and New Earth on the last day.

The prophets who hinted at this salvation, such as Jeremiah, Joel, Isaiah, and Ezekiel (among others) did not know the details of the promises that they preached. Even the angels of God longed to look into these matters.

"Concerning this salvation, the prophets who prophesied about the grace that was to be yours searched and inquired carefully, inquiring what person or time the Spirit of Christ in them was indicating when he predicted the sufferings of Christ and the subsequent glories. It was revealed to them that they were serving not themselves but you, in the things that have now been announced to you through those who preached the good news to you by the Holy Spirit sent from heaven, things into which angels long to look."
(1 Peter 1:10-12)

A LIVING TEMPLE: The Redeemed People of God

Like the letters to the Hebrews and Ephesians, 1 Peter sees the promises of a restored temple as finding their fulfillment in the sacrifice of Jesus on the cross and his resurrection. Jesus taught his disciples that the earthly temple would be destroyed and that he would raise a new temple, a living temple in his body (John 2:19-21). Peter teaches that God has redeemed his people through the offering of Jesus as a sacrificial lamb.

"... conduct yourselves with fear throughout the time of your exile, knowing that you were ransomed from the futile ways inherited from your forefathers, not with perishable things such as silver or gold, but with the precious blood of Christ, like that of a lamb without blemish or spot."
(1 Peter 1:17-19)

As a redeemed people of God, the call is to a life of holiness and mutual love. The believer has been *"born again"* through the *"living and abiding word of God"* (1 Peter 1:23). Quoting Isaiah 8:14, 28:16, and Psalm 118:22, Peter describes Jesus as the chief cornerstone of a living spiritual temple made of human stones. The priests of the new temple no longer need to offer physical blood sacrifices. All the people of God are now priests who offer spiritual sacrifices (1 Peter 2:5).

Those who have been called and believe in Jesus Christ are the redeemed and restored Israel. Using language of the Old Covenant, he identifies them:

"But you are a chosen race, a royal priesthood, a holy nation, a people for his own possession, that you may proclaim the excellencies of him who called you out of darkness into his marvelous light. Once you were not a people, but now you are God's people; once you had not received mercy, but now you have received mercy."
(1 Peter 2:9-10)

Their call is to be the holy people of God in a world that is still in rebellion and under the judgment of God.

A SOJOURN IN EXILE: Glorifying God among Unbelievers

The hope for the unbelieving people of the world is that they will see the witness of holiness, love, and service manifest in the redeemed people of God and be drawn into the praise of God. The Lord will use the *"living and abiding word"* (1 Peter 1:23) spoken by believers. However, the real testimony to unbelievers will come in unusual deeds from a holy life lived in humble submission.

"Beloved, I urge you as sojourners and exiles to abstain from the passions of the flesh, which wage war against your soul. Keep your conduct among the Gentiles honorable, so that when they speak against you as evildoers, they may see your good deeds and glorify God on the day of visitation."
(1 Peter 2:11-12)

Although Christians will be reviled, the character of love and service will be the irresistible counterforce to *"win souls"* for Christ. Christians will bear witness in the context of the public square, in business relationships, and in the household. In the public square, the Christian is to *"honor everyone"* including the secular government! *"Honor the emperor"* (1 Peter 2:17).

In the master-servant relationships, employees and slaves should be submissive to their abusive masters. The model in all of these relationships is Christ Jesus who *"when he was reviled, he did not revile in return ..."* (1 Peter 2:23).

"For to this you have been called, because Christ also suffered for you, leaving you an example, so that you might follow in his steps. He committed no sin, neither was deceit found in his mouth. When he was reviled, he did not revile in return; when he suffered, he did not threaten, but continued entrusting himself to him who judges justly. He himself bore our sins in his body on the tree, that we might die to sin and live to righteousness. By his wounds you have been healed. For you were straying like sheep, but have now returned to the Shepherd and Overseer of your souls."
(1 Peter 2:21-25)

While this is one of the clearest verses on nature of Jesus' substitutionary atonement for us (cf. Isaiah 53:4-6), Peter uses Christ's atonement as a model to follow. It was his actions as a humble servant that led to our conversion and salvation. It will be our humble servant actions that can "win" the souls of the unbelieving. He applies this principle to wives married to unbelieving husbands:

"Likewise, wives, be subject to your own husbands, so that even if some do not obey the word, they may be won without a word by the conduct of their wives, when they see your respectful and pure conduct."
(1 Peter 3:1-2)

The call of the people of God has been to be a blessing to the nations. Jesus' model and Peter's call to the redeemed people of God is to manifest blessing even if we are receiving insults.

"Finally, all of you, have unity of mind, sympathy, brotherly love, a tender heart, and a humble mind. Do not repay evil for evil or reviling for reviling, but on the contrary, bless, for to this you were called, that you may obtain a blessing."
(1 Peter 3:8-9)

A FIERY TRIAL: Suffering in the Flesh for God's Ultimate Glory

The last section of Peter's first letter frames the suffering of the redeemed people of God in the larger context of God's ultimate glory. The *"fiery trial"* that they were enduring was only for a *"little while."* The people who revile and persecute the church will be *"put to shame"* (1 Peter 4:12-5:5).

Just as the people who heard the message of salvation in Noah's day and in their rejection were swept away in a flood of judgment, while Noah and his family were saved, so to the present unbelievers who are swept up in a *"flood of debauchery"* will have to *"give account to him who is ready to judge the living and the dead"* (1 Peter 4:4-5).

In contrast, the people of God should understand that the present trials and sufferings are temporary (1 Peter 4:7). It is a form of testing and refining: *"For it is time for judgment to begin at the household of God; and if it begins with us, what will be the outcome for those who do not obey the gospel of God?"* (1 Peter 4:17). If we are faithful to the example of Christ, when the *"chief Shepherd appears,"* the Christian *"will receive the unfading crown of glory"* (1 Peter 5:4).

THE SECOND LETTER TO PETER
Succession of the New Covenant

Peter's first letter took the hopes and promises of a restored inheritance and applied them to the redeemed New Covenant. At different times, the people had been waiting for the Promised Land, return from exile, a restored temple and a messianic king.

The second letter of Peter serves a similar function for the New Covenant as the Book of Deuteronomy does for the Old Covenant. Like Moses, Peter conveyed the terms of the covenant to the people of God.

Utilizing the general framework of a constitutional treaty between a king and his subjects, Moses set out the terms for the relationship between Yahweh and Israel. While significantly shorter that Deuteronomy, Peter utilizes a similar structure for his final letter to the church. The logic of the treaty breaks into five parts:

1. Preamble
2. Historic Prologue
3. Stipulations
4. Blessing and Curses
5. Succession

The preamble establishes the parties in the covenant relationship: God, his people, and the Covenant Mediator (Moses or Peter). The historic prologue rehearses the mighty acts of salvation and redemption that established the relationship between God and his people. The prologue recounts why the people owe their love and obedience to God.

Having established the relationship, the next section on stipulations outlines the relationship expectations for the people of God. The blessings and curses section provides the positive and negative divine responses to the people's faithfulness.

The final section on succession makes allowance for how the terms of the covenant are to be passed on to future generations. As Moses' personal ministry and leadership was ending, he wrote out the terms of God's covenant with Israel for successive generations. Just as Moses provided a framework for the people of God to continue in faithfulness to God's covenant for successive generations, so too did the apostles.

Consider the following five-part outline of 2 Peter in comparison with the five-part outline for Deuteronomy.

Literary Structure

	Passing on the New Covenant	II Peter	Deuteronomy	Purpose	Application for the Covenant People of God
I	Preamble	1:1-2	1:1-4	*Establishes the origins of the covenant relationship*	*Remember the God who has established a covenant you*
II	Historic Prologue	1:3-4	1:5-4:43	*Rehearses the historical background of God's mercy*	*Remember what God has done on your behalf*
III	Stipulations	1:5-7	4:44-26:19	*Outlines expectations of covenant life*	*Remember God's requirements for life*
IV	Blessings and Curses and Ratification	1:8-11	27:1-30:20	*Presents blessings, curses and ratification of the covenant relationship*	*Remember the blessings curses and ratification of the covenant relationship*
V	Succession	1:12-3:18	31:1-34:12	*Spells out the continuation of covenant administration*	*Remember to listen to the God appointed leaders as bearers of the authoritative word of God*

The New Covenant

The first chapter of 2 Peter establishes the covenant relationship between God and his people with the apostles as mediators. Jesus is the *"God and Savior"* who through his divine nature has granted all things that pertain to *"life and godliness"* (2 Peter 1:1-3). Instead of providing an escape from an earthly bondage and slavery in Egypt, the salvation given by Jesus is escape *"from the corruption that is in the world that is in the world because of sinful desire"* (2 Peter 1:4). The promise offered is not a land flowing with milk and honey, but rather the promise to grant us *"his own glory and excellence"* that we *"may become partakers of the divine nature"* (2 Peter 1:3-4).

In the New Covenant, the stipulations of God are not written on tablets of stone but on the human heart (Jeremiah 31:31). Therefore, the New Covenant call to obedience is in the form of character growth and change, and not an external commandment.

"For this very reason, make every effort to supplement your faith with virtue, and virtue with knowledge, and knowledge with self-control, and self-control with steadfastness, and steadfastness with godliness, and godliness with brotherly affection, and brotherly affection with love."
(2 Peter 1:5-7)

In both the Old and the New Covenant, the believer is justified by faith in the promise of God and not by works. It is God who calls his people and saves them from bondage to evil. However, true faith in the promises of God will manifest itself in fruits of obedience. These fruits displayed in increasing measure provide assurance of salvation. Whoever *"lacks these qualities"* (2 Peter 1:9) does not manifest the fruit of salvation and election.

In the Old Covenant, the consequences for those who did or did not live in faithfulness revolved around blessings and curses. With the New Covenant, the blessings and curses are ultimate. Faithful believers will be *"richly provided for"* with an *"entrance into the eternal kingdom of our Lord and Savior Jesus Christ"* (2 Peter 1:11). The curses are utmost as well. Here, he mentions the potential to fall. Later in Chapters 2 and 3, he is more specific.

Finally, Peter addresses the issue of succession. Like Moses writes of himself at the end of Deuteronomy (see Deuteronomy 32:50), Peter has been given knowledge of his impending exodus from this world (2 Peter 1:15). His primary concern is for the succession of the faith to future generations. The apostles are dying, but the faith does not die with them.

"Therefore I intend always to remind you of these qualities, though you know them and are established in the truth that you have. I think it right, as long as I am in this body, to stir you up by way of reminder, since I know that the putting off of my body will be soon, as our Lord Jesus Christ made clear to me. And I will make every effort so that after my departure you may be able at any time to recall these things."

(2 Peter 1:12-15)

How will Peter make every effort to ensure the church's recall of the faith? It must be written down. So now we are told the reason for the writing of scripture–succession. Peter now moves to the issue of authority of apostolic teaching versus the false teaching of false prophets.

Succession

Succession: II Peter 1:12-3:18			Purpose	Application
V.a	Departure of the Apostles and the provision of the New Covenant scriptures	1:12-15	Provide provision of New Covenant dynastic disposition	Remember the New Covenant through the provision of the New Covenant Scriptures
V.b	Authority of Apostles and the New Covenant scriptures	1:16-21	Ratification of Covenant	Recognize the Authority of the Apostles Call under Jesus Christ and pay attention to the New Covenant Scriptures
V.c	Threat for departure from the New Covenant scriptures	2:1-22	Dire threat to false teachers, and warning against apostasy	Shun apostasy from the New Covenant Scriptures of the Apostles of Jesus Christ
V.d	Promise for faithfulness to New Covenant Scriptures	3:1-18	Promise for covenant faithfulness to the Apostolic Word and Command	Remain faithful to the New Covenant Scriptures commanded by the Apostles of Jesus Christ

Peter explains his intentions in writing; he wishes to provide an accurate record of Christian values that will live on after his death. By recording his wisdom, he can pass it down through apostolic succession to later leadership. He goes on to affirm his witness of Jesus' divinity and validates the New Covenant scriptures by saying that all prophecy comes from God. The early church can trust the scriptures because they are not the words of men, but the word of God delivered through men.

Peter warns against false teachers who will usher in destructive policies and blasphemy. God will not spare those false teachers, and God will not spare sinful people who live without repentance. This dire warning against sin also serves as a warning to believers against apostasy, *"For it would have been better for them never to have known the way of righteousness than after knowing it to turn back from the holy commandment delivered to them"* (2 Peter 2:21). Keeping the faith means remaining vigilant over the morality of the community and one's heart. The reward for this faithfulness is God's promise of salvation: the day of the Lord. Peter reminds his audience that the Lord does not measure time as people do, and so believers cannot anticipate the day of the Lord except in hope. He closes his letter by charging his readers to *"take care that you are not carried away with the error of lawless people and lose your own stability. But grow in the grace and knowledge of our Lord and Savior Jesus Christ"* (2 Peter 3:17-18).

Fig. 3. *The Martyrdom of St Peter* (Martyrdom of St Peter) Painting by Michelangelo Merisi da Caravaggio dit The Caravaggio (1571-1610) 1600-1601 Dim 230x175 cm Chiesa di Santa Maria del Popolo (Church of Santa Maria del Popolo), Cappella Cerasi Rome / Photo © Luisa Ricciarini / Bridgeman Images.

JUDE

The short letter from Jude is written as a follow-up to Peter's second letter. The anticipated false teachers of Peter's letter have arrived. Jude's tone and urgency is several notches higher than the level of alarm sounded in 2 Peter.

If Peter's letter is like a New Covenant version of Deuteronomy, Jude's letter functions as a New Testament prophetic oracle prosecuting the covenantal concerns expressed in 2 Peter.

LETTER TO THE HEBREWS

Unfortunately, there is no way to know who wrote the letter to the Hebrews. Some in the early church attributed it to the Apostle Paul, perhaps because *"our brother Timothy"* is mentioned (Hebrews 13:23) who was Paul's young protégé. But the reference to Timothy could apply to any of the leaders in the early church.

The letter was written by someone highly educated as the letter is some of the highest quality Greek in the New Testament. Other candidates for authorship have included: Luke, Apollos, Priscilla, Aquila, Silas, and Philip. And any of these could have been serving as a scribe to an apostle such as Peter, though Hebrews 2:3 would seem to indicate that the author was not one of the 12 apostles.

It also is not possible to discern precisely to whom the letter was written. Clearly, the recipients would have been Jewish Christians in need of remedial instructions related to the relationship of Jesus to the Mosaic covenant:

"For though by this time you ought to be teachers, you need someone to teach you again the basic principles of the oracles of God."
(Hebrews 5:12)

Much of the letter is devoted to teaching the relationship of Christ to the Mosaic covenant. This would have been a primary concern for Jews. We know they were Christians because they had heard the message (Hebrews 2:3-4), had been baptized, and received the Holy Spirit (Hebrews 6:1-5). There is a concern for their growth in the faith (Hebrews 5:11-6:12). They also had some experience with persecution (Hebrews 12:4).

In the final greetings, we see this line: *"Those who come from Italy send you greetings"* (Hebrews 13:24). Does that mean the letter is from Italy? Or, more likely, is it extending greetings to Italy, probably Rome? Either way, there is a personal connection on the part of the author and readers.

It is quite likely that the letter to the Hebrews was written sometime before 70 A.D. The letter speaks in the present tense of ongoing Levite priestly ministry and temple sacrifice (see Hebrews 7:27; 8:5; 9:6-10). These practices would have ceased following the destruction of the temple by the Romans in 70 A.D.

A letter discussing the temple and priestly practices after 70 A.D. would speak of these in the past tense. If they were Jewish Roman Christians, the recipients may very well have been living during the cruel persecutions of Christians by Emperor Nero (64-68 A.D.) when Peter and Paul were both martyred.

> "It [the message of salvation] was declared at first by the Lord, and it was attested to us by those who heard, while God also bore witness by signs and wonders and various miracles and by gifts of the Holy Spirit distributed according to his will."
> Hebrews 2:3-4

CHAPTER 8 Letters From Departing Apostles

The Literary Structure of Hebrews

The Letter to the Hebrews			Chapters 1-13
The Supremacy of Jesus Christ and the New and Better Covenant Son of God	Pay Attention: The Word of the Covenant: The Son of God	The Supreme Son of God	1:4-2:18
		The Supreme Covenant Mediator	3:1-4:13
	Draw Near: The Sacrifice of the Covenant: The Blood of Jesus	The Supreme High Priest	4:14-7:28
		The Supreme New Covenant	8:1-10:18
The Response: New Covenant Faithfulness	The Life of the Covenant: Faith in Jesus	The Call to Faith	10:19-12:29
		Living Sacrifices	13:1-25

The main message of the book is that Jesus Christ is the supreme mediator of the New Covenant. It is a clarion call to draw near to God through the blood sacrifice of Jesus and follow him by faith and in covenant faithfulness to the end of the age.

The writer argues for Christ's superiority as the climax and fulfillment of God's earlier covenantal mediators, particularly through the creation, through angelic messengers, through Moses, through the Levite priesthood, and through the temple and its sacrifices (see chapters 1:1-10,18). The opening verses of the book assert its central argument:

"Long ago, at many times and in many ways, God spoke to our fathers by the prophets, but in these last days he has spoken to us by his Son, whom he appointed the heir of all things, through whom also he created the world. He is the radiance of the glory of God and the exact imprint of his nature, and he upholds the universe by the word of his power. After making purification for sins, he sat down at the right hand of the Majesty on high, having become as much superior to angels as the name he has inherited is more excellent than theirs."
(Hebrews 1:1-4)

The author of Hebrews is asserting that Jesus is the climactic, final, authoritative, greatest, and supreme revelation of God. The readers may have been tempted to fall back into their Mosaic roots and not continue press forward into the full implications and life of the new and better covenant.

There are of course serious implications with the assertion of Jesus Christ as supreme. This message not only helps to contextualize the prior revelations and commands of God preceding the coming of Jesus Christ, it sets its hearers on a clear path way toward a life of holiness and godliness in the present. It also provides the foundation of a glorious hope in the fulfillment of the promised future for the people of God. The only appropriate response to God's revelation and covenant promise in Jesus Christ is faith (Hebrews 10:19-13:25).

The Supremacy of Jesus Christ and the New and Better Covenant

The first 10 chapters of Hebrews focus on the supremacy of Christ in all things pertaining to salvation and a relationship with God. The author essentially argues that Jesus is the supreme mediator of God in word and deed. Chapters 1-4 focus on Jesus as the covenant word of God in comparison with angelic messengers and Moses. These chapters call the believer to hear and obey the supreme word: Jesus Christ. Chapters 5-10 reflect on Jesus as both priest and sacrifice as the sacramental mediator of the New Covenant. These chapters call the believer to draw near to God through the blood of Jesus Christ shed on the cross.

The Word of the Covenant: The Son of God

The major theme of Chapters 1-4 is a call to pay attention to the Word of God: The Son of God. According to the writer of Hebrews, Jesus is the supreme revelation of God. God has spoken *"at many times and in many ways ... but in these last days he has spoken to us by his Son"* (Hebrews 1:1). The revelation of God's word through Jesus is supreme over all other divine messengers (Hebrews 1-2), even Moses (Hebrews 3-4).

The Supreme Son of God

Angels are clearly important in the divine economy. He has used them in powerful ways to serve the elect of God (Hebrews 1:14). However, it is important to understand their proper relationship to the Lord Jesus. Angels serve Jesus, not the other way around.

They are creatures, while Jesus is the creator, sustainer, and redeemer of all things (Hebrews 1:1-3). His name is greater than theirs (Hebrews 1:4). Scripture has testified consistently that angels serve the Son of God and those who will *"inherit salvation."* The implication of Jesus' supremacy over the angels is that his message supersedes theirs and the people of God must remain attentive to the *"great salvation"* proclaimed *"at first by the Lord"* (Hebrews 2:3):

"Therefore we must pay much closer attention to what we have heard, lest we drift away from it. For since the message declared by angels proved to be reliable, and every transgression or disobedience received a just retribution, how shall we escape if we neglect such a great salvation? It was declared at first by the Lord, and it was attested to us by those who heard, while God also bore witness by signs and wonders and various miracles and by gifts of the Holy Spirit distributed according to his will."
(Hebrews 2:1-4)

Jesus is in the process of bringing *"many sons to glory"* through his and their suffering (Hebrews 2:10). Jesus will deliver us from Satan and the power of death that he holds (Hebrews 2:14). Because Jesus was made like us, even in weakness, suffering, and temptation, he is better equipped to minister to our needs when we are under the same trials (Hebrews 2:18).

The Supreme Covenant Mediator

Just as Jesus is supreme to angelic messengers of God's word, so too is he supreme over all human mediators of God's covenant. Moses is the supreme mediator before the coming of the Lord, but Jesus is greater than Moses.

The people of God have a history of rebelling against the human mediators of God's covenant. As great as Moses was, people hardened their hearts to his message and leadership. Because Jesus is greater than Moses, the danger of hardening our hearts to his message is even greater.

The Israelites who hardened their hearts to Moses lost the privilege of entering the Promised Land, their sabbath rest (Hebrews 3:16-19). Jesus is leading us to an even greater land of promise—an even greater sabbath rest. It remains for the people of God to enter that ultimate promise of God (Hebrews 4:9).

"Let us therefore strive to enter that rest, so that no one may fall by the same sort of disobedience. For the word of God is living and active, sharper than any two-edged sword, piercing to the division of soul and of spirit, of joints and of marrow, and discerning the thoughts and intentions of the heart. And no creature is hidden from his sight, but all are naked and exposed to the eyes of him to whom we must give account."
(Hebrews 4:11-13)

Just as in the days of old, the key to entering into the rest of God is in hearing and obeying the word of God. Jesus is the living and active word of God (cf. Revelations 1:12-16).

THE SACRIFICE OF THE COVENANT:
The Blood of Jesus

The first four chapters give those who are paying attention their eschatological marching orders. Jesus is leading his New Covenant people into God's asbbath rest. That which was hinted at through angels, Moses, and the prophets is now able to be pursued in fullness by those who hear and obey the word of Jesus Christ. Hebrews 1-4 is a call to pay attention to and obey the living and active word. Hebrews 5-10 is a call to draw near to God through the person and work of Jesus as high priest and atoning sacrifice on the cross. He introduces this section with the charge that he will develop through the next five chapters:

"Since then we have a great high priest who has passed through the heavens, Jesus, the Son of God, let us hold fast our confession. For we do not have a high priest who is unable to sympathize with our weaknesses, but one who in every respect has been tempted as we are, yet without sin. Let us then with confidence draw near to the throne of grace, that we may receive mercy and find grace to help in time of need."
(Hebrews 4:14-16)

The challenge for the Hebrews is that they are slipping away from a relationship with God rather than drawing near. There are two reasons for this. One, they are immature. This immaturity is due to an inattentiveness and hardness of heart toward the word (see Chapters 1-4). Two, the root problem is related to human weakness and sin nature. Jesus is the only one who can help us overcome human weakness and sin. He has fought the battle over these two forces and won the victory. He alone can help us; however, only the believer must draw near, not fall away.

The Supreme High Priest

One of the good things about human high priests is they can *"deal gently"* with the struggles of the *"ignorant and wayward"* (Hebrews 5:2) because they too have a human nature and therefore a sinful nature. That is why the Aaronic priesthood had to sacrifice for their own sins before offering sacrifices for the people (Hebrews 5:3). That is why it is not a self-appointed position, but a divine calling (Hebrews 5:4).

Jesus was called divinely to this very position as a high priest in the order of Melchizedek. He too is able to deal gently with us because he suffered in human weakness (Hebrews 5:8-9).

Excursus on Christian Maturity and Apostasy

The writer of Hebrews begins to develop this more fully, but then digresses into some concerns that he has for the readers. They have become *"dull of hearing"* (Hebrews 5:11) because of their lack of diligence in delving deeper into the *"word of righteousness"* (Hebrews 5:13). At this point he would have expected that they become teachers feeding others solid food. Instead, they need remedial training and "need milk, not solid food" (Hebrews 5:11-13).

Despite their immaturity, the writer is going to press on into deeper things for the sake of their growth and salvation.

"Therefore let us leave the elementary doctrine of Christ and go on to maturity, not laying again a foundation of repentance from dead works and of faith toward God, and of instruction about washings, the laying on of hands, the resurrection of the dead, and eternal judgment. And this we will do if God permits."
(Hebrews 6:1-3)

The concern is that the dullness of hearing, and the need for baby milk could be early warning signs of apostasy from the faith. Apostasy is refusing to follow or obey a religious faith, even after hearing and agreeing with it. Is it possible to have just enough external exposure to and experience with the faith to become immune to it?

"For it is impossible, in the case of those who have once been enlightened, who have tasted the heavenly gift, and have shared in the Holy Spirit, and have tasted the goodness of the word of God and the powers of the age to come, and then have fallen away, to restore them again to repentance, since they are crucifying once again the Son of God to their own harm and holding him up to contempt. For land that has drunk the rain that often falls on it, and produces a crop useful to those for whose sake it is cultivated, receives a blessing from God. But if it bears thorns and thistles, it is worthless and near to being cursed, and its end is to be burned."
(Hebrews 6:4-8)

The writer is confident that this is not them. Although there is evidence of apostasy, such as dullness and spiritual stagnation, there are other signs of life. These are *"things that belong to salvation"* (Hebrews 6:9). The evidence he sees is in their good works and loving character toward the saints, the people of God. It is important for these Christians to return their focus and attention to the promises of God.

The struggles facing the Hebrews may have led to a lack of hope. But their hope can be strong as they renew their attention to the promises of God, if they will trust him (Hebrews 6:13-19). Jesus has shown us the way in to a deeper relationship with God.

"We have this as a sure and steadfast anchor of the soul, a hope that enters into the inner place behind the curtain, where Jesus has gone as a forerunner on our behalf, having become a high priest forever after the order of Melchizedek."
(Hebrews 6:19-20)

The Supreme High Priest

> The writer of Hebrews now develops a theological argument for the supremacy of Jesus' high priesthood in the order of Melchizedek over the priesthood of Aaron and Levi. The section has four parts:
>
> 1. **The Challenge to Draw Near to the Throne of Grace Jesus the High Priest.** *(4:14-16)*
> 2. **The Calling of Jesus as a Priest forever in the Order of Melchizedek.** *(5:1-10)*
> 3. **An Excursus on Christian Maturity and Apostasy** *(5:11-6:12)*
> 4. **The Oath of God for a Better Priest that brings a Better Hope than the Law of Moses** *(6:13-7:28)*

The Oath of God for a Better Priest That brings a Better Hope than the Law of Moses

God's stated purpose is a promise made to Abraham. The promise is found in Genesis 22:

"By myself I have sworn, declares the Lord, because you have done this and have not withheld your son, your only son, I will surely bless you, and I will surely multiply your offspring as the stars of heaven and as the sand that is on the seashore. And your offspring shall possess the gate of his enemies, and in your offspring shall all the nations of the earth be blessed, because you have obeyed my voice." (Genesis 22:16-18)

The writer argues that this promise is guaranteed by an oath. Because God does not have anything higher than himself to swear by, he swears by himself. The fulfillment of this promise to Abraham and Abraham's heirs is absolutely guaranteed by the oath of God. Therefore, the heirs of Abraham receive two unchangeable things: the oath and the promise. What is the promise? multiplication and blessing. The blessing for Abraham came in his lifetime through the priesthood of a rather enigmatic figure named Melchizedek. His name means the *"king of righteousness"* and he was the King of Salem (Shalom), which means peace (Genesis 7:1).

The writer argues that the priesthood of Melchizedek supersedes the priesthood of Levi and Aaron for three reasons: the Abrahamic tithe, the change to a new order of priesthood by indestructible resurrection power of Jesus versus week and useless law, the confirmation by oath of God in the promises of scripture.

They use an argument based in Abraham's tithe. First, he is great because the patriarch Abraham offered a tenth of all his wealth and received a blessing from him. The lesser (Abraham) is blessed by the greater (Melchizedek) (Genesis 7:6-7).

Second, he is compared with a priesthood according to the law versus a priesthood according to *"the power of an indestructible life"* (Hebrews 7:16). With Jesus, there has come a change in the priesthood that necessitates a change to the laws. There is nothing the law of Moses relates to anyone other than a Levite serving at the altar of God. Jesus was a member of the tribe of Judah. But the law was imperfect and weak Genesis (7:18). The change was wrought by the power of the resurrection (Genesis 7:16) and that enables the fulfillment of the divine promise of

Psalm 110:4:

"You are a priest forever after the order of Melchizedek."
(Psalm 110:4)

The promise and purpose was confirmed by oath. Just as the Lord God swore an oath to multiply and bless Abraham (Genesis 6:13-20), so has the Lord sworn by oath to anoint the messiah as a priest forever in the order of Melchizedek. The finite, sinful, and tempo-rary priesthood that always would require an endless supply of new priests with continual sacrifices has been replaced by a permanent priesthood in one great high priest.

"... but he holds his priesthood permanently, because he continues forever. Consequently, he is able to save to the uttermost those who draw near to God through him, since he always lives to make intercession for them.

For it was indeed fitting that we should have such a high priest, holy, innocent, unstained, separated from sinners, and exalted above the heavens. He has no need, like those high priests, to offer sacrifices daily, first for his own sins and then for those of the peo-ple, since he did this once for all when he offered up himself. For the law appoints men in their weakness as high priests, but the word of the oath, which came later than the law, appoints a Son who has been made perfect forever."
(Hebrews 7:24-28)

The bottom line is that God has given us a better high priest in Jesus because he is permanent, sinless, and completely effective for all time for all people. Therefore, he can *"save to the uttermost those who draw near to God through him"* (Hebrews 7:25). Because he is the superior high priest, his coming and ministry guarantees a superior New Covenant (Hebrews 7:22).

> Having established the supremacy of the high priesthood of Jesus, the writer now turns his focus to the supremacy of the covenant that comes by the ministry of the great high priest.
>
> The writer's thought progresses:
>
> 1. **Jesus' Priesthood Inaugurates the Ministry of the New Covenant** (8:1-13)
> 2. **Jesus: The Mediator of a New Covenant** (9:11-28)
> 3. **Jesus: The Sacrifice of the New Covenant** (10:1-17)
> 4. **The Call to Enter the Holy Place** (10:18-39)

Jesus' priesthood ushers in the ministry of the New Covenant

Quoting the prophet Jeremiah (Hebrews 31:31-34), the writer argues that God announced his intention to make the first covenant obsolete by superseding it with a new and better covenant. As Moses instituted the construction of the tabernacle, the ministry of the priesthood and the sacrifices, he was making a copy and a shadow of the heavenly things he saw in the glory cloud on the mountain.

Why would the worshiper want the earthly and the temporary priesthood, worship, and temple, when the real and the permanent priesthood and heavenly throne room is revealed and available in Jesus Christ?

The New Covenant makes the first covenant obsolete (Hebrews 8:13). Working inward toward the place of worship and holiness, the writer describes how the shadow and temporary both point toward the New Covenant in Jesus Christ.

The writer describes in detail the earthly tabernacle with its holy place and most holy place. He describes the ministry of the priests and the sacrifices offered. These merely point to the greater realities of Jesus as both priest and sacrifice.

Jesus: The Mediator of a New Covenant

The coming of Christ marked the unveiling of worship in the true holy place.

"But when Christ appeared as a high priest of the good things that have come, then through the greater and more perfect tent (not made with hands, that is, not of this creation) he entered once for all into the holy places, not by means of the blood of goats and calves but by means of his own blood, thus securing an eternal redemption."
(Hebrews 9:11-12)

All the ministry of the earthly priesthood and their sacrifices could accomplish was the *"purification of the flesh"* (Hebrews 9:13). The New Covenant promised to change the state of the heart. So, the *"blood of Christ"* through the *"eternal Spirit"* purifies *"our conscience from dead works to serve the living God"* (Hebrews 9:14).

Purification from sin requires blood sacrifice. The priest's role is to offer blood sacrifices to purify. Jesus' priestly ministry was entirely effective because of the nature of the sacrifice that he offered.

"Thus it was necessary for the copies of the heavenly things to be purified with these rites, but the heavenly things themselves with better sacrifices than these. For Christ has entered, not into holy places made with hands, which are copies of the true things, but into heaven itself, now to appear in the presence of God on our behalf. Nor was it to offer himself repeatedly, as the high priest enters the holy places every year with blood not his own, for then he would have had to suffer repeatedly since the foundation of the world. But as it is, he has appeared once for all at the end of the ages to put away sin by the sacrifice of himself."
(Hebrews 9:23-26)

Jesus: The Sacrifice of the New Covenant

The priestly ministry of Jesus was entirely effective because he offered not the blood of bulls and goats, but a sacrifice of himself *"once for all."*

"And by that will we have been sanctified through the offering of the body of Jesus Christ once for all."
(Hebrews 10:10)

The blood of animals could never remove sin. The proof of that is in the need for continued repetition of the sacrifices (Hebrews 10:2). The benefit of the Old Covenant sacrifices is in the continual reminder of sin (Hebrews 10:3).

Two components promised by the New Covenant in Jeremiah are:

1. **The indwelling Holy Spirit:** The law is written on the heart.
2. **The forgiveness of sins:** God will remember their sins no more.

Jesus has *"perfected for all time those who are being sanctified"* (Hebrews 10:14). Therefore, there is now no more need for any further *"offering for sin"* (Hebrews 10:18).

The Call to Enter the Holy Place

Having taught the promise, the supremacy and the means of the fulfillment of the New Covenant in Jesus, the writer now encourages the people of God to enter into the real holy place.

"Therefore, brothers, since we have confidence to enter the holy places by the blood of Jesus, by the new and living way that he opened for us through the curtain, that is, through his flesh, and since we have a great priest over the house of God, let us draw near with a true heart in full assurance of faith, with our hearts sprinkled clean from an evil conscience and our bodies washed with pure water. Let us hold fast the confession of our hope without wavering, for he who promised is faithful."
(Hebrews 10:19-23)

Jesus has given us full access into the holy place of God. It remains for us to draw near in full assurance of faith and trust in God.

The author of Hebrews has come full circle to the resolution to the concern voiced in Hebrews 5:11-6:12. It is for the members of the church that were falling away rather than moving closer to an intimate communion with God. Their minds had grown dull to the word and they lacked maturity (Hebrews 6). They were going back to the old ways rather than growing in maturity considering their conversion and baptism. Yet because of the great ministry and sacrifice of Christ, our privilege is full access to God. So, he offers three exhortations by way of encouragement:

1. **Let us draw near [to God]** (10:22)
2. **Let us hold fast to the hope without wavering** (10:23)
3. **Let us consider how to stir up one another** (10:24)

Because the New Covenant is final, the consequences in our application of it are final as well. We are reaching the final day (Hebrews 10:25). So now is not the time to shrink back but to hold fast and persevere to the end. Yes, the challenges and struggles with sin and persecution are hard. But the stakes could not be higher both negatively and positively.

"Therefore do not throw away your confidence, which has a great reward. For you have need of endurance, so that when you have done the will of God you may receive what is promised.

Yet a little while, and the coming one will come and will not delay;

but my righteous one shall live by faith, and if he shrinks back, my soul has no pleasure in him."

But we are not of those who shrink back and are destroyed, but of those who have faith and preserve their souls."
(Hebrews 10:35-39)

THE RESPONSE: New Covenant Faithfulness

Life in the New Covenant is one lived by faith. The writer now defines and calls the church to the life of faith (Hebrews 11:1-12:29). He then challenges the people of God to offer themselves as living sacrifices in worship to God (Hebrews 12:30-13:25).

The Call to Faith

Here we find one of the clearest definitions of faith.

"Now faith is the assurance of things hoped for, the conviction of things not seen. For by it the people of old received their commendation."
(Hebrews 11:1-2)

Verse by verse, the author tells the story of redemptive history, making the case that a vibrant relationship with God is based on faith in the promises of God. The faith of the early heroes of God is commendable. Yet they never received, in their lives, the fulfillment of the New Covenant as those living today can.

"And all these, though commended through their faith, did not receive what was promised, since God had provided something better for us, that apart from us they should not be made perfect."
(Hebrews 11:39-40)

The call therefore is to follow their example and witness in embracing by faith the promises of God in the New Covenant through Jesus. Jesus himself shows the way as the perfector of our faith:

"Therefore, since we are surrounded by so great a cloud of witnesses, let us also lay aside every weight, and sin which clings so closely, and let us run with endurance the race that is set before us, looking to Jesus, the founder and perfecter of our faith, who for the joy that was set before him endured the cross, despising

the shame, and is seated at the right hand of the throne of God."
(Hebrews 12:1-2)

Yes, it is hard; yes, there is suffering; yes, the Lord will discipline us to sanctify us that we might share in his holiness. Through it all, the call is to have faith in God through Jesus Christ. They had the Mount Sinai experience that was terrifying. However, we as the heirs of the New Covenant have access to Mount Zion.

"But you have come to Mount Zion and to the city of the living God, the heavenly Jerusalem, and to innumerable angels in festal gathering, and to the assembly of the firstborn who are enrolled in heaven, and to God, the judge of all, and to the spirits of the righteous made perfect, and to Jesus, the mediator of a new covenant, and to the sprinkled blood that speaks a better word than the blood of Abel."
(Hebrews 12:22-24)

The call to the New Covenant believer is to hear the voice of the God and offer our lives in acceptable worship, with reverence, and awe; for our God is a consuming fire (Hebrews 12:28-29).

Living Sacrifice

The sacrifices that please God are not those offered at the temple in Jerusalem (Hebrews 13:10-11). That is to go backward and reject the New Covenant. The sacrifices that please God are those offered in worship by spiritual fruits of love and service (Hebrews 13:1-3); in holiness of life eschewing sexual immorality and honoring marriage (Hebrews 13:4); in not being corrupted by love of money (Hebrews 13:5); and, in following the leadership and example of Christian elders (Hebrews 13:7, 17).

The Christian life in these last days will be one of suffering for the name of Jesus. He suffered so we should be willing to join him in his sufferings (Hebrews 13:13). We can bear anything now, because we have assurance and faith in the hope that is offered in the New Covenant:

"For here we have no lasting city, but we seek the city that is to come. Through him then let us continually offer up a sacrifice of praise to God, that is, the fruit of lips that acknowledge his name. Do not neglect to do good and to share what you have, for such sacrifices are pleasing to God."
(Hebrews 13:14-16)

CHAPTER 8 NOTES:

CHAPTER 9
Pick Up Your Cross and Follow Jesus

OBJECTIVE: The maturing Christian will understand the story of Jesus and the call and costs of discipleship.

INTRODUCTION

As synoptic gospels, Matthew and Luke describe Jesus' life from his miraculous birth, through his ministry, and conclude with his sacrificial death on the cross. Though these gospels present similar accounts of Jesus' words and actions, they have different emphases. Matthew writes from a Jewish perspective, with a Jewish audience in mind, and stresses Jesus' heritage as the son of David. Luke writes to a Gentile audience. However, both Matthew and Luke emphasize the responsibilities, challenges, and divine rewards of following Jesus. They challenge their readers to respond to the Gospel story by believing and committing to eternal fellowship with the Messiah.

The Jewish-Roman Wars and Destruction of the Temple[1]

In 66 A.D., the first Jewish-Roman war took place after the Roman procurator, Gessius Florus, stole money from the Temple and murdered the Jews who opposed him. As tensions between the Jewish population and the Roman authorities rose, this direct affront to the Jewish faith sparked the first of several uprisings that resulted in war. Jerusalem fell into unrest, and the Roman authorities were quick to lash out in violence, crucifying rebels and city leaders. That did little to stop the rebellions.

Despite losing battles to Syrian and Roman forces, the Jewish rebels remained steadfast in their opposition. After the Roman General Vespasian arrived to crush the rebellion, however, it took one year to subjugate Jewish resistance in the north. The leaders of these areas escaped to Jerusalem. However, infighting among Jewish factions sparked a civil war within the city. Although Jerusalem was in turmoil, Jews continued to seek safety in the city because of its fortified walls.

Fig. 1. *Les quatre evangelistes Peinture de Jacob Jordaens* (1593-1678) 17eme siecle. Dim. 1,34 x 1,18 m Paris, musee du Louvre / Photo © Photo Josse / Bridgeman Images.

In 70 A.D., the Roman siege of Jerusalem began. Because they could not breach the city's walls, the Romans constructed a wall as tall as the one surrounding Jerusalem. Anyone caught attempting to escape from Jerusalem was crucified. During the seven-month siege, zealots burned almost all of the dry food supplies for the city, and many people died of starvation. When the defensive wall began to crumble, the Romans burned the city, destroyed the temple, and sold most of the survivors into slavery. Historians estimate that about 1 million people were killed during the siege.

[1] En.wikipedia.org/wiki/first_jewish-Roman_war

THE GOSPEL ACCORDING TO MATTHEW
Who Was Matthew?

Matthew was a Jewish tax collector before Jesus' call to follow him, and later he became one of the 12 disciples. Some modern scholars believe that because the Gospel of Matthew relied on the Gospel of Mark as a source, the author could not have been an eyewitness. However, all the earliest church leaders attribute this Gospel to Matthew the tax collector. Further, if Peter is the source behind Mark, then it would make sense that they would utilize one another's work.

Recipients[2]

Matthew's concern with fulfillment of the Old Testament and his tracing of Jesus' lineage to Abraham mean that his audience was likely Jewish. He does not explain Jewish customs and uses Jewish terminology. Throughout the text, he emphasizes Jesus' role as the "Son of David." He also has more quotations from and allusions to the Old Testament than any other New Testament author.

Date and Place of Writing[3]

Some have argued that based on its Jewish characteristics, Matthew's Gospel was written as the first Gospel in the early church period, possibly in the early part of 50 A.D. It was a time when the church was largely Jewish, and the Gospel was preached to Jews only (Acts 11:19). However, those who have concluded that both Matthew and Luke drew extensively from Mark's Gospel date it later. As a result, some think that Matthew would have been written in late 50 A.D. or in early 60 A.D. Others, who assume that Mark was written between 65 A.D. and 70 A.D., and place Matthew in 70 A.D. or later.

Purpose[4]

Matthew's main purpose is to prove to his Jewish readers that Jesus is their Messiah. He does this primarily by showing how Jesus, in his life and ministry, fulfilled the Old Testament scriptures. Although all the Gospel writers quote the Old Testament, Matthew includes nine proof texts unique to his Gospel (see Matthew 1:22–23; 2:15; 2:17–18; 2:23; 4:14–16; 8:17; 12:17–21; 13:35; 27:9–10), to prove his theme: Jesus is the fulfillment of the Old Testament predictions of the Messiah. Matthew even finds the history of God's people in the Old Testament reflected in some aspects of Jesus' life. To accomplish his purpose, Matthew emphasizes Jesus' Davidic lineage.

---

[2]http://www.biblica.com/niv/study-bible/matthew/
[3]http://www.biblica.com/niv/study-bible/matthew/
[4]http://www.biblica.com/niv/study-bible/matthew/

Outline Based on Missionary Journey and Geography:

- The Early Life of Jesus: Matthew 1:1-4:11
- The Ministry of Jesus in Galilee: Matthew 4:12-18:35.
- The Ministry of Jesus in Judea: Matthew 19:1-28:20

Literary Outline

MATTHEW		Chapters 1-28
Prologue:	Birth and Infancy of the Messiah	1-2
Narrative:	Preparations for Ministry in Galilee	3-4
First Discourse:	The Sermon on the Mount	5-7
Narrative:	Nine Miracle Stories	8-9
Second Discourse:	The Missionary Sermon	10
Narrative:	Diverse Responses to Jesus	11-12
Third Discourse:	The Parables of the Kingdom	13:1-53
Narrative:	More Diverse Responses to Jesus	13:54-17
Fourth Discourse:	The Ecclesial Sermon on Life in the Community	18
Narrative:	Journey to Jerusalem and Controversy in the Temple	19-23
Fifth Discourse:	The Eschatological Sermon	24-25
Epilogue:	The Passion and Resurrection of the Messiah	26-28

INTRODUCTION: THE MESSIANIC KING
Genealogy

The first word of the Gospel is the Greek word *"genesis"*. It means beginning. New creation comes with the advent of the Messiah. The genealogy highlights Abraham, the father of the Jewish people; David, the King of Israel; and, the exile of Israel to Babylon. The Jews of Jesus' day did not believe the exile was over because of their partial return from Babylon; the foreign occupation of the land by the Roman empire; the fact that an Edomite was serving on David's throne; and, the Temple had been rebuilt. They were awaiting the end of exile and the return of Yahweh with the Messiah. They sought the fulfillment of 70 years of Jeremiah and 70 weeks of years (7 X 70 years) in Daniel 9.

Yahweh, the creator of the world, chose and called Israel to be the people through whom he would redeem the world. The covenant promises made to Abraham and David are the only hope for all the people of the world. The point of the Gospel writers is that the life, death, and resurrection of Jesus is the dramatic climax of the story of Israel for the salvation of the world!

INFANCY NARRATIVE
The Naming of Jesus

Jesus is the Hebrew name Joshua, meaning *"Yahweh saves."* To make the point, Matthew (see Matthew 1:23) quotes the prophet Isaiah (see Isaiah 7:14). The Hebrew name Immanuel means *"God is with us"*. Matthew makes it clear that now *"Jesus is with us"*.[5]

With the arrival of the wise men and the announcement of the birth of the Messiah in Bethlehem, Herod the Great felt deeply threatened and pursued the holy family with the intent to kill the child. Just as Israel fled to Egypt, so too did the holy family. Herod's slaughter of the innocent male children of Bethlehem mirrors the evil act of Pharaoh's slaughter of the Hebrew children (Exodus 1:22). Through a series of divine dreams given to Joseph, the Lord protects his holy seed, his son (Mathew 2:15).

---

[5] Ibid, p. 96.

THE GOSPEL OF THE KINGDOM
The Inauguration of the Kingdom

The baptism of Jesus by John is the formal ceremonial moment marking the inauguration of his rule as the anointed one, the messianic king. With the descent of the Holy Spirit *"coming to rest on him"* and divine voice from heaven, *"This is my beloved Son, with whom I am well pleased"* (Matthew 3:17), the reign of Jesus as messianic king began. Jesus is established as the Son of God, the promised heir of David's throne, and the Servant of the Lord (Matthew 3:1-7:29).

The Temptation

Jesus' anointing is immediately tested by the devil. Jesus reveals that his kingdom will not be *"of the world and their glory"* (Matthew 4:8). He will not fall prey to the devil's schemes. Jesus will succeed in resisting Satan's temptations in the wilderness where both humanity and Israel have failed.

Jesus' Kingdom Reign Begins

Jesus' threefold public ministry will consist of teaching, preaching, and healing (Matthew 4:23). Jesus' entire message as the Yahweh Messiah is: *"Repent, for the Kingdom of Heaven is at hand"* (Matthew 3:2). Jesus immediately begins to gather followers who will become his disciples. The first teaching discourse, the Sermon on the Mount, reveals what it means to be a disciple of Jesus.

Fig. 2. *The Baptism of Jesus, Saint Matthew* - Bible, Tissot, James Jacques Joseph (1836-1902) (after) / Lebrecht History / Bridgeman Image.

THE SERMON ON THE MOUNT
Key Themes

Jesus described the blessing of living righteous lives as kingdom citizens. The challenges of righteousness were far greater than the leaders of Judaism had taught or practiced. Indeed, they had misinterpreted the intent of God's law. God is not interested in controlling outward behavior to please others; he wants obedience to begin in the heart to please an audience of one: the father who sees in secret. Jesus assured his faithful followers that the kingdom already belongs to us. Ultimately, we must decide whether to live for God or this world (Matthew 5-7).

A Christian's Character

The Beatitudes emphasize eight principal marks of Christian character and conduct, especially in relation to God and to men, and the divine blessing that rests on those who exhibit these marks. The follower of Jesus Christ is called to be distinct from the prevailing culture. Jesus uses two metaphors, salt and light, to indicate the influence for good that Christians will exercise in the community—but only if they exercise the character and practices taught by him in the Sermon on the Mount (Matthew 5:3-16).

A Christian's Righteousness

What is the Christian's attitude toward the law of God? Did Jesus come to abolish the law? No. He came to fulfill it! The righteousness of a follower of Jesus must exceed the righteousness of the Pharisee. The problem is not the law itself, but rather the bad interpretation of the law and its poor implementation (Matthew 5:17-48).

A Christian's Piety

The followers of Jesus are called to manifest a religious devotional life that neither resembles the hypocritical display of the Pharisee nor the mechanical formalism of the pagans. Christian piety is to be sincere and real, with an awareness of God's audience (Matthew 6:1-18).

A Christian's Ambition

The Christian must have a different attitude toward material wealth and possessions. Following Jesus changes our attitude in both scarcity and abundance. The follower of Jesus is free from self-centered anxiety about food, drink, and clothing. Money is not the chief idol. We cannot worship both God and money. The supreme ambitions of the Christians are for the kingdom of God and the glory of God (Matthew 6:19-34).

A Christian's Relationships

The Christian life is about relationships: first, our relationship to God and, second, to one another. New relationships are created, old relationships are changed. We are not to judge our brother but to serve him. We are to avoid offering the Gospel to those who decisively reject it. We are to manifest an intimate prayer life with God as father. We are to be wary of false prophets who hinder people from finding the narrow gate and the hard way (Matthew 7:1-20).

A Christian's Commitment

The bottom line: It is not enough to call Jesus *"Lord"* or merely to listen to his teaching. If we are to be true followers, we must mean what we say and do what we hear. On this commitment hinges our eternal destiny. Fundamentally, it comes down to the issue of authority (Matthew 7:21-27).

THE SPREAD OF THE KINGDOM
Who Is This Man?

The narrative concentrates on the mighty acts of Jesus. He manifests divine authority over sickness; over nature; over demonic powers and the paralysis of sin; and, over disabilities and death. A question hangs in the narrative: *"What sort of man is this, that even winds and sea obey him?"* (Matthew 8:27).

Reactions

In addition to focusing on Jesus' authority, Matthew calls attention to the Jewish crowd and their leader's reactions to Jesus' power: opposition, fear, and willful rejection (Matthew 8:34, 9:8). Those asking for healing and recognizing their need are affirmed for having great faith. The Roman centurion is commended because as one *"under authority,"* he recognized Jesus as a commander who could just *"say the word"* and his will would be done. The centurion believes, but unfortunately Jesus chides the Jews: *"with no one in Israel have I found such faith"* (Matthew 8:9-10).

The Jewish leadership is skeptical, accusing Jesus of *"blaspheming,"* for exercising the authority to forgive sin (Matthew 9:3). They question his table fellowship with sinners and tax collectors (Matthew 9:11). They accused him of exercising satanic power because he drove out demons. The demons, however, know with whom they are dealing: *"What have you to do with us, O Son of God?"* (Matthew 8:29). The demons knew that they were at war with an overwhelmingly powerful authority.

Regardless of the reactions, word spread about Jesus throughout the region. (Matthew 9:26, 31). *"Never was anything like this seen in Israel"* (Matthew 9:33). One thing that must be noted is that no one could remain neutral on the question of Jesus.

Fig. 3. Fol.49r *Christ Heals a Man Possessed* (vellum), Italian School, (15th century) / Biblioteca Reale, Turin, Piedmont, Italy / Alinari / Bridgeman Images.

There are two categories of people: those who believe and commit to follow and those who do not believe.

Commitment

Following Jesus requires radical and costly submission to his authority. Following Jesus is a radical act because it may cost a disciple basic security, such as a place to live (Matthew 8:18-20). Also, following Jesus is costly because it must take precedence over all social obligations, even those family obligations society and religion consider to be *"ultimate"* (Matthew 8:21-22).

Compassion

Jesus had tremendous compassion for people in need. He cares about a leper, the servant of a Gentile soldier, an old hemorrhaging woman, and a young girl. Matthew ties his ministry of compassion to work of the suffering servant of Isaiah 53:4: *"Surely he has borne our griefs and carried our sorrows."* While Jesus manifests such awesome power and authority, it is the power of a physician. He comes as a doctor for the sinner (Matthew 9:13).

THE SPREAD OF THE KINGDOM
The 12 Disciples Are Commissioned

Jesus extended his kingdom ministry by empowering the 12 disciples with authority *"over unclean spirits, to cast them out, and to heal every disease and every affliction"* (Matthew 10:1). Jesus commanded them to announce and enact the presence of the kingdom (Matthew 10:7-8). The message would be validated by acts and signs of compassion. Jesus' agents are called to live simply and travel light, trusting in the Lord to provide for their needs. *"Whoever receives you receives me, and whoever receives me receives him who sent me"* (Matthew 10:40). The responsibility for accepting the message and the messenger of the Gospel resides with the hearer. To reject the messenger is to reject the message of hope (Matthew 8:1 – 10:15).

Fig. 4. *Christ with the twelve Apostles, illustration for 'The Life of Christ',* c.1886-96 (gouache on paperboard), Tissot, James Jacques Joseph (1836-1902) / Brooklyn Museum of Art, New York, USA / Bridgeman Images.

Persecution Is Promised

Persecution and proclamation are inseparable. Jesus promises to empower his disciples when they come against opposition. In their own strength they are helpless; he is sending them out as sheep in the midst of wolves (Matthew 10:16). However, he promises to provide for their faithful witness in their hour of need. They will endure physical suffering and shame on account of Jesus. The persecution will divide families. There will be betrayals by those closest, brothers, sisters, and parents—even children *"will rise against parents and have them put to death"* (Matthew 10:21). There will be no safe refuge from persecution (Matthew 10:16-25).

Promises for the Persecuted

The disciples are called to fear God rather than men. The promised persecution should make the disciple of Jesus more bold. He told them: *"What I tell you in the dark, say in the light, and what you hear whispered, proclaim on the housetops"* (Matthew 10:27). God will not be mocked—his disciples are precious to him, and he will vindicate them. God is ultimately sovereign and in control: not one sparrow falls to the ground apart from the sovereignty of God. The Lord intimately knows his disciples and their situations *"… even the hairs of your head are all numbered"* (Matthew 10:30).

SIGNS AND PARABLES
Doubts and False Expectations

The section begins with John the Baptist asking, *"Are you the one who is to come, or shall we look for another?"* (Matthew 11:3). The question raised in this narrative is this: Are the expectations of Israel for their coming Messiah correct? While Jesus reassures John, the Jewish crowds and religious leaders remain unconvinced.

Jesus pronounces a prophetic *"woe oracle"* on the Jewish towns in Galilee for their lack of faith despite his mighty acts. He compares them with Gentile cities that would have repented *"long ago"* if the people of those cities had seen what these towns have seen. God has hidden the revelation of the kingdom from those who are *"wise and understanding"* and has revealed them to *"little children"* (Matthew 11:25). But the invitation to the kingdom is open to those who are weary and heavy laden. Also, Jesus faced rejection by the religious leaders for his behavior, especially when his disciples harvested grain and ate on the Sabbath (Matthew 12:1).

Lord of the Sabbath

The disciples were accused of doing what was *"not lawful to do on the Sabbath"* (Matthew 12:2). The response of Jesus argues for the validity of their actions on the basis of three arguments:

I. David and his followers ate the bread from the temple. Implication: Jesus is king, like David, only greater.

II. The priests are allowed to work in temple service on the Sabbath. Implication: Jesus is priest, only something greater than the temple itself.

III. What could be greater than the temple itself? Implication: The Son of Man is Lord of the Sabbath.

To reveal his sovereignty over the Sabbath, Jesus performs a mighty act by healing a man's hand (Matthew 12:13). Matthew then ties the entire work of Jesus to the servant song of Isaiah 42, which was connected to the divine voice at Jesus' baptism.

Can This Be the Son of David? – Or Is It Satan?

The healing of the demon-oppressed blind and mute man causes people to wonder whether Jesus is the Messiah, *"the Son of David,"* but the Pharisees determine that Jesus is doing the work of *"the prince of demons"* (Matthew 12:24). Jesus puzzles why Satan would work at cross-purposes with his own evil kingdom. But, then again, why would someone supposedly working for the kingdom of heaven work against the Son of Man and blaspheme the work of the Holy Spirit? People can determine who a teacher of the kingdom of God is and who is not by the fruit they bear and the treasure they bring forth (Matthew 12:33-37). The demand for a sign by *"an evil and adulterous generation"* would be met by the sign of Jonah: discipline and judgment for themselves and repentance and mercy for the Gentiles (Matthew 12:38-42). Those who would become Jesus' disciples must be loyal to *"the will of my Father in Heaven"* higher than even above their most cherished social conventions, friends and family (Matthew 12:49-50).

KINGDOM PARABLES

The prevailing Jewish expectation was a desire to see the kingdom of heaven immediately consummated with the coming of the Messiah. However, Jesus taught through his parables of the kingdom that their expectations were mistaken. While the coming of the Messiah did bring forth the kingdom of heaven, it would take time to develop and mature before the final consummation. (Matthew 13:1-53)

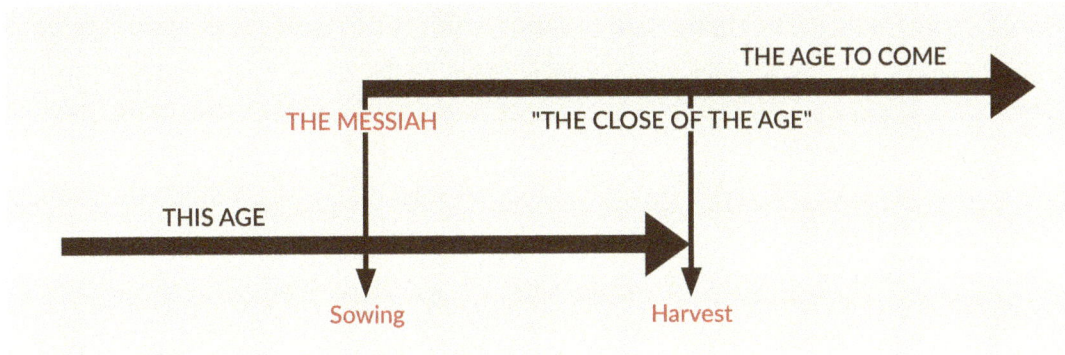

The Son of Man would come first to plant the seeds of his kingdom. Later, he would return for a great harvest. In the parable of the sower, Jesus taught that the seed of the *"word of the kingdom"* (Matthew 13:19) would bear great fruit in the good soil of *"He who has ears, let him hear"* (Matthew 13:9). Many would not respond in faith to the call of the kingdom of heaven because of trials, worries of life, and the work of the evil one (Matthew 13:1-23).

Jesus taught that the nature of the kingdom of God was progressive, like leavening working through dough, and in accordance with the Word of God. It would begin small *"like a grain of mustard seed"* (Matthew 13:31). But over time it would grow into a massive tree. While the kingdom was developing, the good and bad would grow and develop together, like weeds in the midst of a vibrant wheat field. Make no mistake, however, the harvest will come. At *"the end of the age"* (Matthew 13:49) the righteous sons of the kingdom will be gathered as wheat, and the evil and wicked will be judged like bundles of weeds being burned in the *"fiery furnace"* (Matthew 13:50).

Jesus taught that the kingdom of heaven was of supreme value and was to be sought at all cost. If it were a pearl or a treasure in a field, it would be wise to sell everything you possess to buy that field (Matthew 13:44-46).

FALTERING FAITH AND TRUE GREATNESS
Great Faith Versus Little Faith

Matthew records 13 stories that share the major theme of faith in Jesus. The focus is on the faith of the disciples, in particular those who consistently falter. This lack of faith is in direct contrast to the Canaanite woman who is commended, *"O woman, great is your faith!"* (Matthew 15:28).

In the first two stories, Jesus is rejected. First, in his home town of Nazareth, Jesus was recognized as one of *"wisdom and these mighty works"* (Matthew 13:54), and yet they still took offense at him. *"And he did not do many mighty works there, because of their unbelief"* (Matthew 13:58). Second, the story tells where Herod does not dispute Jesus' fame in doing mighty works. However, Herod is under judgment for murdering John the Baptist, God's prophet.

The next three stories focus on the disciples who need to grow in their faith. With the feeding of the 5,000, Jesus challenges the faith of the disciples, *"… you give them something to eat."* But they replied, *"We have only five loves here and two fish"* (Matthew 14:16-17). Next, Jesus sent them out on the lake and came to them walking on water. Peter demonstrates a measure of faith but then he doubts, to which Jesus responds, *"O you of little faith, why did you doubt?"* (Matthew 14:31).

Jesus gets into a conflict with the Pharisees over internal and external righteousness. When Peter asks for a simple clarification about Jesus' teaching, he is questioned: *"Are you also still without understanding?"* (Matthew 15:16). And, as already noted, … the Canaanite woman is commended for having *"great faith"* (Matthew 15:28). The disciples continue to show a lack of it. Even with another feeding of the 4,000, they show the same doubts.

Fig. 5. The Feeding of the 5,000 in the Gospel of John reports that five barley loaves and two small fish supplied by a boy were used by Jesus to feed a multitude. ***The miracle of the five loaves and two fish*** (oil on wood), Cranach, Lucas, the Elder (1472-1553) / Nationalmuseum, Stockholm, Sweden / Bridgeman Images.

In Matthew 16:8, he says his disciples have *"little faith."* Peter expresses tremendous faith in his bold confession of Jesus as the Christ and then immediately is rebuked as *"Satan"* for *"not setting your mind on the things of God, but the things of man"* (Matthew 16:23), and later for his three denials before the cock crowed. He sees the glory of Jesus during the transfiguration and yet mistakenly wants to set up a shrine to Jesus on the mountain. In Matthew 17:14-23, Jesus explains the reason why the disciples could not excise the demonic spirit, *"because of your little faith."* If only they had *"faith like a grain of a mustard seed,"* nothing would be impossible for them (Matthew 17:20).

Who Do You Say I Am?

The climactic turning point of the Gospel of Matthew is Peter's confession in answer to the question: Who do you say that I am? The focus of the Gospel to this point has been to answer this question through the teachings and mighty acts of Jesus and show the various reactions of faith, doubt, fear, and rejection. Peter concludes the matter with a dramatic confession that Jesus is *"... the Christ, the Son of the living God"* (Matthew 16:16). With the confession of Peter, the Gospel shifts to answer the question: What is the Messiah going to do? From that time on, Jesus begins to teach (Matthew 16:21).

Jesus will teach his disciples three times that: *"... he must go to Jerusalem and suffer many things from the elders and chief priests and scribes, and be killed, and on the third day be raised"*

(Matthew 16:21; see also Matthew 20:18). Peter and the other disciples completely fail in their understanding of the mission of the Messiah. *"Far be it from you Lord! This shall never happen to you!"* (Matthew 16:22). As far as Jesus' identity is concerned, Peter is rock solid—it is the nature of Jesus' mission that causes Peter to become a stone of hindrance. Satan offered Jesus a kingdom without a cross at the temptation in the desert, now his offer returns on Peter's lips.

The Transfiguration

The Mount of Transfiguration is compared to Mount Sinai (see Exodus 24:15-18). There the inner three of the New Covenant, Peter, James, and John, meet the inner two of the Old Covenant, Moses and Elijah. The Shekinah glory (a form of the Hebrew word that means *"he caused to dwell,"* used by Rabbis but not found in the Bible) of Yahweh is manifest. Only the Glory is radiating from the personhood of Jesus. The divine voice again confirms the kingly identity of Jesus (see Psalm 2) and commends obedience to Jesus as they would to God's law.

ECCLESIAL SERMON:
True Greatness Within Kingdom Family Life

As Jesus travelled from town to town, small groups of followers began to form. If the Sermon on the Mount was preached to communicate how they should live as the righteous and reconstituted Israel being the *"salt of the earth,"* *"light of the world,"* and the *"city set on a hill"* (Matthew 5:13-14), the ecclesial sermon taught how his disciples should live as brothers and sisters—as Jesus' *"children"* (Matthew 18:3). Likewise, the author of Matthew recognizes that the movement begun in Jesus' day has expanded and connects directly to his own. The congregations of believers in his day also need direction living together faithfully in community.

Humility as Children

One of the many challenges for Jesus' followers was pride. Being personally called by the king, the Son of God, was quite heady. The disciples came to Jesus asking, *"Who is the greatest in the kingdom of heaven?"* (Matthew 18:1). He rebuked them, as pride had no place in his community. Greatness in the people of God is attained by becoming *"like children"* (Matthew 18:3). While the disciples were thinking of themselves as great ones, Jesus challenged them to consider themselves as little ones. *"Whoever humbles himself like this child is the greatest in the kingdom of heaven"* (Matthew 18:4). Paradoxically, by decreasing self-importance, other importance is heightened. Humility about self enables the disciple to become serious about his own sin (Matthew 18:7-9).

Dealing with Sin

Jesus established within the community of disciples a very practical approach to dealing with sin. He provides steps that not only preserve the integrity of the individual who has sinned, but also the needs of the one who has been sinned against. By having a progressive approach, both can maintain the highest hopes for preserving the relationship. The goal in any level of confrontation of sin within the church is never to win the issue, but rather win the brother. Jesus promises that in these very challenging and difficult situations for the family, he will be present (Matthew 18:15-20).

Forgiving Sin

Peter raises the issue if there are any limits to reconciliation. *"'Lord, how often will my brother sin against me, and I forgive him? As many as seven times?' Jesus said to him, 'I do not say to you seven times, but seventy-seven times'"* (Matthew 18:21-22). In a society that is concerned about personal honor, offense is taken easily, and relationships are ended sharply as a result. Seeing yourself as a servant forgiven of an insurmountable debt should be sufficient encouragement to *"forgive your brother from your heart"* (Matthew 18:35).

PRESENT OPPOSITION AND FUTURE VICTORY

As the story of Jesus moves geographically from Galilee to Judea (Matthew 19:1), it moves dramatically toward its culmination in the cross and resurrection. Matthew tells the story of the intensified conflict between Jesus and his opponents. The discourse in this section reveals Jesus' ultimate victory (Matthew 19:1 – 25:46).

INTENSIFYING OPPOSITION
Opposition from the Pharisees and Sadducees

Early in the Gospel, Matthew revealed the beginning of tensions with the Pharisees and other Jewish leaders. They had come to the conclusion that Jesus was in league with the *"prince of demons,"* (Matthew 9:34) and Matthew records that after he proclaimed: *"For the Son of Man is Lord of the Sabbath"* (Matthew 12:8), they *"… went out and conspired against him, how to destroy him"* (Matthew 12:14). At this point in the Gospel narrative, the Pharisees are openly hostile in their interactions with Jesus. They ask questions designed to trap Jesus, as in Matthew 19:3-8; 21:15, 23; and 22:15-40. They plotted using questions related to controversial subjects such as divorce, paying taxes to Caesar, the resurrection of the dead, and the law to test him and *"to entangle him in his words"* (Matthew 19:3-8 & 22:15).

Jesus Opposes the Pharisees and Sadducees

At the same time, Jesus challenged the Jewish leaders. Not only did he play solid defense by using their own questions against them, he went on a theological offensive, asking a Royal Riddle of his own: *"What do you think about the Christ? Whose son is he?"* (Matthew 22:42). And then he references Psalm 110:1 with this:

"The Lord said to my Lord,
'Sit at my right hand,
until I put your enemies under your feet'"?
(Matthew 22:44)

Psalm 110 refers to the enthronement of the Messiah, the victory of the Messiah over the nations of the world, and the eternal priesthood of the Messiah in the order of Melchizedek. The implication of the riddle is that the Messiah is more than just a descendant of David. By David calling him LORD, the Messiah will take the throne of Yahweh (see Daniel 7:13-14). His priestly calling supersedes and replaces the Levite priesthood, and his victory over the nations will include all enemies of Yahweh—even the nation of Israel, if it proves to be his enemy.

Condemning Parables

Beyond the direct verbal sparring, Jesus also told stories about and against the Jewish leadership. We see this in the parables of the two sons, the tenant farmers, and the wedding banquet in Matthew 21:28–22:15. The parable of the two sons reveals the difference between lip service and life service; when the call to prepare for the kingdom came through John the Baptist, the Pharisees give lip service but did not change their minds and believe, *"but the tax collectors and prostitutes believed him"* (Matthew 21:32).

With the parable of the tenants, Jesus tells a story of a land owner, his vineyard, and wicked tenants. The parable is a crushing condemnation of the Jewish leadership for their rejection of the prophets and their open hostility for the Messiah. In this story, the wicked tenants plot to kill the son (Hebrew, ben), but they find that the Son has come not only to lay claim to the vineyard but also to build the new temple. However, instead of receiving the foundation stone (Hebrew and Aramaic, eben) of the temple, the builders have rejected it … and they are crushed by it!

In the third parable, the wedding feast, the king sees only a man without a *"wedding garment"* (Matthew 22:12). He had the man bound and he *"cast him into the outer darkness"* (Matthew 22:13). The king did not realize he was no ordinary man.

The Prophet Jesus

The crowds believed Jesus was a prophet: *"And when he entered Jerusalem, the whole city was stirred up, saying, 'Who is this?' And the crowds said, 'This is the prophet Jesus, from Nazareth of Galilee'"* (Matthew 21:10-11). Jesus placed a prophet's judgment against the chief priests and scribes when Jesus overturned the tables of the money changers and drove them out of the temple in Matthew 21:12-16. He then announced seven *"woe oracles"* in Matthew 23:13-35.

"Woe to you, scribes and Pharisees, hypocrites! For you travel across sea and land to make a single proselyte, and when he becomes a proselyte, you make him twice as much a child of hell as yourselves."
(Matthew 23:15)

The hostility of the Jewish leaders was aggravated by the way the crowds continued to honor Jesus on occasions such as the triumphal entry in Matthew 21:15: *"But when the chief priests and the scribes saw the wonderful things that he did, and the children crying out in the temple, 'Hosanna to the Son of David!' they were indignant …."* And in Matthew 21:46, *"And although they were seeking to arrest him, they feared the crowds, because they held him to be a prophet."* The entire confrontation would reach its culmination with the crucified Messiah.

The Last Will Come First

Jesus encouraged his disciples to put this confrontation with the religious leaders into perspective. The kingdom of heaven requires absolute and total sacrifice: an impossible task for any person without God's intervention (Matthew 19:6). Peter acknowledged, *"See, we have left everything and followed you. What then will we have?"* (Matthew 19:27). Jesus promised that one day they would sit with him in glory. But in Matthew 20:17-19, he also warned them that those glorious days would come after his own death.

Moreover, Jesus insisted that his disciples would reach glory only after a life of humble suffering. Jesus drove home this point three different times. In Matthew 19:30, Jesus said, *"But many who are first will be last, and the last first."* He repeats this phrase again in Matthew 20:16 and Matthew 20:26-28. Jesus' kingdom is not like the kingdoms of this world where *"… the rulers of the Gentiles lord it over them, and their great ones exercise authority over them"* (Matthew 20:25). The servants of Jesus' kingdom would suffer, and the true king of Israel himself would be killed by the leaders of Israel and Rome. Apparent defeat would come before victory; the last will be first.

PRESENT OPPOSITION AND FUTURE VICTORY
Eschatological Sermon: Future Victory

Jesus taught that the judgment of God would begin with a judgment on the corrupt Jewish leaders and institutions such as the Temple. He also prophesied that there would be a final judgment of all people that would come at an unknown hour. It would take a long time, but the righteous of the kingdom of heaven would be ready.

The entire discourse falls into the category of prophetic speech. Prophecy in the Bible is used to communicate the present application of the promises of God to his people, both the promises to bless for covenant faithfulness and the promises to judge for unfaithfulness. One way to look at prophets is as God's prosecuting attorneys who bring lawsuits against the people for violation of God's covenant and hold out hope of restoration for repentance. Theologians speak of the time in which we live as the *"now"* but *"not yet."* We realize some blessings and judgments of the end times in light of the cross, resurrection, and ascension of Jesus, but the kingdom of heaven on Earth is *"not yet"* here in its fullness. (Matthew 24:1 – 25:46)

The Seven Woes

This discourse focuses on the Pharisees. It takes the form of a prophetic lawsuit against the Pharisees and scribal leaders. He begins with a general indictment on them for their pursuit of self glorification at the expense of others. First, they put heavy burdens on others that they themselves were not willing to bear. Jesus taught exactly the opposite about himself. *"Come to me, all who labor and are heavy laden, and I will give you rest. Take my yoke upon you, … and you will find rest for your souls. For my yoke is easy, and my burden is light"* (Matthew 11:28-30). Second, they loved to do things in order to receive praise from men. Jesus taught that we should only practice our religion for the Father who sees in secret (Matthew 6:1-18). Finally, he moves to a sevenfold woe oracle for the following hypocrisies: making salvation hard for other people, corrupting converts, trivializing religion, neglecting what is important, self-indulgence, wickedness within, and the murder of God's prophets. (Matthew 23:1-38)

Lament Over Jerusalem and the Prophecy of Its Destruction

As with all pronouncements of judgment in the Scriptures, it is not the desired outcome for Yahweh. Jesus laments what must come upon the city as a consequence of unfaithfulness on the day of his (Yahweh's) visitation. Jesus expresses his feelings about Jerusalem in Matthew 23:37-38. While Jesus' disciples are impressed by the Temple complex, Jesus is not. *"But he answered them, 'You see all these, do you not? Truly, I say to you, there will not be left here one stone upon another that will not be thrown down'"* (Matthew 24:2).

Signs of the "Now" End of the Age

The disciples questioned Jesus on the timing of these prophecies of judgment and destruction of Jerusalem and the Temple. He answers that they will know the signs of the judgment of Jerusalem. It would happen within *"this generation"* (Matthew 24:34), but they would not be able to time that day when *"Heaven and earth will pass away"* (Matthew 24:35-36).

The Abomination of Desolation

The main sign that the time of Judgment was upon them was the *"abomination of desolation."* The reference is from Daniel 9:27 and refers to some type of pagan symbol or idolatry set up within the Jewish Temple. Matthew hints to his readers with the parenthetical comment, *"let the reader understand"* (Matthew 24:15), that these things were happening in their day. Indeed, in 70 A.D. the Romans sacked Jerusalem and destroyed the Jewish Temple.

The Coming of the Son of Man

In the Old Testament, Yahweh uses foreign powers, natural disasters, and economic collapse to execute his judgments. These things are acting as his agents. Nevertheless, he is sovereign over these powers and they are doing his will and bidding on the day of judgment. The same is true for the judgment of Jerusalem, the Romans are the earthly instruments of judgment for the Son of Man. Nev-ertheless, it is he who comes on the day of judgment. The judgment of Yahweh always comes not only with earthly disasters and agency, but also apocalyptic signs and por-tents in the heavens.

The Lesson of the Fig Tree

"From the fig tree learn its lesson: as soon as its branch becomes tender and puts out its leaves, you know that summer is near. So also, when you see all these things, you know that he is near, at the very gates" (Matthew 24:32-33). The judgment will be severe. Jesus reminds them that *"this generation will not pass away until all of these things take place"* (Matthew 24:34). Jesus' words are sure: they also will not pass away! But Jesus holds out *"that day and hour"* are a mystery held in the secret council of God the father (Matthew 24:36). He now turns to a reflection on the final judgment that remains a *"not yet"* but is promised. In the interim, there will be much tribulation (Matthew 24:9).

THE TIMING OF THE "NOT YET" FINAL JUDGMENT

While the judgment on Israel, Jerusalem, and the Temple would be accompanied by signs so that it could be discerned and predicted by the faithful and righteous, the time of the final judgment is not known. It will arrive one day, like the flood in Noah's day or a thief who arrives unannounced in the middle of the night.

Fig. 6. *The Wise and Foolish Virgins,* c.1822 (w/c and pen on paper), Blake, William (1757-1827) / Yale Center for British Art, Paul Mellon Collection, USA / Bridgeman Images.

Therefore, the righteous followers of the kingdom of heaven need to be alert and always prepared for the final judgment. The parables of the 10 virgins and the talents serve as a warning to procrastination when it comes to repentance. The delay of the final judgment provides precious time to get ready and be faithful stewards of the time and resources given. But one does not want to be caught by that day unprepared or unfaithful to God's call on our lives (Matthew 24:32-30).

Final Judgment the Sheep and the Goats

At the final judgment, Jesus is the ultimate judge of everyone and everything. There may be some surprises on that day for both the blessed and the cursed. Lip service is not enough: Stewardship of the kingdom is related to how well we minister to the *"least of these my brothers"* (Matthew 25:40). Who are the humble siblings of the king? The poor? The larger context of the Gospel would seem to warrant considering these *"least of these my brothers"* as the Gospel messengers of Jesus (cf. *"my brothers"* Matthew 12:50; 28:10 cf. *"the least"* Matthew 5:19, 11:11, 18:3-6). As Jesus said to the 12 when he sent them out in Matthew 10:32-33:

"So everyone who acknowledges me before men, I also will acknowledge before my Father who is in heaven, but whoever denies me before men, I also will deny before my Father who is in heaven."
(Matthew 10:32)

CULMINATION OF JESUS' MINISTRY

The Gospel of Matthew reaches a dramatic and climactic culmination in Jesus' arrest, crucifixion, and resurrection. The conflict with the Jewish authorities reached a crisis point, the disciples faltered, and yet the rebellion and failure of humanity served to exalt Jesus. With Jesus' vindication in his resurrection, all authority in heaven and Earth are given to him. However, Jesus taught through his parables of the kingdom and his ecclesiastical discourse that the Jewish expectation of imminent final restoration and judgment were mistaken. While the coming of the Messiah did bring forth the kingdom of heaven, the kingdom would take time to develop and mature before the final restoration and judgment (Matthew 26:1 – 28:20).

The resulting reality is the inauguration of an unanticipated age or period in history where the kingdom of this world (This Age) and the kingdom of heaven (The Age to Come) not only are overlapping but also in deadly conflict. The Jewish expectation was that the king and kingdom of the age to come would destroy the powers and kingdom of this world and age. In an apparent worldly rejection and defeat, God vindicates his king and kingdom in a display of power this world and age do not possess or know—resurrection.

The Kingdom of Heaven and The Age to Come

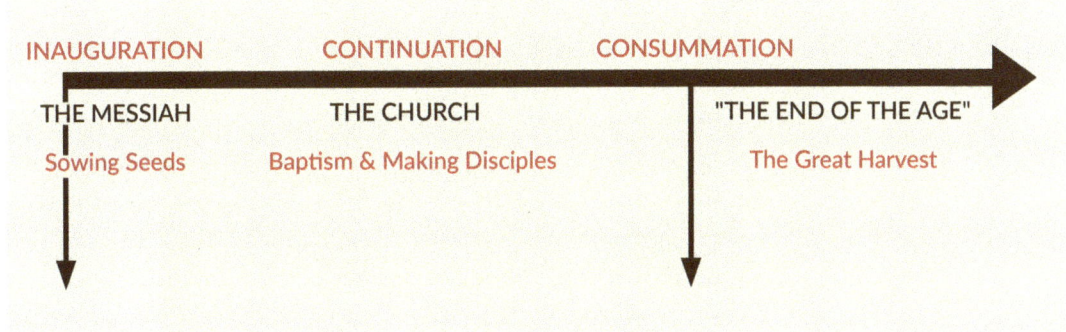

Kingdoms in Conflict

First, the Son of Man would come to plant the seeds of his kingdom. Second, he would return for a great harvest. Not only would there be a phased approach with the coming of the final restoration, but also for the final judgment. The cross and resurrection of Jesus reveal both the nature of the conflict and the victory.

THE GOSPEL OF LUKE
Introduction

The Gospel of Luke was written by a Gentile physician and the traveling companion of the apostle Paul. It was written to Theophilus, translated as lover of God, as a way of encouraging certainty in the spoken word delivered by an eyewitness of Jesus. The Gospel of Luke and the Book of Acts form a two-part work with the aim of telling *"an orderly account"* of all of the things related to the beginning of Jesus ministry through the apostolic acts of the early church. (Luke 1:3-4)

The Tradition of the Early Church

The early church fathers were unanimous in ascribing authorship to Luke. Irenaeus, Tertullian, Clement of Alexandria, Origen, and the Muratorian Canon agreed on Luke as the author of the Gospel and the Book of Acts. Neither Eusebius of Caesarea, nor any other ancient writer, mention other traditions about authorship.

A Traveling Companion of Paul

As the missionary journeys of the apostle Paul are recorded in the Book of Acts, there is a grammatical change of voice regarding the members of Paul's party, moving from third person plural *("they")* to first person plural *("we")*: (see Acts 16:10–17; 20:5–15; 21:1–18; 27:1–28.) It is believed that this is when the author of Luke/Acts joins the missionary party in person and participates in the events he is describing. In the prologue of the Gospel, he alludes to "many have undertaken to compile a narrative of the things that have been accomplished among us." (Luke 1:1). The *"among us"* implies that the author began writing the Book of Acts following his completion of his Gospel narrative of Jesus. If we take this to be the case, he would be one of the many traveling companions of Paul on his missionary journeys.

ORIGINAL AUDIENCE

While Luke addressed his Gospel to Theophilus, he may have had in mind any individual who wanted to be in a personal relationship with God. The narratives of Luke and Acts record nothing of the destruction of the Temple or the martyrdom of any of the apostles other than Stephen, events that certainly would have figured prominently in any narrative about the apostles. So, it likely that these works were both completed prior to 70 A.D. and sometime after the completion of the Gospel of Mark. That Gospel seems to be a source for some of Luke's material.

The Structure of Luke

   A. Preface (1:1-4)
   B. The Birth of the Savior Messiah Lord (1:5-2:52)
   C. The Inauguration of Jesus' Kingdom (3:1-4:13)
   D. Jesus' Kingdom Begins in Galilee (4:14-6:49)
   E. Who is this Jesus? (7:1-9:51)
   F. The Journey to the Throne (9:51-19:27)
   G. Jesus in Jerusalem of Israel (19:28-21:38)
   H. The Climax of the Kingdom: Passion Death and Resurrection (22:1-22:53)

Preface

The Gospel of Luke begins with a preface that reveals the purpose for writing: to set forth an *"orderly account"* of the teachings of the eyewitnesses and ministers of the word of the Gospel of Jesus. It likely represents the body of Paul's Gospel presentation (cf. Romans 16:25-27). Paul had a two-part gospel mission, *"to the Jew first and also to the Greek"* (Romans 1:16). It could be that the content of Luke's Gospel was the same presentation Paul would make to the synagogue leaders and then to the Gentile public. A traveling companion with Paul would have heard this message again and again. By recording it, Paul's sermons could be copied, shared, and memorized.

THE BIRTH OF THE SAVIOR (Luke 1:5-2:52)
Angelic Announcements

As in the Gospel of Matthew, the Gospel of Luke contains a birth narrative. In a largely Roman context, this would have been an essential component for Paul's missionary presentation of the Gospel in both the Jewish synagogues and to Greek and Roman citizens. For the Jews, it was critical to establish that Jesus, as the Messiah, was *"descended from David according to the flesh"* (Romans 1:3) and was in fulfillment of the Jewish expectation of the anointed Son of God (Luke 1:5-38).

John the Baptist would be the spirit-filled embodiment of Elijah, who fulfills the prophetic expectations spoken through the prophet Malachi (especially 2:6-7; 3:1, 18; 4:5-6). His primary mission would be to *"turn many from iniquity"* (Malachi 2:6). John's role is one of preparation and announcement. The people would be called to repent and turn back to the Lord, away from sin and rebellion. He marks the advent of one greater: the LORD (Yahweh) himself.

Gabriel's announcement to Mary parallels the announcement to Zechariah with some significant differences. Both angelic scenes function together, as the sons will in their ministries: John as the preparer, Jesus as the fulfillment. Both parents are told that they will be with child, both question the earthly possibility of such a thing, and both are told that God, through the workings of the Holy Spirit, will take care of the details—he is looking for faithful servants. To which Mary responds to the call: *"Behold, I am the servant of the Lord; let it be to me according to your word"* (Luke 1:38).

Blessings and Magnification!

Just as Elizabeth blesses Mary, so to does John the Baptist acknowledge Jesus by leaping *"in her womb."* The blessing of Mary by Elizabeth is a preview of John's future acknowledgement of Mary's son. Mary's song is a celebration of the salvation of God through great reversals: For Mary personally, he has taken a *"lowly servant"* and done *"great things for her."* She calls him *"My Savior."* (Luke 1:39-56)

Through the gift of the Messiah, the Lord has dethroned the powerful, lifted up the lowly, filled the hungry, and sent the rich away empty. Mary's humility and exaltation mirrors what God is promising to do for Israel.[6]

The central claim of the Gospel is that Jesus is the Messiah, Lord, and Savior for all people—Jew and Gentile alike. With that salvation, the current state of affairs will not stand. The Lord has "turned the world upside down" (Acts 17:6), and it began with the birth of the Messiah.

Fig. 7. *The Adoration of the Shepherds*, detail of the group surrounding Jesus (oil on canvas), Reni, Guido (1575-1642) / Museo Nazionale di San Martino & Certosa, Naples, Campania, Italy / Bridgeman Images.

MARY		ISRAEL
v. 48	*"his servant"*	v. 54
vv. 48, 50	*object of favor & mercy*	v. 54
v. 48	*"lowly"*	v. 52
v. 50	*"perpetuity of mercy"*	v. 55

The Birth of the John the Baptist

With the dramatic and insistent naming of John by his parents, in obedience to the angel Gabriel (Luke 1:13), Zechariah is filled with the Holy Spirit (Luke 1:67) and prophesied:

"Blessed be the Lord God of Israel, for he has visited and redeemed his people and he has raised up a horn of salvation for us... whereby the sunrise shall visit us from on high to give light to those who sit in darkness and in the shadow of death, to guide our feet into the way of peace."
(Luke 1:68-79)

---

[6]Green, Joel, The Gospel of Luke (Grand rapids, MI: Eerdmans Publishing Co., 1997) p. 101.

The heart of the prophecy is that Yahweh is faithful and is fulfilling his promises and covenants with Israel by personally visiting his people. Zechariah's son, John, is the prophet of the Most High, who will go before Yahweh and prepare his ways. Yahweh has come to save his people, and John's role is to get them ready for their Lord's advent. Do not miss the explicit point that Luke is making in recording Zechariah's prophecy: Jesus is Yahweh, God in the flesh, who has come to save and forgive his people Israel. The narrative is written to make precisely that point.

However, the Gospel of Luke has a second purpose, of bringing about the *"obedience of faith for the sake of his name among all the nations"* (Romans 1:5). While the birth narrative establishes the Messiah as a descendant of David according to the flesh, it also serves as a polemic against the Roman imperial theology (Romans 1:3). The Roman Caesars had created a mythology where the emperor was divine and worthy of temple worship. For example, a 9 B.C. inscription attributes a divine status to Caesar and describes his birth as being the birth of a god: *"The birthday of the god [Augustus] has been for the whole world the beginning of good news (euangelion) concerning him [therefore let a new era begin from his birth]"* (Orientis Graeci Inscriptiones Selectae, OGIS 2. #458).[7]

The birth of Caesar Augustus is heralded as *"good news"* for *"a god"* has been born who would bring a *"new era"* of peace and welfare to the *"whole world."* This is the very Caesar who called for the census that would force Jesus' mother out of Nazareth to Bethlehem, the city of David, because of her ancestry from the tribe of Judah.

In a dramatic irony that would not be lost on Luke's readers, Caesar Augustus, by his exercise of earthly power and authority, unwittingly had fulfilled the Jewish expectation of the true Messiah who would rule over him. Notice the similarity of the inscription concerning birth of Caesar Augustus to Luke's recounting of the angelic announcement to the shepherds of the birth of Jesus:

"And the angel said to them, 'Fear not, for behold, I bring you good news of great joy that will be for all the people. For unto you is born this day in the city of David a Savior, who is Christ the Lord.'" (Luke 2:10-11)

Luke is masterful at telling the Messianic story in such a way that would speak to both Jewish and Greek readers with a single message. The Jewish Messiah has been born in the person of Jesus and he is not just the Lord and savior of Israel, but he fulfills the hopes

---

[7] Horsley, Jesus and Empire: The Kingdom of God and the New World Disorder, (Minneapolis, MN: Augsburg Fortress Press, 2003) p. 23-24.

and expectations for all of the people of the world: Jew and Gentile, shepherds and kings.

Presentation in the Temple

In fulfillment of the Law of Moses, Jesus, as the firstborn son, belonged to the Lord because of the Exodus and the Passover redemption (Exodus 13:1-2). The firstborn was *"redeemed"* by appropriate sacrifice in the Temple that Mary and Joseph fulfill (Luke 2:22-24). However, the appearance of the infant child savior activated two prophets in the Temple, Simeon and Anna, who were both waiting for the *"consolation of Israel"* and the *"redemption of Jerusalem"* (Luke 2:38).

Anna's prophecies are not recorded. We know only that she encouraged the expectant mother. Both serve as faithful testimonies to the action of Yahweh in Messiah. But Simeon's prophecy reminds Luke's readers of God's larger plan of salvation for Israel and the Gentiles: *"… for my eyes have seen your salvation that you have prepared in the presence of all peoples, a light for revelation to the Gentiles and for glory to your people Israel"* (Luke 2:30-32). This was in fulfillment of Isaiah 49:6 *("I will make you as a light for the nations, that my salvation may reach to the end of the earth.")*. Through Simeon, God revealed that Jesus was the Messiah who would bring salvation and glory to Israel. And more than this, he would extend the Gospel of God's kingdom to the Gentile nations, so that they might also be saved.

Jesus Comes of Age

Jesus fulfilled Jewish righteousness in every way. When a young Jewish boy came of age, he was to recite the commandments of the Lord before the rabbis. This demonstration showed he knew the law. According to the Talmud, he would *"at age 13 become subject to the commandments and release of the father's responsibility."* The key question in this story is: Who is Jesus' father? Jesus' response: *"Did you not know that I must be in my Father's house?"* (Luke 2:49).

THE INAUGURATION OF JESUS' KINGDOM

The birth narratives set the stage for the formal inauguration of Jesus' Kingdom ministry. Luke has three parts in this section: The Baptism of Jesus, the Genealogy of Jesus, and the Temptation of Jesus. He frames the baptism of Jesus in relationship to the larger political scene in Luke 3:1-2. Jesus' kingdom is in direct contrast to the prevailing Roman and Jewish leadership. Jesus' baptism marks a new political reality for the kingdoms of this world. The true and rightful leader of the world is stepping on to the scene of history. How will the people of the world respond (Luke 3:1-4:13)?

At the heart of John's message is prophetic announcement of judgment and a call for immediate repentance. He warns against presumptive faith in genealogical heritage rather than the *"good fruit"* of faithfulness to Yahweh. Jesus is told with a display of divine authority: *"You are my beloved Son; with you I am well pleased."* (Luke 3:22) This divine utterance establishes the identity and authority of Jesus as the king according to 2 Samuel 7, Psalm 2 and Isaiah 42:1. However, Luke emphasizes through his review of Jesus' genealogy that he is the Son of God for all of mankind.

The Genealogy of Jesus

Matthew and Luke both have a genealogy for Jesus. Matthew emphasizes Jesus as the restorer from exile, the son of David, and heir of the promises to Abraham. Luke traces Joseph's line through David and Abraham, taking the line back to Adam, the son of God. Luke is laying the groundwork for Paul's teaching, that Jesus is the second Adam.

The Temptation of Jesus

Just as Satan questioned the veracity of God's words with the first Adam, *"did God really say"*, he does so again. God said, *"You are my beloved son ..."* (Luke 3:22) to which Satan counters, *"If you are the Son of God ..."* (Luke 4:3, 9 cf. 4:41). Where the first Adam failed, the second Adam prevailed. The temptation mirrors Adam's temptation. The story also carries with it the remembrance of Israel's failure to trust in God's word and its spending 40 years in the wilderness.

ISRAEL		JESUS
Deuteronomy 8:2	*Divine Leading in the Wilderness*	Luke 4:1
Deut. 8:2: Exodus 16:35, Numbers 14: 34	*"Forty" (Years/Days)*	Luke 4:2
Exodus 4:22-23	*Israel/Jesus as God's Son*	Luke 4:3, 9
Deuteronomy 6:13	*Temptaton: Idolatry*	Luke 4:8
Deuteronomy 6:16	*Tempation: Testing God*	Luke 4:12

Clearly where Adam and Israel have allowed Satan to dominate and control through manipulation, Jesus has authority over Satan through the Word of God and the Spirit of God. As Luke's readers contemplate their own relationships with the powers that be, they learn that the Word and the Spirit are stronger than any other force in heaven or on Earth. Soon, this will be demonstrated in Galilee.

JESUS' KINGDOM BEGINS IN GALILEE
The Sermon in Nazareth

Luke frames the Gospel ministry of Jesus by first recounting the sermon he preached in Nazareth. In Luke 4:16-21, Jesus quotes from Isaiah 61:1-2 where the prophet announces a Jubilee, the year of the Lord's favor, where the consequences of sin and bondage are reversed. Luke's Gospel (and Acts) emphasizes this Jubilee program as the heart of Jesus' ministry. The residents of Nazareth embrace the announcement of Jubilee but apply it only to themselves. Jesus challenges them to see that Jubilee is a gift not only for the people of Israel, but also for the whole world. The people of Nazareth react violently to Jesus' challenge of their provincialism (Luke 4:14-6:49).

The narrative progresses to Capernaum, where Jesus liberates a man oppressed by an unclean demon. He then heals Simon's mother-in-law of a fever. The year of the Lord's favor had begun, and the liberation was manifest in astonishing authority and power. For Luke, the power is in the Word and the Spirit, proclamation and action. The Good News of the kingdom is announced, and the evil must depart.

Fishing for People

Through a demonstration of fishing expertise and a massive catch, Jesus calls Simon Peter, James, and John: *"And Jesus said to Simon, 'Do not be afraid; from now on you will be catching men'"* (Luke 5:10). But first, Jesus would have to teach them how to do it. The first catches of people would be equally as powerful: a leper is healed and made clean (see Luke 5:12-14) and a paralytic is forgiven of his sins and empowered to walk. Through these actions, Jesus reveals that he is the master fisherman for people—God in the flesh. By manifesting the kingdom in word and power, Jesus gained a band of followers. These disciples increasingly became the target of the religious leaders. The Pharisees questioned the inclusion of the tax collector Levi and other sinners. When asked why Jesus openly ate with these sinners he replied, *"Those who are well have no need of a physician, but those who are sick. I have not come to call the righteous but sinners to repentance"* (Luke 5:31-32).

The question of table fellowship would be in Luke's readers' minds as well. Jubilee applies to the socially outcast, the sick, and the poor. A restructuring of social relationships must take place in the kingdom. Jesus finally calls 12 apostles from all the disciples. These 12 would be equipped to be the *"fishers of men"* who would be sent out to catch people for the kingdom. The number 12 is significant in that through these 12, Jesus is reconstituting the 12 tribes of Israel.

The Sermon on the Plain

The Sermon on the Plain has many similar elements to the Sermon on the Mount recorded in Matthew's Gospel. Both of these sermons represent consolidations of Jesus' teachings. It is likely that he taught these messages repeatedly, in various contexts and times. The similarities and differences are accounted for by the repetition of the themes and both Jesus' and the Gospel writer's emphases based on their context and audience's needs (Luke 6:17-6:49).

In this sermon, Jesus is defining the kingdom worldview and life. There is a pattern of the world to which people conform and there is the transformed life in Jesus to which the disciple is transformed (cf. Romans 12:1ff). The content of the sermon focuses on blessings and woe; generosity toward the poor and needy; mercy and love toward enemies; reconciliation and restoration; forgiveness and repentance; and the need for total internal transformation. Jesus calls his followers not only to be hearers of the word, but also doers of it. The great multitude *"… came to hear him and to be healed"* (Luke 6:18), but Jesus is looking for commitment and action (Luke 6:46-49).

Jesus Demonstrates His Teaching

The call to be merciful to enemies is one of the more difficult teachings of Jesus. Following the sermon, Jesus puts his own words into practice by showing love and concern to a centurion's servant and a poor widow's son. Both episodes reveal issues of power, authority, and status. It is the powerful centurion's humility and faith that impresses Jesus; it is the widow's grief for her only son that moved him to compassion. The kingdom of God recognizes lowly humility and human need, and it responds with power (Luke 7:1-50).

Unresponsiveness to the Kingdom's Call

Jesus compared the Pharisees and Scribes to a then-popular children's song: *"We played the flute for you, and you did not dance; we sang a dirge, and you did not weep"* (Luke 7:32). The song invites the hearer to respond, but no response is given. That generation was skeptical of the invitations of God offered through John the Baptist and Jesus. Hence, they did not dance, and they did not weep. The Gospel writer says that they had *"rejected the purpose of God for themselves"* (Luke 7:30). John the Baptist called them to a baptism of repentance, but they refused. The prophet sang the dirge, but they did not weep. Jesus proclaimed the Good News of forgiveness and restoration for the sinner and the broken-hearted. He celebrated and ate with them, but they refused to come to the party table. The Lord played the flute, but they did not dance (Luke 7:18-35).

A Right Response: The Sinful Woman

The sinful woman who anoints Jesus' feet with ointment reveals the true response that leads to salvation in the kingdom. She is contrasted with the Pharisee and owner of the home who failed to show any hospitality to the Lord and only showed a critical spirit. Jesus identifies the heart of the issue between the two: *"Therefore I tell you, her sins, which are many, are forgiven—for she loved much. But he who is forgiven little, loves little. And he said to her, 'Your sins are forgiven'"* (Luke 7:47-48). The depth of a disciple's understanding of God's forgiveness leads to a depth of love in the disciple. Salvation transforms character.

Hearing the Good News of the Kingdom

In Luke 8:1-21, we see the emphasis on hearing and responding to Jesus' word. He is building a group of faithful followers who will grow and yield abundant fruit for the kingdom. The underlying issue is the people's response to his word, and his authority and power. Jesus is like a sower planting seeds. He is looking for a fruitful harvest. However, powerful forces such as the devil, oppressive persecutions and testing, and the worldly allure of riches and cares, threaten to prevent belief and salvation. Jesus is looking for family members *"… who hear the word of God and do it"* (Luke 8:21).

Power and Authority
Who Then is this? Jesus, Faith, and Fear

More than anything else, people were amazed by Jesus' works of power and authority. The responses of those who encounter Jesus move rapidly between fear and faith, faith and fear. In Luke 8:22-56, Jesus demonstrates power and authority over the active presence of diabolic agents and influence in the natural and spiritual realms, over sickness and unclean conditions, and even over death. Jesus is called "Master" (Luke 8:24, 45) and *"Son of the Most High God"* (Luke 8:28).

When the disciples are faced with the terror of the chaotic force of the sea, Jesus asks his disciples, *"Where is your faith?"* (Luke 8:25). At issue is the locus of the disciples' faith and fear. When Jesus demonstrates his authority over *"the wind and the raging waves"* (Luke 8:24). Jesus gives them something truly to fear—Him. In the meantime, the legions of demons know with whom they are dealing: The Son of the Most High God. And they beg him for mercy (Luke 8:26-33, cf. James 2:19). The crowd's reactions are mixed. The people of the Gerasenes region asked Jesus *"to depart from them, for they were seized with great fear"* (Luke 8:37). Those who are healed desire to be with him and proclaimed his greatness to others.

The contrast with fear is faith. The woman with a discharge problem is commended because she fearlessly reached out and touched the hem of Jesus' cloak, believing in his power to heal. Her faith is transformed to reverent awe as she falls down before him and declares his power. Jarius' fear due to the untimely news of his daughter's death is transformed to faith with Jesus encouragement, *"Do not fear; only believe, and she will be well"* (Luke 8:50).

Who Then Am I? Disciples, Faith, and Faltering

If Luke 8:22-56 is about the power and authority of Jesus over nature, demons, sickness, and death, Luke 9:1-50 is about the power and authority given to the apostles for ministry. They begin with some success in preaching and healing (Luke 9:6). This work caught the attention of King Herod (Luke 9:7-9).

However, the disciples' strong start in mission quickly degenerates as they are called to exercise extraordinary faith in ministry. When faced with a large, hungry crowd and inadequate resources, Jesus urges them: *"You give them something to eat"* (Luke 9:13). Their worldly solution was to *"send the crowd away to go into the surrounding villages and countryside to find lodging and get provisions"* (Luke 9:12). Jesus' kingdom solution would demonstrate the abundance of the kingdom. He broke the loaves and fishes *"and gave them to the disciples to set before the crowd"* (Luke 9:16). The lesson was to allow Jesus' power and authority to work through them. The 12 apostles each held a basket of leftovers in their hands.

With Peter's correct understanding of the identity of Jesus, Luke turns his story to the 12 apostles' growing understanding of their own identity and roles in the kingdom of Jesus. From this point on, it becomes clear why the apostles need to learn how to minister in power and authority. Jesus would teach them: *"The Son of Man must suffer many things and be rejected by the elders and chief priests and scribes, and be killed, and on the third day be raised"* (Luke 9:22). The critical task for the apostles (and for Luke's readers) is to learn what it means to *"come after"* Jesus through cross-bearing self-denial and daily devotion to Jesus (Luke 9:23).

Glory and Suffering

One of the most difficult things for the apostles to grasp is the paradoxical connection between suffering and glory, humility and greatness. Not only do they have a difficult time grasping how this paradox applies to Jesus, but also how he would have them apply the paradox to themselves. Jesus certainly had proclaimed and revealed his glory to the apostles.

But he emphasized that in gaining the whole world, one forfeits himself. And that when a disciple denies self and takes up his cross daily and follows Jesus, the result is the salvation of one's soul and the kingdom of God. The powers and authorities of this world are not going to recognize the glory of the Son. The disciple must make a choice between the world and the kingdom of God—to gain one is to forfeit the other.

Jesus knew his disciples needed reassurance of his majesty and glory, so he took Peter, James and John on the mountain of transfiguration where he revealed his glory. But the discussion was about *"his departure, which he was about to accomplish at Jerusalem"* (Luke 9:31). Peter, wanting to remain in the goodness of the glory, misspoke. Again, the divine voice of the father affirms the Messianic lordship of Jesus (cf. Psalm 2, Samuel 7). However, this time the divine voice is directed at the disciples rather than Jesus: *"Listen to him!"* (Luke 9:35). The way of the cross is a spiritual battle, the disciples need to trust and obey the way of the master.

The next day after the transfiguration glory, the disciples falter in the battle against demonic powers. Jesus expresses growing impatience with the denial and corruption in the hearts of the disciples comparing it with the faithlessness and corruption of the Israelites in the wilderness after the Exodus (cf. Deuteronomy 32:4-5): *"Jesus answered, 'O faithless and twisted generation, how long am I to be with you and bear with you? Bring your son here'"* (Luke 9:41).

The power of the divine mission comes from humility, obedience, and faith in the crucified way of the Lord. The majesty of God is revealed in humility and lowliness. Jesus needed this one fact to *"sink into their ears."* He is the example: *"The Son of Man is about to be delivered into the hands of men"* (Luke 9:44). Suffering is the path to glory. But they were dense in their understanding. In contrast, they continued to have majesty and glory on their minds as they were arguing about *"which of them was the greatest"* (Luke 9:46). Jesus again emphasized that the one who is the greatest is the one who is the least among them.

THE JOURNEY TO THE THRONE:
To Jerusalem and the Cross

The largest section in the Gospel of Luke is often called the travel narrative. Luke uses this portion of his Gospel to address several important issues and theological challenges for his readers.

INTRODUCTION: On the Way

In Luke 9:51, he highlights the nature of Jesus' ministry as the fulfillment of the absolute commitment to the enduring obedience of Isaiah's suffering servant. Jesus is singularly focused on his vocation to suffer and die as the savior of the world. While Luke is telling the story of Jesus' dedication to his call, he makes the application of the call of the disciple to the singularly-focused, costly vocation of servant ministry for the kingdom of God (Luke 9:51-56).

James and John misunderstood their kingdom vocation as one of prophetic judgment. They were eager to *"tell fire to come down from heaven and consume"* the Samaritans, but Jesus rebuked them (Luke 9:54-55). Luke uses this episode to set the stage for the entire travel narrative. The call of the disciple is to endure earthly suffering, rather than incite violence and glory. The Messiah and the kingdom of God will be rejected by the Jewish leaders. But their rejection means salvation for the world.

The Cost of Following Jesus

Through the travel narrative, Luke emphasizes the difficulty of following Jesus on the path of discipleship. Jesus is asking for total commitment and focus from his followers. Many would say to Jesus, *"I will follow you wherever you go"* (Luke 9:57). However, the would-be disciple must understand that following Jesus is a total and absolute commitment to the kingdom, come what may. There will be suffering, persecution, and rejection. If the king faced a cross at the hands of the Jewish and Roman leadership, so too would the disciples. The disciple may find his own family members set against him (Luke 14:26). Discipleship requires a total dedication to the kingdom:

there can be no looking back once the commitment to follow has been made. Therefore, all who are contemplating the call to follow Jesus must count up all of the costs involved and make certain of their absolute commitment.

On the Christian Life

The first section in the travel narrative focuses on the nature of discipleship, both the positive and the negative. First, Luke tells stories that consider what the committed disciple of Jesus should do: proclaim the Gospel (Luke 10:1-24); do good (Luke 10:25-37); be devoted to God's word (Luke 10:38-42); pray (Luke 11:1-13); cast out demons (Luke 11:14-32); and, be holy (Luke 11:33-36). Second, he considers attitudes, practices, and behaviors the disciple should avoid: hypocrisy (Luke 11:37-12:3), fear of persecution (Luke 12:4-12), greed (Luke 12:13-21), worry (Luke 12:22-34), and complacency (12:35-48).

On the Jewish Rejection

The second section of Luke's travel narrative focuses on the Jewish rejection of Jesus and the announcement of the kingdom. Many failed to see and interpret correctly the times in which they were living. Jesus points out how savvy they are at recognizing the patterns in weather, but how inept they are at recognizing the coming of the kingdom when it is clearly before them (Luke 12:54-59). Part of the reason for the Jewish rejection is that they were looking for a dramatic fulfillment of the kingdom rather than a gradual coming of the kingdom, like a growing mustard seed or leavening dough (Luke 13:18-21).

The Lord has defined the entrance into the kingdom of God as a *"narrow door."* There is a limited time to respond to the invitation, but once the master of the house has *"risen"* and shut the door, it may be too late for the mass entrance of the Jewish people (Luke 13:24-25). The patriarchs may be welcomed, but many of their descendants will be "cast out" (Luke 13:28). Their rejection of the kingdom will lead to a mass entrance of people *"from east and west, and from north and south"* (Luke 13:29).

This section ends with the Lord lamenting over Jerusalem for its unwillingness to gather into the kingdom at the day of visitation of its Lord and King (Luke 13:34). The Jewish rejection of the Messiah means that their presumption of pride is completely off (Luke 14:7-11). Their rejection of the wedding invitation meal has resulted in an invitation to everyone else (Luke 14:15-24).

On the Repentance of New Believers

The third and final section of Luke's travel narrative expands on the invitation to the wedding feast. The Messiah was rejected due to his own people's failing to take seriously the call to discipleship and repentance—with a lot of excuses (Luke 14:18-20). So the invitation to discipleship has come to the poor, crippled, blind and lame, and then to the ends of the Earth. Again, this is a costly call (Luke 14:25-35), but it is nevertheless an invitation to be a member of the kingdom of God by the king himself.

The Lost Sheep, Coin, and Son

The inclusion of the repentant of Israel (e.g., tax collectors and sinners) is the first stumbling block to the Jewish leadership. Jesus compares these sinners to a precious lost sheep, coin, and son. The argument is from the lesser to the greater. The joy and celebration felt at finding a lost sheep or coin does not compare with a parent's delight at the repentance and return of a lost child. However, the Jewish problem is they are looking at the sinner through the eyes of a resentful brother rather than a forgiving father.

Expectations for Repentance

The Lord is looking for repentance and holiness of life in stewardship of earthly possessions and wealth (Luke 16:1-15); in staying faithful to the commandments of God; in the honoring of marriage and eschewing divorce (Luke 16:16-18); in caring for neighbor and the poor (16:19-31); and, in reconciliation through repentance and forgiveness (Luke 17:1-10). The invitation to salvation is open to all people, however, all are called to a transformed life of faithfulness to Jesus.

RESPONDING TO THE KINGDOM[8]
A Grateful Heart: The 10 Lepers

Fig. 8. *The lost sheep*, illustration from 'Harold Copping Pictures: The Crown Series', c.1920's (colour litho), Copping, Harold (1863-1932) / Private Collection / Bridgeman Images.

The story of the ten lepers reveals the proper attitude and response to the call of the kingdom—gratitude. The fact that the one leper who returns is a Samaritan strikes at the heart of the dilemma of the Jewish rejection and resentment of Gentile repentance and inclusion—a sense of entitlement versus humility at grace (Luke 17:11-19).

---
[8] This portion of the outline comes from Joel Green, The Gospel of Luke

Faithfulness at the Coming of the Son of Man

Jesus is looking for a consistent quality of faithfulness from his people. There is not going to be any type of last-minute warning signs so a would-be disciple can get himself right with the Lord at the last minute. As in the days of old (e.g., the flood, Sodom and Gomorrah), judgment comes. It is best to be prepared and expectant by persistently showing repentance consistent with the kingdom. The persistent widow is representative of the *"elect who cry out to him day and night."* (Luke 18:7). The unanswered question is: *"… when the Son of Man comes, will he find faith on earth?"* (Luke 18:8).

How to Enter the Kingdom: Faith

Luke closes the travel narrative with stories that demonstrate the faith that the Son of Man is hoping to find. The first example is of a repentant tax collector who cries, *"God, be merciful to me, a sinner!"* (Luke 18:13). Humility leads to kingdom exaltation (Luke 18:14). The second example is a child. The disciples seek to prevent the children from coming to Jesus, but he lifts them up as examples of the faithful who can enter the kingdom of God. One has to *"receive the kingdom of God like a child"* (Luke 18:17).

The blind beggar has it right, we need to be asking Jesus to have mercy on us. Jesus asks the beggar, what do you want me to do for you? Notice he does not ask for material provision, he says: *"Lord, let me recover my sight"* (Luke 18:41). This is the type of faith the Son of Man seeks. He says to the man: *"your faith has made you well"* (Luke 18:42).

The final example of the type of faith the Son of Man is looking for is in the repentance of Zacchaeus. He is a man short in stature and reputation—someone others considered unworthy of the kingdom as he was a sinner. Yet, like the blind man, he wanted to see Jesus. And as a result, he was granted salvation and repentance.

JESUS' MINISTRY IN JERUSALEM

Jesus' arrival in Jerusalem is an occasion to celebrate the arrival of the king. However, as the king finds the city in a state of rebellion to its rightful God and king, he laments. The primary movement in the structure of this section is summarized as follows:

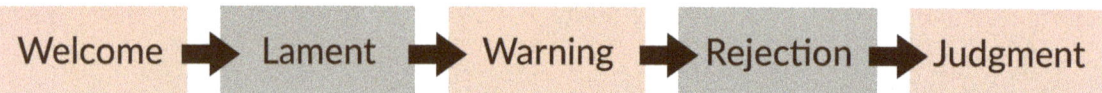

The prophetic action of warning in the Temple leads to an increased confrontation and rejection with the Jewish leadership, culminating with a prophetic oracle of judgment. The followers of Jesus are warned to be watchful and mindful of the judgment on Jerusalem that will usher in the *"times of the Gentiles"* (Luke 21:24).

Jesus' Arrival in Jerusalem

The travel narrative ends with the Parable of the Minas (Luke 19:11-27), the story of a hostile citizenry rejecting its king out of hatred. The arrival of Jesus in Jerusalem reveals the parable has become reality (Luke 19:28-47).

The Triumphal Entry

Jesus' entrance into Jerusalem points to prophecy in the Old Testament, Zechariah 9:9, that describes the Messiah's entrance into Jerusalem. The symbolism is not lost on the Jewish leadership, only they reject its application to Jesus. As the disciples cry out, *"Blessed is the King who comes in the name of the Lord!"* Some of the Pharisees reply, *"Teacher rebuke your disciples"* (Luke 19:38-39).

Jesus Weeps Over the City and Its Future

The heart of Jesus is for the Jewish people to welcome their God and Messiah. But Jesus only finds an occasion to lament. The entirety of the Zechariah 9:9 prophecy is one where Yahweh comes to save his people. However, the rejection of God on the day of his visitation results in judgment for Jerusalem and its leaders (Luke 19:41-44).

The first place Jesus goes when he enters Jerusalem is to the Temple. His coming was prophesied as one of purification in Malachi 3:5. That judgment is enacted by over turning the tables of the Temple. The indictment is stinging: *"My house shall be a house of prayer, but you have made it a den of robbers"* (Luke 19:46). The Temple was to be a place where the people and the nations could come and find healing, salvation, and reconciliation with God. The present leaders of Jerusalem and Israel had made it a house of thieves and insurrectionists. Those leaders did not heed the prophetic warning, but rather hardened in their resolve to *"destroy"* Jesus (Luke 19:47).

Teaching in the Temple and Growing Hostility to Jesus

Jesus' teachings and actions in the Temple became a flash point for confrontations with those leaders. They questioned his authority and he revealed their lack of authority (Luke 20:1-8). First, Jesus told the parable of the vineyard, a story about the rejection of the servants of the vineyard by its stewards culminating with the rejection of the vineyard owner's son. The key to understanding the story is in recognizing that Yahweh is the owner and Israel's leaders are the tenants. Jesus then uses Psalm 118:8 to bring home the point. There is a play on words with the original Aramaic that Jesus spoke. The Aramaic word for son is *'ben'* and stone is *'eben.'* In rejecting the Son, the leaders of Israel have rejected the stone. Jesus continues to answer the leaders' increasingly dishonest questions about resurrection and whether the Messiah is the son of David (Luke 20:27-44). The encounter culminates in Jesus' warning against pride and self-righteousness and the ensuing judgment of the leaders if they do not change (Luke 20:45-21:4).

The Coming Devastation

The final section in Jesus' ministry is a prophecy of judgment on Jerusalem and the Temple. As Jesus indicated in the Parable of the Vineyard, a new cornerstone was to be laid. In order for that new Temple to begin construction, the old one must be destroyed. The question the disciples raise is *"When?"* Jesus describes many signs and portents that will accompany the siege of Jerusalem and its destruction. He warns his disciples of their coming persecution, their need for endurance; and he graphically describes the fall of Jerusalem and coming of the *"times of the Gentiles."* The teaching for Jesus' disciples and Luke's readers is to be watchful and ready for the coming judgment (Luke 21:5-38).

THE CROSS AND THE CROWN

Throughout the Gospel story, the conflict between Jesus and the Jewish leadership has been building to a climax. In the final chapters of the Gospel, the barriers that have been preventing this conflict from reaching its dramatic resolution gradually start to fall. The forces of evil, both spiritual and worldly, unintentionally fulfill the plan and purposes of God. With Satan's infiltration to Jesus' inner 12 (Luke 22:3), the priests looked for the *"opportunity to betray him"* in the "absence of a crowd" (Luke 22:6). Fear is the governing force behind everyone but Jesus.

The New Covenant

Luke explicitly names the feast of Unleavened Bread and the night of the Passover sacrifice. He is not one to emphasize Jewish scriptures and customs. However, in this case he does. Jesus' pending crucifixion finds its significance in this festival and ritual: his body is the bread, and his blood is the Passover sacrifice. Ironically, as Jesus is explaining his own sacrificial death, the disciples begin arguing over who is the greatest. Luke is bringing this teaching in at this point as a contrast for his readers—particularly leaders. The leader is to be one who serves (cf. Romans 12:1-3). Jesus sets himself as an example to be followed in servant leadership. In this world, it is humility and perseverance in suffering that will be rewarded (Luke 22:28-30).

THE TIME OF TRIAL

Sandwiched between the prediction of Peter's denial and his actual denial stand several scenes that highlight the wrong way to be a disciple at the critical moment of trial. Jesus models the right response. When considering one's own time of trial, the first task is to pray. Jesus models a prayer for deliverance and protection in the temptation and calls them to wrestle with God over their own witness to the truth. This is their first failure, for they had fallen asleep while they were supposed to be praying (Luke 22:25-46). The disciples' second failure is to act out of their own human strength. When the crowd came to arrest Jesus at Judas' betraying kiss, the first instinct was to resort to the sword. However, Jesus used the moment to reveal that violence was merely the power of darkness.

The third failure of the disciples was manifest in Peter's three denials at the moment of truth. The disciple of Jesus is called to face the time of trial with bold confession that Jesus is Lord. But Peter denies knowing him (Luke 22:31-62). Consider that Luke's readers would face many trials of their faith. The temptation is to respond to force with force or denial. The Gospel response is to find strength in prayer first and stand boldly in the power of God rather than the power of darkness. Jesus shows us the way of the Kingdom in his bold and faithful witness.

THE INNOCENT TRANSGRESSOR

Understanding the way of the cross is to follow Jesus. As he is placed on trial for his actions, the theme in Luke's Gospel is in his innocence. Jesus maintained absolute integrity in boldly facing the trial and remaining faithful to the kingdom. His transgression was his innocence.

The judgment of the world was to crucify the innocent. Both Pilate and Herod find no basis for any charges against him (Luke 23:4, 14, 22; cf. 23:41, 23:47). Clearly for Luke, the nature of the crucified life is to boldly face persecution in humility and innocence. Jesus showed complete trust in the Father's plan for his own life.

THE RESURRECTION AND VINDICATION

The resurrection narratives in Luke emphasize two things for the disciples of Jesus and Luke's readers. The first is that Jesus' resurrection is not an idle tale. The second, the Road to Emmaus story illustrates how faith is strengthened (Luke 23:50-24:53).

No Idle Tale

Throughout Luke's Gospel, he has presented a serious call to a costly discipleship that requires giving up everything for Jesus, even life. The only reason why anyone would pick up such a cross is because of the hope of resurrection life. The story of the women and Jesus' tomb illustrates that even the first disciples struggled with believing the testimony of the women: that Jesus tomb was empty and, as the angel said, *"He is not here, but has risen"* (Luke 24:6).

The Road to Emmaus

On the road to Emmaus, two disciples interact with the risen Jesus —only in their despair and discouragement, they do not recognize the Lord. The Lord reveals himself to the disciples in two ways: First, he explains the Old Testament scriptures to them and connects Jesus' life to the Word of God. The second way he reveals himself is through the breaking of bread.

Remember, Luke's point is to help his reader, Theophilus, to *"have certainty concerning the things you have been taught"* (Luke 1:4). The heart of the disciple is set on fire through the study of the scriptures. Jesus makes himself known to his disciples through the breaking of the bread. In Acts 2:42, Luke describes the practices of the early church:

"And they devoted themselves to the apostles' teaching and the fellowship, to the breaking of bread and the prayers."
(Acts 2:42)

CHAPTER 9 NOTES:

CHAPTER 10
The Last Apostle: The Writings of John from Patmos

OBJECTIVE: The maturing Christian will understand the writings of the John, the Last Apostle, to live abundant life in Jesus, the Word made flesh.

INTRODUCTION

Following the destruction of the Temple in 70 A.D., John was one of the few remaining apostles. He was the only apostle to die of old age. As the Roman Empire became more violent against Christians, followers of Christ needed encouragement to stay strong in their faith, and those who had not yet decided to follow Jesus needed a Gospel with a different approach. John's Gospel, letters, and the Book of Revelation are intended to convert new audiences and strengthen the faith of those already converted. John's witness of Jesus provides stories and sermons not mentioned in other Gospels, though his letters address common issues the early church faced, including apostasy and false teachers. Revelation is the most unique book of the New Covenant because it has a tone and imagery completely different from any other work. All of John's writings, however, create a compelling witness for the divinity of Jesus and the eternal life possible only through him.

Fig. 1. *The Death of Jesus*, illustration for 'The Life of Christ', c.1884-96 (w/c & gouache on paperboard), Tissot, James Jacques Joseph (1836-1902) / Brooklyn Museum of Art, New York, USA / Bridgeman Images.

Roman Empire 70 A.D. - 100 A.D.

The years after the destruction of the Temple were difficult for the Jewish communities and the growing Christian movement. The Romans continued to persecute the Jews, and a great many Jewish people were sold into slavery. The rest scattered to outlying provinces and countries. The Christians began to face more intense persecution as well. They were crucified, fed to lions, or otherwise tortured unless they renounced their faith in Jesus. During the last years of the empire, the rapid transfer of power from one emperor to the next continued: There were five emperors during that time span. Vespasian was succeeded by his son Titus, who died of a fever. His younger brother Domitian took over, but he was assassinated 15 years later, and Nerva became emperor for two years. In 98 A.D., Trajan became the Roman emperor. This constant turnover of power contributed to an uptick in the chaos and violence that characterizes this period of history.

THE GOSPEL OF JOHN
Introduction

Purpose of the Book

The Gospel of John states its purpose in John 20:30-31:

"Now Jesus did many other signs in the presence of the disciples, which are not written in this book; but these are written so that you may believe that Jesus is the Christ, the Son of God, and that by believing you may have life in his name."
(John 20:30-31)

The author's aim in writing it is to encourage belief in Jesus as the Messiah, the Son of God. His intent is not only to inform but also to convert those who hear the Gospel into eternal life.

Author

The Gospel writer does not specifically name himself, however he does identify himself as one of the 12 who were present at the last supper:

"Peter turned and saw the disciple whom Jesus loved following them, the one who also had leaned back against him during the supper and had said, 'Lord, who is it that is going to betray you?' When Peter saw him, he said to Jesus, 'Lord, what about this man?' Jesus said to him, 'If it is my will that he remain until I come, what is that to you? You follow me!' So the saying spread abroad among the brothers that this disciple was not to die; yet Jesus did not say to him that he was not to die, but, 'If it is my will that he remain until I come, what is that to you?' This is the disciple who is bearing witness about these things, and who has written these things, and we know that his testimony is true."
(John 21:20-24)

Six times throughout the Gospel, the author calls himself "the disciple whom Jesus loved," or the beloved disciple. It is the beloved disciple who reclines at the table next to Jesus at the Last Supper, and asks Jesus to reveal the identity of his betrayer (John 13:23-25). At the foot of the cross, Jesus tells his mother, "Woman, here is your son," and to the beloved disciple he says, "Behold, your mother" (John 19:26-27). When Mary Magdalene is confronted with the empty tomb, she immediately runs to tell the beloved disciple and Peter. The two men rush to the empty tomb and the beloved disciple arrives first but defers to Peter to enter first (John 20:1-10).

In the last chapter of the Gospel of John, the beloved disciple, is one of seven fishermen involved in the miraculous catch of 153 fish (John 21:1-25). Also in this chapter, Simon Peter is reprimanded after he inquiries about the fate of the beloved disciple (John 21:20-23). Finally, the author shares that this is the testimony of the disciple whom Jesus loved (John 21:24). In the entirety of the Book of John, the son of Zebedee is never named, and the reader is left to consider John as the author.

The Tradition

In the first centuries of the Christian Church, authorship of the fourth gospel was attributed to Jesus' disciple John, the brother of James and the son of Zebedee. Early records suggest John as the author when Bishop Irenaeus wrote:

"Afterwards, John, the disciple of the Lord, who also had leaned upon his breast, did himself publish a Gospel during his residence at Ephesus in Asia."
(Irenaeus, Against Heresies 3.1.1)

According to the early church historian Eusebius (325 A.D.), Irenaeus was a disciple of Polycarp, who was a disciple of the apostle John. This makes this early reference a very reliable personal testimony. There were groups that opposed the content of the Gospel, such as the followers of the Gnostic heresies of Marcion. However, they never called into question the authorship of the Gospel.

John the Beloved Disciple

Because John was one of the inner three of Jesus' 12 disciples (cf. Matt. 17:1), we know a great deal about him. John and his brother are known as the sons of Zebedee. They were fishermen. Along with Simon Peter, they were called by Jesus from the shore of the Sea of

Galilee to become *"fishers of men."*

It is possible that John was a cousin of Jesus, one commentator writes:

"A comparison of Mark 15:40 and Matthew 27:56 indicates that their mother's name was Salome and that she also followed Jesus at least some of the time. At one time she asked Jesus to give her sons preferential treatment in his kingdom, according to Matthew 20:21. Going a step further, a comparison of John 19:25 and Matthew 27:56 may indicate that Salome, the mother of the sons of Zebedee, was actually the sister of Mary the mother of Jesus. This would have made John the cousin of Jesus. If this was true it helps explain why Jesus speaking from the cross in John 19:25-27 asked John to take care of his mother."[1]

James and John were called *"Sons of Thunder"* (Mark 3:17). The two brothers had a zealous militant streak. In the Gospel of Luke, we read about how they wanted to *"call down fire"* on a Samaritan village for rejecting Jesus (Luke 9:54-56). It is this strong emotion that Jesus transfigures in the person of John. He becomes zealous for love.

As a member of the inner three, Peter, James, and John were with Jesus all the way to the cross. They were present on the Mount of Transfiguration and they were with Jesus when he sweat blood in the Garden of Gethsemane. They received special attention and teaching from Jesus. For this reason, these three are considered the primary pillars of the early church (see Galatians 2:9).

Tradition holds that John had a lengthy ministry in Ephesus. As Irenaeus provided reports of his ministry in Ephesus through his disciple Polycarp:

"John, the disciple of the Lord, going to bathe at Ephesus, and perceiving Cerinthus within, rushed out of the bath-house without bathing, exclaiming, 'Let us fly, lest even the bath-house fall down, because Cerinthus, the enemy of the truth, is within.'"[2]

From the Book of Revelation, we know of John's exile to Patmos for holding fast to the word of truth in Jesus (Revelation 1:9). Tradition tells us that John died of old age but not until suffering persecution, including being thrown into boiling oil at the Latin Gate.

---

[1] The Gospels: The Gospel according to John (Third Millennium Ministries, 2012) p. 5.
[2] Irenaeus, Against Heresies, III.3.4

Original Audience

As the quotation from Irenaeus indicates, the original audience of the Gospel of John was the region of Asia Minor. As with Luke's and Mark's gospels, John gives some explanation to his readers that indicates that they were not from Israel.

It is likely that his audience included both Jewish and Gentile readers. He is careful to distinguish Jews from Israelites. John uses the term Jews more than any other Gospel, 70 times compared with 20 for the other three gospels combined. Whenever he uses the term, it usually has a negative connotation. However, he is careful to identify Jewish believers as Israelites.

John's Gospel is written well after the destruction of the Temple in 70 A.D. He places prophesies of that destruction at the beginning of the Gospel, and they are not emphasized as they are in the synoptic gospels. He was writing around 85-90 A.D. during a time when believers were being persecuted.

Structure

The structure of the Gospel is:
- Prologue: The Word Made Flesh (John 1:1-18)
- The Book of Signs: The Signs of the Messiah (John 1:19-12:50)
- The Book of Glory: Jesus Preparation of the Messianic Community and his Passion (John 13:1-20:31)
- Epilogue: Witnesses to Glory: Resurrection and Witness (John 21:1-25)

The Prologue: The Word Made Flesh

The first chapter introduces the major themes of the Gospel. Some commentators see a chiastic structure to the Prologue:[3]

The Word Made Flesh

A The Divine Word was with God eternally. (1-2)
  B All things came into being through it/him (the Word). (3)
    C In him were life and light, which darkness did not overcome. (4-5)
      D [John was not the light, but came to testify about the light.] (6-8)
        E The true light was in the world, but the world did not recognize him. (9-10)
          F He came into his own realm, but his own people did not accept him. (11)
            (G THOSE WHO DO BELIEVE IN HIM BECOME CHILDREN OF GOD. 12)
          F' These believers are not ordinary human offspring, but are born of God. (13)
        E' The Incarnate Word reveals God's glory, full of grace and truth. (14)
      D' [John testified about the priority of the one coming after him.] (15)
    C' Out of his (the Word's) fullness, we all received grace upon grace. (16)
  B' Grace and truth came into being through Jesus Christ. (17)
A' The only-begotten.

The hinge of the chiasm at G) highlights the main purpose of the Gospel. John is writing to encourage the belief that leads to adoption as children of God. Indeed, this is the theme summarized by John in the Epilogue (cf. John 20:30-31).

Jesus is the revelation of God's life and glory. Here, glory is the visible manifestation of the true nature of God in all of his attributes. Throughout the Gospel, John describes signs of Jesus' glory. There are seven "I am" statements that connect the Divine Name (Yahweh) to Jesus' self-disclosure as the Word made flesh. The number seven plays prominently in the Gospel as a symbol of a new creation and new covenant in Jesus.

---
[3] http://catholic-resources.org/John/Outline-John01.html

> **"I Am" Statements:**
> 1. *I am the bread of life* (6:35, 48, 51)
> 2. *I am the light of the world* (8:12; 9:5)
> 3. *I am the door of the sheep* (10:7, 9)
> 4. *I am the good shepherd* (10:11, 14)
> 5. *I am the resurrection and the life* (11:25)
> 6. *I am the way, the truth, and the life* (14:6)
> 7. *I am the true vine* (15:1)

The rejection of the Messiah by his own will form the major plot line of Jesus' interaction with the Jewish leaders throughout the Gospel culminating in his trial and crucifixion. In addition, the themes of belief and receiving the Lord will form important plot lines and a call into action.

Another significant theme is the idea of bearing witness or testimony. The role of John the Baptist is highlighted in the prologue. It sets a theme and testimony about Jesus that is called into question by the Jews and Romans; it is a call to action for the disciples of Jesus Christ.

INTRODUCTION
Structure

The structure of the Gospel is:[4]
- Prologue: The Word Made Flesh (John 1:1-18)
- The Book of Signs: The Signs of the Messiah (John 1:19-11:54)
- The Book of Glory: Jesus Preparation of the Messianic Community and his Passion (John 11:55-20:31)
- Epilogue: Witnesses to Glory: Resurrection and Witness (John 21:1-25)

THE BOOK OF SIGNS: THE SIGNS OF THE MESSIAH

The overarching purpose of the Gospel is to tell the story of the Messiah, Jesus Christ. John wants to show him to us using stories that reveal his glory through—signs, works, and words. He uses the testimonies of others to reveal Jesus' identity and call.

---

[4] Adapted from the outline by Andreas Kostenberger, John: Baker Exegetical Commentary on the New Testament, (Baker Academic: Grand Rapids, 2004) pgs. 10-11.

This first half of the Gospel divides into four main sections:

THE BOOK OF SIGNS: The Signs of the Messiah	1:19-12:50
1. Prelude to Jesus' Public Ministry	1:19-51
2. Early Ministry: The Divine Groom and the New Temple	2:1-4:54
3. Rising Opposition: More Signs, Works, and Words	5:1-8:11
4. Radical Confrontation: Climactic Signs, Works, and Words	8:12-10:42

John structures his Gospel not only to reveal Jesus as the Messiah, God in the flesh, but also to show increasingly hostile opposition to that revelation. Before Jesus' public ministry begins, we see hints of the Jewish rejection in the questions to John the Baptist.

PRELUDE TO JESUS PUBLIC MINISTRY
The Testimony of John the Baptist

As the prologue highlights, the Messiah has a forerunner named John whose role bears witness to the coming of the *"true light, which gives light to everyone"* (John 1:9). John's witness is a testimony to three main aspects of Jesus' nature: his divinity, his humiliation, and his anointing (John 1:9-34).

John was not the light, but he reflects it like a mirror. The Jews interrogate John about his identity and role. As the questioning progresses, John becomes increasingly curt, revealing impatience with their hostility. John is clear on his own identity: He is the prophesied one announced in Isaiah, *"the voice of one crying out in the wilderness, 'Make straight the way of the Lord,'"* (John 1:23). The word translated in English as "LORD" in the Isaiah quotation is the Hebrew proper name for God—Yahweh. John understood that he was the one whose job was to ready Israel for the visitation of her God, Yahweh in the flesh.

John also understands that his function is that of a sign that points to Jesus, the Lamb of God. In identifying Jesus as the Lamb of God, he connects Jesus' coming humiliation with the Passover and the Temple sacrifices that propitiated divine judgment, to accomplish divine mercy and grace. The Gospel will develop this connection as the story unfolds and builds toward Jesus' sacrificial death on the cross to take *"away the sin of the world!"* (John 1:29).

The third component of John's testimony highlights the anointing of

Jesus by the Holy Spirit and Jesus' ministry as one who anoints. The word Messiah means *"Anointed One."* John bore witness that Jesus was indeed the spirit-filled one. The preparatory and physical water baptism in John's ministry will give way to a more powerful baptism by the Holy Spirit on Jesus.

Responding to the Testimony

If the Jews were skeptical of the witness of John, there were others who responded positively. The opposition grows as the Gospel unfolds, but so does the belief of those who follow Jesus.

Two of John's disciples respond by following Jesus, Andrew and an unnamed disciple (possibly the Gospel writer John). The two quickly become three when Andrew testifies to his brother Simon. Three then becomes five after Jesus calls Philip and Nathaniel. Jesus is building a core group of those who believe that Jesus is the Messiah.

Belief in Jesus spreads for two main reasons: the testimony of other believers to their own personal experience with him and Jesus' own self-revelation to them. Jesus invites them into a personal relationship, *"Come and you will see."* (John 1:39). These men's own questions are resolved by the testimony of their peers and the welcome and divine foreknowledge of Jesus.

Fig. 2. *Christ and the Woman of Samaria,* c.1700 (oil on canvas), Franceschini, Marco Antonio (1648-1729) / Museum of Fine Arts, Houston, Texas, USA / museum purchase funded by "One Great Night in November, 2009" / Bridgeman Images.

The story of Jacob's ladder (see Genesis 28:12) was to be fulfilled in Jesus. The patriarch was given a vision of a ladder from heaven to Earth, where the angels of God ascended and descended. Jesus informs Nathaniel that he will see Jacob/Israel's role as mediator of the divine to the world fulfilled in him, the divine Son of Man (cf. Daniel 7:13-14). The place of that divine mediation in Genesis 28 was called Bethel, or *"house of God."* This location will become a discussion point with the Samaritan woman later in the Gospel (cf. John 3: 13-22 and 4:20). The Gospel is beginning to make the case that Jesus is the New Temple.

THE DIVINE GROOM AND THE NEW TEMPLE!
Glory: Here Comes the Groom

Critical to John's storyline is that Jesus is Yahweh, the bridegroom who has come to claim his bride. John chooses to tell the story of the first sign that manifests Jesus' glory in the setting of a wedding at Cana of Galilee. The statement to Jesus' mother, *"My hour has not yet come,"* (John 2:4) begins a common theme of Jesus' self-awareness of a messianic timing and divine providence. His hour of glorification where the divine wedding banquet overflows with wine is a future reality yet to reach its consummation (e.g., Jeremiah 31:12; Hosea 14:7; Amos 9:13-14; cf. Revelation 19:6-8; 21:2). Every action of Jesus is purposeful, toward the fulfillment of the will of his divine father. Yet here, it is the will of his human mother that prevails! In changing water in to the best wine the text tells us:

"This, the first of his signs, Jesus did at Cana in Galilee, and manifested his glory. And his disciples believed in him."
(John 2:11)

Glory is the visible manifestation of the attributes of God. Jesus reveals in this sign the divine word made to dwell among us. We have seen his glory. Yahweh has come to claim his bride.

The New Temple

In Israel, God's glory dwells in the Temple. John, however, is telling the story of how the presence of God is making his dwelling in the flesh. The old physical structure is corrupt, irrelevant, and inappropriate. Jesus prophecies its judgment and declares his own body to be the new temple:

"Jesus answered them, 'Destroy this temple, and in three days I will raise it up.' The Jews then said, 'It has taken forty-six years to build this temple, and will you raise it up in three days?' But he was speaking about the temple of his body. When therefore he was raised from the dead, his disciples remembered that he had said this, and they believed the Scripture and the word that Jesus had spoken."
(John 2:19-22)

There were mixed responses to Jesus' signs, deeds, and words. Many believed (John 2:23), but the Gospel reveals that there was an aspect of Jesus' self-disclosure that that would be withheld because *"he him-*

self knew what was in man" (John 2:25). The prophets of the Old Testament recognized that the problem of humanity is a corrupt heart. They anticipated a coming day when Yahweh would provide the gift of a new heart through a new covenant (Jeremiah 31:31-33). They specified that there would be a heart transplant needed that would be given through the Holy Spirit of God (Ezekiel 36:26-27).

Here the wedding and the temple theme come together. Yahweh's presence among his people was no longer to be in a building made by human hands, but in human hearts recreated by the Lord. Israel's teachers knew these passages yet were too hard-hearted to accept them as the Gospel's next story illustrates.

The Need to be Born Again

The fundamental quality necessary to *"see the kingdom of God"* (John 3:4) is to be reborn of the Spirit of God. Nicodemus illustrates the need by his denseness; he is a teacher of Israel, yet he is blind to the testimony of Jesus (John 3:10). Jesus is the fulfillment of all of Israel's salvation stories. This time, he connects the story of salvation offered in the *"lifted serpent"* by Moses in the desert to the Son of man being *"lifted up"* (John 3:14; cf. Numbers 21:8-9). Everyone who looks to the son will be saved! In believing in Jesus, one is given eternal life. But men love the darkness because their deeds are evil.

Jesus is the one who baptizes with the Holy Spirit. Those who would have life will put their trust in him. John tells his disciples that his role is to announce the coming of the divine husband: he is here and will give *"the Spirit without measure"* (John 3:34).

Jesus and the Unlikely Samaritan Bride

The Gospel has introduced several themes that come together beautifully in the story of Jesus and the Samaritan woman: Jacob/Israel, Marriage, Messiah, and Temple. The context is Jacob's well, quite possibly the location where Jacob met his bride (Genesis 29; cf. Genesis 24 Isaac and Rebekah; Exodus 2:16 Moses and Zipporah).

The discussion begins with an acknowledgement of the estrangement between Jews and Samaritans. Nevertheless, Jesus invites the interaction with an offer of *"living water"* (John 7:38). In the Old Testament, living water is a symbol of God's life, abundance, and the promise of the New Covenant restoration (cf. Jeremiah 2:13; Zechariah 14:8; Ezekiel 47:9). Living water develops within the Gospel of John as a sign of the Holy Spirit and Eternal Life (see John 3:5; 4:10-15; 7:38; 19:34). The woman is amazed at the offer and the one offering: *"Are you greater than our father Jacob?"* (John 4:12). She accepts the offer (John 15).

Jesus then changes the subject to marriage. When he reveals that he knows of her five husbands, she then changes the subject to worship! Now she feels she has met her true husband, the Messiah Jesus—at Jacob's well of all places!

The worship issue that the woman raises concerns a long-standing debate between Jews and Samaritans as to whether the Temple should be located in Jerusalem or on Mount Gerizim. Jesus settles the debate in two moves. First, he affirms the Jewish line of interpretation as being authoritative for salvation. Samaritans only accepted the first five books as Scripture. Second, he ends the debate by announcing:

"Jesus said to her, 'Woman, believe me, the hour is coming when neither on this mountain nor in Jerusalem will you worship the Father. You worship what you do not know; we worship what we know, for salvation is from the Jews. But the hour is coming, and is now here, when the true worshipers will worship the Father in spirit and truth, for the Father is seeking such people to worship him. God is spirit, and those who worship him must worship in spirit and truth.'"
(John 4:21-24)

Jesus the husband, new temple, spirit baptizing, anointed one of Israel has found his bride. The worship of the Lord will be in the person of Jesus through spirit and truth. Jesus is the one who offers and gives the Word and Spirit—the Living Water.

A direct contrast can be made between Nicodemus and the Samaritan Woman:

"He was learned and powerful, respected, orthodox, theologically trained; she was unschooled, without influence, despised, capable of only a folk religion. He was a man, a Jew, a ruler; she was a woman, a Samaritan, a moral outcast. And both needed Jesus."[5]

We might add: he came at night, she met Jesus in the light of day at high noon. Nicodemus' faith in Jesus is questionable, her zeal and belief in Jesus was explosive. She testified to her entire village concerning Jesus.

---

[5] DA Carson, The Gospel According to John, The Pillar NT Commentary (Eerdmans Publishing Company, Grand Rapids, 1991) p. 220.

> *"Many Samaritans from that town believed in him because of the woman's testimony, 'He told me all that I ever did.' So when the Samaritans came to him, they asked him to stay with them, and he stayed there two days. And many more believed because of his word. They said to the woman, 'It is no longer because of what you said that we believe, for we have heard for ourselves, and we know that this is indeed the Savior of the world.'"*
> *(John 4:39-42)*

Additional Signs Amid Mounting Unbelief

Jesus continues to manifest signs that reveal his nature and provide occasions to teach and explain his purpose and work in the world. The unbelief and skepticism of the Jews is countered with extended teaching in the form of discourses on the nature and work of the Messiah. In the same way, the positive seeking and clamoring crowds become an occasion to teach about the call of the disciple and character of true belief.

The Father and the Son are Equal: The Healing of a Lame Man

John explains that the pool in Bethesda was a place where many invalids gathered, including the blind, lame, and paralyzed. The belief was that an angel of the Lord would come and stir the waters of the pool and if a sick person entered the waters the moment when it stirred, he would be healed. Jesus identifies a man who wants to be healed but his own disability prevents him from making it to the pool's water in time. In a display of his power and glory, Jesus bypasses the pool and simply tells the man to *"Get up, take up your bed, and walk"* (John 5:8). He does.

The sign becomes an occasion for a Jewish objection because the healing was done on the Sabbath. Jesus overcomes the objection with: *"My father is working until now, and I am working"* (John 5:17). This answer sets the stage for a more significant Jewish objection: Jesus was *"calling God his own father, making himself equal with God"* (John 5:18). Their two objections led to condemnation—they were persecuting Jesus (John 16) and seeking to kill him (John 18). The objection provides the occasion for an extended discourse on Jesus' relationship to God the Father. Amazingly, Jesus does not contradict their conclusion, but affirms them and provides reasons to validate them.

Jesus first identifies himself as doing the same work as God the Father (John 5:19). The works that he highlights are giving life, raising the dead to life, and executing judgment. Jesus teaches that works have been delegated to the son by the father. So, the imperative is on hearing *"the voice of the Son of God"* (John 5:25). *"Do not marvel at this, for an hour is coming when all who are in the tombs will hear his voice and come out, those who have done good to the resurrection of life, and those who have done evil to the resurrection of judgment"* (John 5:28-29).

Jesus then gives three testimonies that validate the assertion of equality between the Father and Son. The first testimony is that of John the Baptist, a testimony that was generally welcomed (John 5:33-35). An even greater testimony are the works that Jesus is doing. They are demonstrations of the Father's power working through the Son. This is the Father's testimony. As with John the Baptist and God, the Jews accept and delight in these authorities, and yet they are not listening to them with regard to the Son. Therefore, they do not accept the voice of the Son.

The Bread of Life

The miraculous feeding of the multitude also provides an occasion for an extended teaching: this time on the blessing and challenge of believing in Jesus for those who do receive him. Certainly, the feeding of the 5,000 with five loaves and two fishes was an occasion that engendered belief and hope in Jesus. While the crowds exalted Jesus, and sought to *"make him king,"* they misunderstood the nature of his kingdom to be about earthly rule and earthly provision (John 6:15). Jesus confronts this misunderstanding:

"Jesus answered them, 'Truly, truly, I say to you, you are seeking me, not because you saw signs, but because you ate your fill of the loaves. Do not work for the food that perishes, but for the food that endures to eternal life, which the Son of Man will give to you. For on him God the Father has set his seal.'"
(John 6:26-27)

His offer to the crowds was of a spiritual nature. The bread that he had to offer was not to fill the stomach temporarily but to fill the soul eternally. The questions the crowd asked him are' correct. *"What must we do, to be doing the works of God?"* (John 6:28). The answer from Jesus is simple: *"This is the work of God, that you believe in him whom he has sent"* (John 6:29).

Jesus is the bread of God come down out of heaven that gives life. Echoing the Samaritan woman's request, they respond, *"Sir, give us this bread always!"* (John 6:34) This request then expands into an extended discourse on the first of seven "I am" statements in the Gospel.

The proper Hebrew name for God, *"Yahweh,"* is translated as *"I am."* The seven discourses expand on the incarnation theme from the prologue, *"the Word became flesh and dwelt among us"* (John 1:14). Jesus' sign points to an eternal reality. His flesh and blood are the very life of God. Whoever feeds on this bread will not die but live. In the disciple's wrestling over this *"hard saying,"* Jesus explains that true belief in Jesus is a gift from God and a work of his spirit in the human heart (John 6:35, cf. 6:42). God the Father knows and draws his people into true, spirit-filled, life-giving relationship with the Son. There are others who do not believe and take offense. The steadfastness of the 12 is evidence of the divine election unto life by Jesus (John 6:70).

JESUS AT THE FEAST OF THE TABERNACLE

In Chapters 7 and 8, the Gospel setting changes from Galilee to Jerusalem and the Festival of the Booths. As the last festival of the Jewish year, this festival not only looks back toward the gracious provision of Yahweh in the wilderness during the 40 years, but also looks forward, as a festival of eschatological, or future hopes, for restoration.

Festival of the Booths

The first interaction concerning the feast is whether Jesus would attend. His brothers urged him to use the festival to make a public display of his signs *"… that your disciples also may see the works you are doing"* (John 7:3). Jesus will not be influenced by his brothers as he was by his mother. There is a divine timing to his unveiling. While he differentiated himself from the will of his brothers, he nevertheless went to the feast in private. The opinions concerning Jesus were already being formed in the minds of the people. *"He is a good man"* and *"No, he is leading the people astray"* (John 7:12) provide a range of popular opinions about Jesus. He begins to teach in the Temple.

The Jewish teachers used the authority of others to build their cases. Jesus claimed God the Father as his authority. *"My teaching is not mine, but his who sent me"* (John 7:16). The opposition to Jesus on the part of the Jews was building as they continued to seek his arrest (John 7:30).

Living Water

On the final day of the Temple festivities, the high priest would pour water at the base of the altar in order to anticipate symbolically the flowing of living water from Jerusalem to the Dead Sea as prophesied in Ezekiel 47. Jesus stands up on this celebrated day and proclaims that he is the source of the living water through the outpouring of the Holy Spirit. Earlier in the Gospel, we learned that Jesus' body would be raised as the New Temple (John 2:19-22; cf. 4:7-14). The responses to this teaching were mixed. Some believed, others doubted based on prevailing interpretations of the prophesies of the Messiah.

I Am the Light: Truth and Lies, Slavery and Freedom

The second "I am" statement is:

"I am the light of the world. Whoever follows me will not walk in darkness, but will have the light of life."
(John 8:12)

In the exchanges that follow, we see the Jews clamoring to invalidate Jesus' claims. Their objections continue to be addressed, yet they persist in unbelief:

"So Jesus said to the Jews who had believed him, 'If you abide in my word, you are truly my disciples, and you will know the truth, and the truth will set you free.' They answered him, 'We are offspring of Abraham and have never been enslaved to anyone. How is it that you say, "You will become free?"'"

"Jesus answered them, 'Truly, truly, I say to you, everyone who practices sin is a slave to sin. The slave does not remain in the house forever; the son remains forever. So if the Son sets you free, you will be free indeed.'"
(John 8:31-36)

Light and darkness are metaphors for truth and lies. Jesus confronts the Jews in their falsehood. How can they say they are free if they do not believe in the Son who gives freedom? How can they say they are Abraham's children if they are following the devil? Jesus speaks of a spiritual slavery to sin, and he offers freedom to those who will walk in the light. The Jews are in slavery, in the dark, in sin, following lies.

The focus becomes Jesus' claims about his relationship with Abraham. The Jews rightly infer from his teaching that he is saying he is greater than Abraham and that he personally knew Abraham (John 8:53). The statement in John 8:58 is a clear self-revelation that Jesus is Yahweh (the *"I Am"*). The Jews knew he was claiming to be God and sought to stone him for blasphemy.

Jesus Heals a Blind Man

The healing of the man born blind becomes the occasion to highlight the blindness of the Pharisees. In their interrogations of the man and his parents, they look foolish for their unbelief. Yet, they persist.

"'We know that God has spoken to Moses, but as for this man, we do not know where he comes from.' The man answered, 'Why, this is an amazing thing! You do not know where he comes from, and yet he opened my eyes.' We know that God does not listen to sinners, but if anyone is a worshiper of God and does his will, God listens to him."
(John 9:29-31)

This issue clearly is that the current shepherds of Israel are illegitimate. The chief shepherd has arrived and found them wanting. Jesus, in his third and fourth *"I am"* statements, announces: *"I am the door of the sheep,"* and *"I am the good shepherd"* (John 10:7, 10:11). These *"I am"* discourses serve as a commentary on the Jewish leadership. They are called *"strangers"*, *"thieves"*, *"robbers"* and *"hired hands."* They do not know the sheep. They do not love the sheep. The sheep do not recognize their voices (John 10:5-14).

Clearly, as John is telling the story of Jesus and his teachings, he is encouraging his readers to be discerning with regard to the spiritual authorities in their lives. Jesus has their best interests at heart. He proves this when he says: *"and I lay down my life for the sheep"* (John 10:15).

THE CLIMACTIC SIGN—THE RAISING OF LAZARUS

The stage is set for a climactic revelation of Jesus' glory through the resurrection of a dead man. The disciples are very much aware that a return trip to Judea could result in Jesus' persecution and death. Jesus persists in his determination to return to Bethany because *"Lazarus has died."* Jesus hints at some great sign he will perform *"that you may believe."* Thomas has his doubts as he prepares to go and die with Lazarus (John 11:14-16).

The miraculous raising of Lazarus after being dead for three days becomes not only a demonstration of Jesus' divinity, but also his humanity. *"Jesus wept"* is both the shortest verse in the Bible and perhaps the most profound (John 11:35). Jesus is described as being *"deeply moved in his spirit and greatly troubled"* (John 11:33). Not only is Jesus acquainted with human sorrows and grief, but he shares in them. He also is the one who can reverse them. In a display of the *"glory of God,"* Jesus calls Lazarus to *"come out!"* (John 11:40-43).

The fifth "I am" statement is:

"Jesus said to her, 'I am the resurrection and the life. Whoever believes in me, though he die, yet shall he live, and everyone who lives and believes in me shall never die. Do you believe this?'"
(John 11:25-26)

Jesus is God in the flesh. He holds the power of life and death in his sovereign hands. He is the bread. He is light. He is the source of living water. He is the gate. He is the Good Shepherd who lays down his life for the sheep. He is the great *"I am."*

The people who hear these claims in the Gospel understand them clearly. Some say he is a demon, some call him a fiend and blasphemer, others call him Messiah.

THE BOOK OF GLORY: Jesus' Preparation of the Messianic Community and His Passion

We have reached a transition section of the Gospel of John. The Book of Signs comes to a close with the most profound and glorious sign, raising Lazarus back to life. Many of those who witnessed this believed in Jesus. However, the more Jesus' glory was on display, the more the corrupt Jewish leadership sought to bring him down.

"So the chief priests and the Pharisees gathered the council and said, 'What are we to do? For this man performs many signs. If we let him go on like this, everyone will believe in him, and the Romans will come and take away both our place and our nation.' But one of them, Caiaphas, who was high priest that year, said to them, 'You know nothing at all. Nor do you understand that it is better for you that one

man should die for the people, not that the whole nation should perish.' He did not say this of his own accord, but being high priest that year he prophesied that Jesus would die for the nation, and not for the nation only, but also to gather into one the children of God who are scattered abroad. So from that day on they made plans to put him to death." (John 11:47-53)

Things have reached a point of no return, and *"the Jesus question"* must be resolved one way or another—so the Gospel must move to its conclusion. While the Jewish leadership may have believed they were solving the Jesus question with their plans, the reader is informed that it is the divine plan they are fulfilling. The stage is set for John's Book of Glory. In this next section of the Gospel, the focus turns to the preparations for Jesus' passion and his death on the cross.

THE BOOK OF GLORY	John 12-20
1. *Preparations for Glory*	John 12
2. *The New Passover*	John 13
3. *The Farewell Discourse*	John 14-16
4. *The High Priestly Prayer*	John 17
5. *The Passion: Betrayal, Arrest, Trial, Crucifixion, and Burial*	John 18-19
6. *The Resurrection*	John 20

PREPARATIONS FOR GLORY
The Anointing for Burial

Jesus retreats to Bethany where he dined with Mary, Martha, and Lazarus. Mary had purchased an expensive perfumed ointment and began to anoint Jesus feet with the *"pure nard"* and her hair. *"Jesus said, 'Leave her alone, so that she may keep it for the day of my burial. For the poor you always have with you, but you do not always have me.'" (John 12:3)* The entire home was filled with the beautiful aroma of Mary's extravagant love. However, Judas (the soon-to-be betrayer) objects on pious grounds of serving the poor. Jesus explains that Mary's action is correct. The reader of the Gospel should begin to understand that Jesus is going to Jerusalem with one purpose—to die.

The Triumphal Entry

Jesus' entry into Jerusalem is poignant for the reader, even though the disciples still do not see the glory of the cross (John 12:16). Jesus' crucifixion is a triumph over evil, and sin and an exaltation of Jesus as Messiah. Ironically, the exaggerated fears of the Pharisees would be realized.

The disciples are approached by Greeks who desire to see Jesus. This is the occasion for Jesus to explain to the disciples that his hour of glorification has arrived at last. Paradoxically, glory manifests in death. Like a grain of wheat that dies in order to produce an abundance of fruit; Jesus' fruit of glory is wonderful, it is the dying that is troubling. Jesus taught his disciples:

"Now is the judgment of this world; now will the ruler of this world be cast out. And I, when I am lifted up from the earth, will draw all people to myself."
(John 12:31-32)

The reader is told that by *"lifted up,"* Jesus was indicating his type of death. Jesus' glorification would divide all of humanity into two groups: believers and unbelievers. Unbelievers will reject the glory of the Son of Man because they love *"the glory that comes from man more than the glory that comes from God"* (John 12:43). Believers recognize that in the person of Jesus they are seeing the glory of God the Father. Belief in and obedience to the glory of Jesus is eternal life (John 12:50).

THE NEW PASSOVER
The Foot Washing

The washing of the disciple's feet illustrates what it means to believe in Jesus. Belief is about having the humility to receive the grace of God offered through the actions of the Son of God. Jesus' humility in taking the role of a servant points dramatically to his gift on the cross (cf. Philippians 2:7-8).

Peter receives a lesson in being served by his master that his pride would prevent him from receiving. But as Jesus taught him: *"If I do not wash you, you have no share with me"* (John 13:8). Jesus is offering grace and salvation, but it must be received humbly. Once a disciple is a recipient of grace, he must give it as well. The next lesson for the disciples is to live a life of grace. Jesus says,

"If I then, your Lord and Teacher, have washed your feet, you also ought to wash one another's feet. For I have given you an exam-

ple, that you also should do just as I have done to you. Truly, truly, I say to you, a servant is not greater than his master, nor is a messenger greater than the one who sent him."
(John 13:14-16)

The Farewell Discourse

Jesus' last teachings are recorded in greater detail in John's gospel than the synoptic gospels. John takes three chapters to provide some of the most rich and profound teaching in the New Testament. Here we find the last two *"I am"* statements. Also, Jesus offers an extended teaching on the role of the third person of the Godhead, the Holy Spirit.

I am the Way, the Truth, and the Life

With Jesus' announcement of his imminent departure, discouragement sets in among the disciples. However, Jesus reassures them in his sixth *"I am"* statement. Ultimately, his departure from the disciples will be for their triumph and glory—if they do not lose their bearings. And they know the way to glory. Jesus reminds them: *"I am the way, and the truth, and the life. No one comes to the Father except through me"* (John 14:6). They know the way to glory because they know Jesus. As long as they keep their faith in him, they will never be led astray. Jesus indicates that it will be better for him to depart so that the Holy Spirit can come.

The Helper

While Jesus' physical presence is glorious, he is able to empower the disciples by indwelling them spiritually. Jesus teaches his disciples about the helper, the *"Spirit of Truth"* (John 16:13). Again, Jesus makes a distinction between the unbelieving world and his disciples. The world will not be given the Spirit of Truth, but the one who keeps the commandments of Jesus and loves him will be given the Holy Spirit (John 14:17). It will have certain roles and functions to help the disciples remain faithful to Jesus while they are living in the world. The primary role Jesus highlights is that the Holy Spirit will be a surrogate by providing continuing help and instruction after Jesus departs.

I am the True Vine

Understanding the relationship to the Father, Son, Holy Spirit, and the disciple comes in the last *"I am"* statement. The role and nature of the Holy Spirit in the lives of the disciples is illustrated by the metaphor of the vine.

"I am the vine; you are the branches. Whoever abides in me and I in him, he it is that bears much fruit, for apart from me you can do nothing."
(John 15:5)

Throughout the Gospel, Jesus makes the point that he is the source of life. In the seventh *"I am"* statement he reveals that the way to remain connected to that life is through the indwelling of his Holy Spirit. The way a disciple can be assured of the connection is by the manifestation of fruitfulness. The fruit of the Father is seen in the lives of the disciples through obedience to the commands of Jesus.

Jesus clearly states that his primary command is to love (John 15:16-17). Assurance of connectedness to Jesus comes with the manifestation of the fruit of the Holy Spirit. Jesus delights to do his Father's will and so will his disciples (John 15:10).

The Hatred of the World

The love that Jesus has for his disciples and that his disciples have for him will cause persecution by the world. Because the world hates Jesus; it hates God the Father; therefore, it will hate Jesus' disciples. The disciple must remember that the world and Jesus are enemies. The disciple must not be naive to this enmity. This is where the helper, the Spirit of Truth, is beneficial to the disciples. The Holy Spirit will bear witness against the world through the disciples (John 16:8-11). The Holy Spirit will give the disciples the right words to speak and provide reassurance (John 16:12-15).

Victory Over the World

Jesus reassures the disciples that he will return and triumph over the evil powers of this world. One day the disciples will be like a woman who has given birth to a baby. She will forget the pain and rejoice in the new life. In the meantime, the disciples will suffer, but they should take heart in the ultimate victory in Jesus Christ. The suffering and tribulation facing the disciples looks very different through the lens of the cross and resurrection of Jesus Christ.

THE PRAYER OF JESUS: The High Priestly Prayer

The conclusion of the farewell discourse leads to the throne room of intercession. After giving final instructions to his disciples, he now offers a final prayer. Traditionally, the prayer has been referred to in the church as the High Priestly Prayer. This is because Jesus is making intercession on behalf of his followers to God the Father. The prayer breaks neatly into two sections. First, Jesus prays for himself and his disciples. Second, Jesus prays for all believers and the world.

Jesus Prays for Himself and his Disciples

Jesus is a finisher. In completing the work he has been given to do, glory will shine. However, this last work requires the strength and working of the Father in him. Jesus prays for himself.

"Father, the hour has come; glorify your Son that the Son may glorify you, since you have given him authority over all flesh, to give eternal life to all whom you have given him."
(John 17:1-2)

The content of the farewell discourse becomes a collected prayer of intercession to God on behalf of the disciples. Jesus prays for their protection and provision through the sanctifying work of the helper, the Spirit of Truth.

"I do not ask that you take them out of the world, but that you keep them from the evil one. They are not of the world, just as I am not of the world. Sanctify them in the truth; your word is truth."
(John 17:15-17)

Jesus prays that his disciples would be made holy through the revealed word of God and his truth. The disciple would be in the world but not of it. In order to maintain that distinction, the disciples need help from the Holy Spirit and the truth.

Jesus Prays for All Believers and the World

The second half of the prayer focuses on the church that will come to exist because of the work of the disciples. One of the most important characteristics of believers in Jesus is that they remain united in him. There is only one God; the Father and the Son are one. The unity of all believers in the word of God under the Son of God is the only hope for the conversion of the world.

THE PASSION AND RESURRECTION OF JESUS

The final three sections in the Gospel of John are the climactic events surrounding his passion and resurrection.

THE PASSION AND RESURRECTION	John 18-21
The Passion Narrative	John 18-19
The Resurrection	John 20
Epilogue: Peter and the Disciple Whom Jesus Loved	John 21

The Passion Narrative

The passion narrative emphasizes the sovereign control of Jesus and his Father over the affairs of men. Many people and groups will be involved in the crucifixion of Jesus, all asserting power and control. However, God remains firmly in control (John 18-19).

The Betrayal and Arrest

Jesus predicted his betrayal at the last Passover (John 13:21). In the High Priestly Prayer, he prayed that not one of his disciples would be *"… lost except the son of destruction, that the Scripture might be fulfilled"* (John 17:12). Now the time has come for the betrayal and again we see the divine foreknowledge in Jesus *"knowing all that would happen to him"* (John 18:4). John sees the fulfillment of Jesus' High Priestly Prayer in his plea for immunity for his disciples (John 18:9).

Peter stands ready to use force to prevent Jesus' arrest. He strikes the high priest's servant. However, Jesus rebukes Peter for seeking to prevent the Father's plan. *"So Jesus said to Peter, 'Put your sword into its sheath; shall I not drink the cup that the Father has given me?'"* (John 18:11).

The Denials of Peter

Like the betrayal, Jesus had predicted that Peter would deny him three times (John 13:36-38). Peter would have the opportunity to lay down his life for Jesus, but not before his own character was refined by failure. Later in the Gospel, Jesus restores Peter by giving him the opportunity to confess his love for Jesus three times. Jesus' faithful witness should be compared with Peter's denials.

The Trials

Jesus underwent two trials: one Jewish and one Roman. The trial before the Jewish leadership had a formal and an informal hearing. First, Jesus is brought to Annas, the father-in-law of the current high priest Caiaphas. Although he had been deposed from office by the Romans, he was still powerful and clearly in charge.

The second trial mentioned in the Gospel is before the Roman Governor Pontius Pilate. John's account of the Roman trial is the most detailed of the four Gospels. First, Jesus is interrogated (John 18:28-40) and, second, he is sentenced to be crucified (John 19:1-16a). The trial is narrated in seven sections following an oscillating pattern of Pilate's movement inside and outside the Roman governor's headquarters, the Praetorium.

The Interrogation before Pilate

The story reveals a delicate dance of evil and corruption. Politically, neither the Jewish leaders nor Pilate wanted to take responsibility for putting Jesus to death. Both powers preferred to see the other bear the blame. Yet both make clear their own positions: the crucifixion of Jesus must happen.

The primary charge before Pilate that would carry weight would be an assertion of rival kingly authority to Caesar's throne. The crux of Pilate's questioning centers on Jesus' royal claim. Pilate asks, *"Are you the King of the Jews?"* (John 18:33). Jesus denies that he is mounting an insurrection against Caesar, but at the same time, he makes an absolute claim to his authority as the transcendent king of a kingdom:

"Jesus answered, 'My kingdom is not of this world. If my kingdom were of this world, my servants would have been fighting, that I might not be delivered over to the Jews. But my kingdom is not from the world.' Then Pilate said to him, 'So you are a king?' Jesus answered, 'You say that I am a king. For this purpose I was born and for this purpose I have come into the world—to bear witness to the truth. Everyone who is of the truth listens to my voice.' Pilate said to him, 'What is truth?'"
(John 18:36-38)

This question is left hanging unanswered in this scene, but not in the Gospel. Has not the reader already been given the definition of truth when Jesus said, *"I am the way, and the truth, and the life"* (John 14:6)? John addressed the issue of truth repeatedly in the Gospel.

"You will know the truth, and the truth will set you free" (John 8:32).

The Sentence

Jesus has full control over the situation and Pilate is losing control. He is powerless because of his own fear (John 19:8). The Jews are the ones to make the case that Jesus set himself up to be a king. Using Jesus, Pilate ruthlessly mocked their charges, even clothing Jesus in kingly garments and showing him to be a weak king. Pilate acquiesced and charged Jesus, and the Jewish leadership revealed their apostasy by claiming to be more a friend to Caesar than was the Roman governor.

The Crucifixion

The issues of Jesus' royal status and his authority continue to be at the forefront of the narrative when Pilate posted a sign over Jesus crucified body that read, *"Jesus of Nazareth, the King of the Jews."* The chief priests petitioned, *"Do not write, 'The King of the Jews,' but rather, 'This man said, I am King of the Jews.'* Pilate answered, *'What I have written I have written'"* (John 19:19-22).

The irony for the Jews and Romans is that Jesus is the legitimate sovereign over both. His is the fulfillment of the divine plan revealed in the scriptures (John 19:24, 28, 36, 37). The other emphasis in John's gospel is on the completion of the Father's will. Jesus says, *"It is finished"* (John 19:30). Jesus faithfully completed the work that his Father had given him to do. In doing so, he brought glory to the Father.

THE RESURRECTION

The preceding chapter closes with Jesus' hasty burial in the tomb of Joseph of Arimathea (John 19:38-42). Chapter 20 begins with Mary Magdalene going to the tomb, seeing the stone has been rolled away, and running to report to the disciples. Her report contains a false notion: Someone has stolen the body. Mary's story would be corrected by the Lord himself (John 20:16-17).

Peter and *"the other disciple"* (probably John) also inspected the empty tomb and yet did not grasp fully the implications of resurrection, though the text says the other disciple *"saw and believed"* (John 20:8). What exactly did he believe about the empty tomb? The tomb was empty, but Jesus began to appear to the disciples; first to Mary and then to the others. His appearances also contain an apostolic com-

Fig. 3. *The Incredulity of St. Thomas,* 1602-03 (oil on canvas), Caravaggio, Michelangelo Merisi da (1571-1610) / Schloss Sanssouci, Potsdam, Brandenburg, Germany / Bridgeman Images.

missioning.

"Jesus said to them again, 'Peace be with you. As the Father has sent me, even so I am sending you.' And when he had said this, he breathed on them and said to them, 'Receive the Holy Spirit. If you forgive the sins of any, they are forgiven them; if you withhold forgiveness from any, it is withheld.'"
(John 20:21-23)

The work that Jesus instructed the disciples in the farewell discourse recorded in John 15-16 is now complete. The promised Spirit of Truth is given. The disciples now must become apostles and be witnesses to the truth. Their first opportunity to bear witness is to one another. Mary witnesses to the 10, and the 10 witness to Thomas. He becomes the archetypal doubter converted to believer. Here we see the fruit of liberation by the truth. Doubt transforms to worship.

"Then he said to Thomas, 'Put your finger here, and see my hands;

CHAPTER 10 The Last Apostle: The Writings of John from Patmos

and put out your hand, and place it in my side. Do not disbelieve, but believe.' Thomas answered him, 'My Lord and my God!' Jesus said to him, 'Have you believed because you have seen me? Blessed are those who have not seen and yet have believed.'"
(John 20:27-29)

EPILOGUE: The Commission of Peter, and the "Other Disciple"

Jesus' last appearance on the shore of the Sea of Galilee becomes an occasion of restoration and commission. Peter is given three opportunities to reverse his three denials. *"Do you love me more than these?"* Jesus asks him. *"Yes Lord; you know that I love you"* is the reply. With each restorative question comes a charge: *"Feed my lambs"*, *"Tend my sheep"*, *"Feed my sheep"* (John 21:15-17).

Peter played a pre-eminent role in the early church, leading the flock following Jesus' ascension. Ultimately, Peter was martyred for his strong faith and confession. Indeed, Peter would obey Jesus' final command to *"follow me"* (John 21:18-19).

The *"other disciple"* reveals that he has a special role to play as one commissioned to bear witness through the testimony of the Gospel.

"This is the disciple who is bearing witness about these things, and who has written these things, and we know that his testimony is true. Now there are also many other things that Jesus did. Were every one of them to be written, I suppose that the world itself could not contain the books that would be written."
(John 21:24-25)

THE FIRST, SECOND, AND THIRD LETTERS OF JOHN

The three letters of John are located at the back of the New Testament, and often reason do not receive as much attention as the Gospel and letters of Paul. However, they are important and offer practical relevance to the church.

These three letters were written around 85-100 A.D. They represent some of the final thoughts of the apostle as he addresses theological and practical matters in the church. The concern among the apostles, as they were approaching their deaths, was that the message and practice of the faith did not die with them.

John has been associated with the church in Ephesus. It is likely that these letters were written from there and sent to churches in Asia Minor. Each of the letters address a specific subject but they are consistent in one area, insisting that authentic Christianity be manifested in the life of the church.

1 John: Assurance for the Authentic Christian

The first letter lacks the typical identifiers of a letter that would name to whom and from whom it is written. The original audience is often assumed to be the churches in the region of Asia Minor listed in the Book of Revelation. The book is often compared with the Gospel of John for its similarities in thematic content and literary structure.
The letter provides discernible knowledge regarding the nature of authentic and inauthentic Christianity. John writes *"that you may know that you have eternal life"* (1 John 5:13). He uses the two Greek words for *"know"* in more than 30 verses. Knowledge of the identity and practice of the true Christian is defined by knowledge of the nature and actions of God. God's character attributes and divine actions define the true and authentic Christian character and walk. Simply put, if you know the true God, then you know a true Christian. The two main characteristics of God that John identifies are Light and Love. His first letter can be divided simply along these two major themes.

Prologue: The Word of Life

Like the Gospel of John, 1 John begins with a prologue. His first letter opens with:

"That which was from the beginning, which we have heard, which we have seen with our eyes, which we looked upon and have touched with our hands, concerning the word of life—the life was made manifest, and we have seen it, and testify to it and proclaim to you the eternal life, which was with the Father and was made manifest to us—that which we have seen and heard we proclaim also to you, so that you too may have fellowship with us; and indeed our fellowship is with the Father and with his Son Jesus Christ. And we are writing these things so that our joy may be complete."
(1 John 1:1-4)

The word of God in the world has moved from the incarnation to proclamation and inscription. Through the word of life proclaimed and written, believers may have fellowship with the apostles and with the Father and his Son, Jesus Christ. That divine human connectedness will manifest itself primarily in two ways: in fellowship with the light of God and in fellowship with the love of God.

PART ONE: God is Light—Walk in the Light

For John, the world is divided in two: light and dark. There are no shades of gray. Either a person is walking in the light of God or he is walking in darkness. *"God is light and in him is no darkness at all"* (1 John 1:5). Therefore, authentic Christians walk in the light by confessing with honesty the reality of sin in one's life (1 John 1:6-10); repenting of their sins and walking in obedience to the word of God (1 John 2:1-6); obeying the command to love (1 John 2:7-11); not loving the world or things (1 John 2:15-17); and, knowing and confessing the truth of the anointing of Jesus in him (1 John 2:18-25) and from him (1 John 2:26-27).

John's desire is that the authentic believers in Jesus will have confidence without shame in him and in their own status as those born of him. Essentially, being a child of God is to be one who walks in the light of God. God is holy and his holiness will be revealed in the character of those who are in his fellowship and family. The character of the believer will be one of sanctified obedience and righteousness.

PART TWO: God is Love—Walk in Love

The second essential characteristic of the believer flows from the character of God's love.

"Beloved, let us love one another, for love is from God, and whoever loves has been born of God and knows God. Anyone who does not love does not know God, because God is love."
(1 John 4:7-8)

The love of God in the Christian will be manifest in: eschewing hatred or murder (1 John 3:12-15); loving sacrificially in the form of generosity and helping brothers in need (1 John 3:16-18); enjoying the heart assurance of our salvation by God's atoning grace (1 John 3:19-4:12); abiding in his Holy Spirit and love (1 John 4:13-21); overcoming the world by our love for God and his commandments (1 John 5:1-5); and, believing the testimony of God concerning his Son (1 John 5:6-12).
The supreme manifestation of God's love is in the action of Jesus, who

died as the propitiation, as the payment to satisfy the just demands of God's wrath and His judgment of our sins (1 John 4:9). For John, we love because Jesus first loved us (1 John 4:19). The quality, character, and actions of our love are defined by the character and actions of a loving God who has come in the flesh to redeem his people from sin. Authentic Christians will, without fear of condemnation or shame from God or men, walk in the light and love manifest by Jesus Christ in the flesh. Authentic Christians will manifest that same light and love in their daily walk in the fellowship of believers.

CONCLUSION: That You May Know

It is possible to be Christian born of God, saved unto eternal life, and not truly know it. John would have us believe that we are children of God if we are truly walking with him. The purpose of the letter is to provide deep assurance to the authentic Christian.

It also is a letter that will serve as a test for inauthentic Christians. Making a declaration that they love God, or they are a follower of Jesus is not enough. There is only light and darkness; truth or lies; love or hatred; life or death; and, God or the devil. There is no middle ground.

2 JOHN 1

John's second letter is written specifically to *"the elect lady and her children"* (2 John 1:1). This could be a female minister, but more likely it is referring to a congregation as *"the wife of the Lamb"* (see Revelation 21:9-11), and members are the children. In 2 John 13, he sends greetings from *"the children of your elect sister."* This implies the letter is for two sister congregations.

Building on the themes of the first letter, 2 John expresses his concerns for practical reinforcement and accountability in the life of the church. The main charge is found in verses 10 and 11: *"If anyone comes to you and does not bring this teaching, do not receive him into your house or give him any greeting, for whoever greets him takes part in his wicked works"* (2 John 1:10-11).

The concern is not as much for showing love to the people of this world, but for extending the type of hospitality that would provide a false teacher who promotes false teachings. Such teachings should be denied. The authentic marks of the faith should be reinforced as in 1 John.

3 JOHN 1

If 2 John is a charge not to extend hospitality to a false teacher, 3 John is written to encourage hospitality and support for those who manifest an authentic Christianity.

"Beloved, it is a faithful thing you do in all your efforts for these brothers, strangers as they are, who testified to your love before the church. You will do well to send them on their journey in a manner worthy of God. For they have gone out for the sake of the name, accepting nothing from the Gentiles. Therefore we ought to support people like these, that we may be fellow workers for the truth."
(3 John 1:5-8)

In particular, a certain member of the congregation, Diotrephes, had been denying fellowship to brothers in Christ. In 3 John, there are three names mentioned, Gaius, Diotrephes, and Demetrius. Gaius is a leader who needs encouragement to hold the arrogant Diotrephes accountable for his inhospitable character. Demetrius is a test case for Gaius and the congregation. The call is to not be like Diotrephes or controlled by him, but rather to be like Demetrius and welcome him.

Gaius is a commendable Christian (3 John 1-8): for walking truthfully (3 John 3-4); being encouraged to show hospitality (3 John 5-6); and, ministering generously (3 John 7-8) in the face of a fellow member who desires do the opposite.

Diotrephes is a conceited Christian. He is driven by prideful ambition that manifests in insubordination to spiritual authority (3 John 9). He talks a *"wicked nonsense"* about the apostles and all of this gives rise to the marked inhospitable behavior of a controlling bully (3 John 10).

Demetrius is a consistent and true Christian (3 John 11-12) who pursues a godly example (3 John 11) and possesses a good testimony (3 John 12). He is to be welcomed. The heart of the matter is that fellowship is important. If we choose to fellowship with inauthentic Christians, it could very well lead to broken fellowship among true believers.

A THEMATIC COMPARISON OF 2 AND 3 JOHN[6]

2 JOHN	3 JOHN
Written to a lady and her children	Written to a man and his acquaintances
Written to one who was entertaining entertain the right visitors	*Written about one who was refusing to the wrong visitors*
Need was for love to be balanced by truth	Need was for truth (?) to be balanced by love
Truth is the key	*Love (hospitality) is the key*
No personal names (1 John also)	Three personal names: Gaius, Diotrephes, Demetrius

THE BOOK OF REVELATION
Part 1 of 2 Parts - Chapters 1-3

The Book of Revelation is one of the most mysterious books of the Bible. As the last book, it often receives a great deal of attention and study. It is filled with heavenly perspectives, tales of two cities, beasts and dragons, otherworldly and heavenly visions of the past, present, and the future.

The Apostle John wrote it from prison on the island of Patmos. It concerns the prophetic revelations that he received from the risen Lord, Jesus Christ. This is the last of his works. Many of the theological themes found in his earlier works are found here. However, Revelation has more in common with the prophetic literature found in the Old Testament. As a literary genre, it contains visions and revelations of future judgment, future restoration, and uses metaphorical language.

As with the prophetic books, this book serves not only as a handbook for predicting the details of the future but also as motivation and instruction for living faithfully in the present. The future orientation of judgment and hope helps to provide a present perspective to the trials and temptations for faithful Christians living in a corrupt and fallen world. The prophet's job is to provide the larger context of what God is doing in the world and in the heavenly realms; the prophet is interpreting history from God's perspective.

Fig. 4. *St. John the Evangelist on the Island of Patmos*, c.1618 (oil on canvas), Velazquez, Diego Rodriguez de Silva y (1599-1660) / National Gallery, London, UK / Bridgeman Images.

---

[6]http://www.danielakin.com/wp-content/uploads/old/Resource_511/3%20John.pdf (p. 4).

Options for a Christian in 96 A.D.

Being a Christian in a hostile culture where one owed absolute allegiance to Caesar and was expected to worship false gods made life difficult politically, socially, economically, and emotionally. How did people of that time deal with the pressure? They could:[7]

Quit. They could capitulate under the pressure and as a good Roman citizen, renounce Jesus Christ, and bow before the almighty Caesar and Rome.

Lie. This is the situation ethics option. Sometimes, it is called choosing the lesser of two evils. Christians would lie about their allegiance to Rome, but with mental reservations, all the while keeping their true faith and beliefs private.

Fight. They could organize, take up arms and resist oppressive powers with force. Many Jewish Zealots chose this—and they were squashed.

Change the Law. Christians could work within the system to change the political situation and laws. While this ultimately would become what happened to the Roman Empire over the next several hundred years, this was not a great short-term solution.

Adjust. Some Christians incorporated beliefs and practices of the other Roman cults to fit in. For those who advocated syncretism, the intolerance and exclusiveness of faithful Christians must be avoided, so that Christians should do nothing that would indicate disrespect for the religion of other people. Many did this.

Martyrdom. The faithful path was to be an enduring witness to faith and loyalty to Jesus. For many faithful Christians the implications of faithfulness meant persecution and temptation. Many would die at the hands of the Romans. John indicates that faithful endurance to the end is the only appropriate Christian response to the threat and allures of the evil powers of the present age.

---

[7] Adapted from Boring, M. Eugene, Revelation, Interpretation: A Bible Commentary for Teaching and Preaching (Louisville: John Knox Press, 1989) pgs. 21-23.

Literary Structure

GENERAL OUTLINE OF REVELATION

I.	*The King Speaks to the Church in the City*	Chapters 1–3
II.	*The King Judges the "Great City"*	Chapters 4–18
III.	*The King Vindicates the "Holy City"*	Chapters 19–22

EXPANDED OUTLINE OF REVELATION

I.	***The King Speaks to the Church in the City***	*Revelation 1–3*
	A. The Prophet's Call in the Presence of the King	1:1–20
	B. Seven Letters to Seven Churches	2:1–3:22
II.	***The King Judges the "Great City"***	*Revelation 4–18*
	A. Heavenly Throne Room: Who is Worthy?	4:1–5:14
	B. Opening the Scroll: The Seven Seals	6:1–8:1
	C. Seven Angels sounding the Seven Trumpets	8:2–11:19
	D. Seven Signs: Exposé of the Powers of Evil	12:1–14:20
	E. Seven Bowls: The Last Plagues	15:1–16:21
	F. The Fall of the Great City: Babylon	17:1–18:24
III.	***The King Vindicates the "Holy City"***	*Revelation 19–22*
	A. Throne Room: Praise of Lamb's Victory	19:1–10
	B. Seven Visions of the End	19:11–21:8
	C. The Advent of the Holy City: The New Jerusalem	21:9–22:11
	D. The Letter Ends	22:12–21
	F. The Fall of the Great City: Babylon	17:1–18:24

The Primary Question of Revelation

Will the Christians who must decide how to live their lives in the 'Mundane Cities of Asia' (Part I) orient themselves to the *'Great City'* that will inevitably receive God's Judgment (Part II) or to the *'Holy City'* that will be redeemed by God (Part III)?

The Spiritual Dilemma of Revelation

It is easy to understand when unfaithful people experience the consequences of sin and rebellion to God. But how are we to understand the call to endure trial, persecution, and suffering with faith in the reality of God? Is God being faithful to his promises to the prophets of old? Does trusting God and the Messiah make any difference? What is God going to do about all this evil mess?

I. THE KING SPEAKS TO THE CHURCH IN THE CITY

The Book of Revelation is written to address how to understand the call to be faithful and obedient to Jesus Christ in a world that appears to be under the control of the evil one. The revelation given to the apostle John provides the struggling and persecuted Christians in the world with an eternal perspective on their present condition. John receives a vision of the present and future realities taking place in both the earthly and heavenly realms. *"Write therefore the things that you have seen, those that are and those that are to take place after this"* (Revelation 1:19).

The vision provides needed context for the larger and grander story playing out on the stage of redemptive history. First, Jesus is walking among the lampstands, representing the seven churches. The Christians in these local contexts are playing an integral role in the larger story. John writes in the tradition of the great prophets of the Old Testament. He is an ambassador of the King of Heaven. His message is *"from the throne"* (Revelation 21:3).

The first three chapters establish John's call to speak as a prophet and address the immediate concerns of the church living in the world. Chapters 4-18 provide a spiritual picture of Jesus' sovereignty over evil and reveal the ultimate fate of the evil powers in the earthly and spiritual realms. Chapters 19-22 describe the ultimate redemption, vindication, and establishment of the people of God by Jesus at the end of the age. For the persecuted and struggling church, this knowledge of the fate of evil provides the motivation and passion for faithful endurance in the present.

II: THE KING JUDGES THE GREAT CITY
The Heavenly Throne Room: Who is Worthy?

"After this I looked, and behold, a door standing open in heaven! And the first voice, which I had heard speaking to me like a trumpet, said, 'Come up here, and I will show you what must take place after this.' At once I was in the Spirit, and behold, a throne stood in heaven, with one seated on the throne."
(Revelation 4:1-2)

All three units of John's revelation begin with an interaction with the king. As in the first section (Revelation 1-3), both the judgment section (Revelation 4-18) and the vindication section (Revelation 19-22) begin with a vision of the heavenly throne room.

In the judgment section, the question is: *"Who is worthy to execute the judgment of God?"* That is not a simple question. In both heaven and Earth, the stewards of justice and righteousness have proved themselves to be unworthy executors. Rather than leading and maintaining justice, the kings of this world and angelic princes of heaven have become beastly in their tyranny of those under them. Only one in heaven and on Earth has proved worthy: *"the Lion of the tribe of Judah," the lamb who was slain"* (Revelation 5:1-6).

Opening the Seven Seals

A seal conveys a guarantee of authenticity. It is a mark of authority and places one's reputation on the line. In addition, it conveys inaccessibility to the inappropriate and unworthy. An unbroken seal represents a mystery waiting to be revealed, and a broken seal represents a command implemented. As the lamb opens each seal, it unleashes a different power. The first four seals release the conqueror on a white horse, chaos on a red horse, greed and perversion on a black horse, and death on a pale horse (Revelation 6:1-8). The fifth seal reveals the unavenged martyrs. And the sixth seal unleashes the wrath of God (Revelation 6:8-17).

After the sixth seal is released and the day of God's wrath begins, the angels give 12,000 of each tribe of Israel the mark of the Lord. Twelve is a symbolic number repeated throughout the Bible: there were 12 tribes of Israel and 12 disciples. The people bearing the mark of the Lord worship him and will not suffer any harm: *"They shall hunger no more, neither thirst anymore; the sun shall not strike them, nor any scorching heat. For the Lamb in the midst of the throne will be their shepherd, and he will guide them to springs of living water"* (Revelation 7:16-17). Those who remain faithful will be spared the horrors of God's anger at humanity's disobedience and evil.

The Seven Angels Sounding Seven Trumpets

The seventh seal unleashes seven angels, each bearing a trumpet which, when blown, brings a disaster on the Earth. The first angel summons *"hail and fire, mixed with blood"* that burns a third of the Earth and trees (Revelation 8:7). The second angel's blow kills a third of the sea creatures when *"... something like a great mountain, burning with fire, was thrown into the sea, and a third of the sea be-*

came blood" (Revelation 8:8-9). The third angel unleashes a falling star from heaven that turns a third of the water bitter (Revelation 8:10-11). The fourth angel darkens a third of the sun, moon, and stars (Revelation 8:12). The fifth angel opens a bottomless pit created by a falling star, and smoke and locusts rush out of the pit (Revelation 9:1-3). These supernaturally violent locusts torment the people without the seal of God for five months, with their scorpion stings (Revelation 9:4-10). The sixth angel released the four angels bound to the Euphrates, who kill a third of mankind (Revelation 9:13-18). Despite the carnage, the surviving population did not repent of their sins (Revelation 9:20-21).

Before John could record the seventh seal in his vision, an angel stopped him. Instead, he wrote, *"… in the days of the trumpet call to be sounded by the seventh angel, the mystery of God would be fulfilled"* (Revelation 10:7). He goes on to describe the two witnesses who will make prophesies for 1,260 days while the holy city is trampled (Revelation 11:1-3). Then the prophets will be killed by a beast, but they will rise after three days, at which point an earthquake will kill 7,000 people in the holy city (Revelation 11:4-13). Then, John describes the mystery of God revealed at the seventh trumpet. The 24 elders fall before God and worship him, and the ark of the covenant appears in the Temple (Revelation 11:15-19).

Fig. 5. *The Adoration of the Mystic Lamb,* from the Ghent Altarpiece, lower half of central panel, 1432 (oil on panel) (see 472324), Eyck, Hubert (c.1370-1426) & Jan van (1390-1441) / St. Bavo Cathedral, Ghent, Belgium / © Lukas - Art in Flanders VZW / Bridgeman Images.

THE SEVEN SIGNS: The Exposure of Evil

John describes *"a woman clothed with the sun, with the moon under her feet, and on her head a crown of twelve stars"* giving birth to a child who is taken by God (Revelation 12:1-6). She represents Israel and Mary, the mother of Jesus. She is circled by a red dragon who tries to eat the child, and this dragon represents Satan. The archangel Michael casts the red dragon down to Earth, and John goes on to describe metaphorically Satan's pursuit of Israel and then Jesus (Revelation 12:13-17).

An evil beast rises out of the sea and is allowed to rule; there are people on Earth who worship it. The beast controlled by the dragon represents despotic rulers, but it's likely that it specifically represents the Roman emperor. This interpretation is confirmed in Revelation 13:6-8, as John describes how the beast conquered all the nations, just as the Roman Empire conquered three continents. A second beast rises out of the Earth. This beast represents false prophets and also operates under the power of Satan. It marks those who follow it as the Lord marked those who follow him, but it is a perversion. Those bearing the mark of the beast face God's wrath (Revelation 14:14-20).

The Seven Plagues

Chapter 15 describes seven angels, each with a bowl full of God's eternal wrath in the form of plagues. The first plague gives sores to those with the mark of the beast (Revelation 16:2). The second turns the sea into blood, and the third turns the rivers and lakes into blood (Revelation 16:3-4). The fourth plague makes the sun scorch people, and the fifth plunges the Earth into darkness (Revelation 16:8-10). Still, the plagued people do not repent (Revelation 16:11). The sixth plague dries the river Euphrates and brings unclean spirits from the mouths of the dragon, beast, and false prophet, and they gather at Armageddon (Revelation 16:12-16). The seventh plague causes an earthquake that levels the Earth and sends 100-pound hailstones down: but still, the people do not repent (Revelation 16:17-21).

The Fall of the Great City Babylon

In his vision, John personifies Babylon as the *"mother of prostitutes and of earth's abominations"* (Revelation 17:5). She is seated on a red beast, and the beast represents corrupt authorities that have been and will be. These corrupt authorities will fight the Lord, but they will be destroyed. Babylon will be destroyed by the beast. John uses the city Babylon as a metaphor for rampant and widespread sexual and political immorality. She is vice, personified and objectified, and when she is destroyed, those who worshipped her will mourn (Revelation 18:20-24).

THE KING VINDICATES THE HOLY CITY
The Throne Room

Once the last bastion of sin is destroyed, heaven rejoices (Revelation 19:1-5). Now, the marriage supper of the lamb can begin. The angels captured and destroyed the beast and the false prophet in a lake of fire (Revelation 19:19-21). Then, the angels bind Satan in a pit for a thousand years (Revelation 20:1-3).

Visions of the End

John prophesies that the martyrs who died for Jesus were the first to be resurrected and reign with Jesus for 1,000 years (Revelation 20:4). The rest of the dead will be resurrected after 1,000 years (Revelation 20:5). When Satan is released after his 1,000-year imprisonment, he will deceive humanity again, but God will defeat him and throw him into the lake of fire.

Then John describes the judgment of man. Before the great white throne of God, the book of the dead and the book of life were opened, *"And the dead were judged by what was written in the books, according to what they had done… And if anyone's name was not found written in the book of life, he was thrown into the lake of fire"* (Revelation 20:12-15). Death and Hades will be thrown into the lake of fire (Revelation 20:14).

The Advent of the Holy City

At the end of judgment, the holy city of Jerusalem will be ready for God to live among his people. Because this transcendent world is indescribable, John speaks about what it is not. There will be no more death, mourning, crying, or pain (Revelation 21:4). He does, however, describe it in visual terms. It has a city wall, 12 gates, each named for a tribe of Israel, and 12 foundations, each named for the apostles. *"The wall was built of jasper, while the city was pure gold, like clear glass. The foundations of the wall of the city were adorned with every kind of jewel"* (Revelation 21:18-19). The city of God is the made of the most precious materials because it is the most precious place. It is utterly and completely holy and pure. A river of life runs through it, and it will flow forever (Revelation 22:1-5).

Conclusion

John's vision ends with the word of Jesus: *"I, Jesus, have sent my angel to testify to you about these things for the churches. I am the root and the descendant of David, the bright morning star"* (Revelation 22:16). Before John closes his letter, though, he issues a warning against changing the words of his book:

"I warn everyone who hears the words of the prophecy of this book: if anyone adds to them, God will add to him the plagues described in this book, and if anyone takes away from the words of the book of this prophecy, God will take away his share in the tree of life and in the holy city, which are described in this book. He who testifies to these things says, 'Surely I am coming soon.' Amen. Come, Lord Jesus!"
(Revelation 22:18-20)

John's revelation provides strong imagery and detailed warnings against sinfulness and unfaithfulness. Only those who stay strong in the Lord will live—everything and everyone else will perish. Jesus is the only path to eternal life in the holy city.

CHAPTER 10 NOTES:

www.ingramcontent.com/pod-product-compliance
Lightning Source LLC
Chambersburg PA
CBHW042013120526
44592CB00043B/2849